SPEECHES THAT CHANGED THE WORLD

SPEECHES THAT CHANGED THE WORLD

Compiled by Owen Collins

Foreword by Andrew Young

Westminster John Knox Press
Louisville, Kentucky

First published in Great Britain in 1998 by HarperCollinsPublishers

Published in the United States in 1999 by
Westminster John Knox Press
Louisville, Kentucky

This book is printed on acid-free paper that meets the American National
Standards Institute Z39.48 standard. ♾

PRINTED IN THE UNITED STATES OF AMERICA
99 00 01 02 03 04 05 06 07 08 — 10 9 8 7 6 5 4 3 2 1

A catalog record for this book is available from the Library of Congress.

ISBN 0-664-22149-1

Contents

Foreword

"Nothing is more powerful than an idea whose time has come." When that idea is expressed in the context of a crisis situation, the world is changed.

I wish I had been taught the history of ideas rather than the chronology of events and geography. I would have probably been a historian. I had no love for history until I saw it as an unfolding of human consciousness and the development of our raison d'être.

"The pen is mightier than the sword." But the spoken word has the capacity to ignite human consciousness for good or ill. It cannot be ignored.

I am not sure what people felt at Gettysburg as Lincoln spoke. They were probably relieved that the President's speech was so brief after a long day of rather empty oratory. I know that was the immediate reaction to Martin Luther King Jr. at the 1963 March on Washington.

We had heard him say many of the same phrases on previous occasions, but never had 200,000 people been lifted to the heavens on the dream which poured from his fount of eloquence like the waters over Victoria Falls.

I was not excited about the March. I had been in Birmingham, Alabama, where youth stood tall with *real* courage in the face of dogs, fire hoses, and jail. This was a picnic in the park, a moderate, bourgeois expression of support for our actions in the South. It seemed like a waste of time to young militants. But suddenly the world was made to understand that this was a "revolution of values." No longer would we acquiesce to the second-class status accepted by previous generations. We expected, we demanded, complete access to the American Dream. This was no Marxist challenge, as many had suggested. This was the prophetic Judeo-Christian tradition. This was a demand for the fulfillment of the Constitutional promise of Jefferson and a completion of the legacy of Lincoln.

It took several days for us to appreciate the impact of Martin Luther King's words on the world. We knew it was a great speech. We knew that it was heard and understood by the Kennedy White House as well as by Congress. The power and eloquence, the simple faith and powerful idealism of his dream captured churches, intellectuals, liberals, and conservatives. But none could anticipate it being played almost a half-century later, or the dream of a black American preacher spreading like a forest fire from Ireland to Poland to South Africa to Brazil to China and back again. Indeed, this speech may well define the latter half of the twentieth century.

Each of the speeches compiled by Owen Collins has demonstrated a similar capacity to galvanize the heights or depths of the human spirit in response to a contemporary situation. As we listen, we hear time marching on. We sense the hopes and fears that shape our history and foretell the future.

Most of these speeches have already touched our lives. They form a part of the "collective unconscious" that makes us who we are and determines much of the pattern of prejudice or vision that creates our time.

It is extremely helpful to have so much of our history of ideas and ideals in one volume. This is our heritage. In understanding the words that shape us, we better understand ourselves.

This book can be read as history but it is also a tribute to the spirit of humanity, with occasional lapses into fear and hatred. Somehow, the poetic phraseology of these speeches rises above the record of bloodshed and tragedy which is human history. And as we read the great expanse of courage and vision from these orators, it is impossible not to believe that "we shall overcome someday."

Andrew Young

Atlanta, Georgia

PART I

The Ancients

Moses:

Second millennium BC

The Ten Commandments

The Ten Commandments, or the Decalogue, are the summary of the law given by God to Moses on Mount Sinai. They are paramount in the ethical systems of Judaism, Christianity, and Islam.

And Moses called all Israel, and said unto them, 'Hear, O Israel, the statutes and judgments which I speak in your ears this day, that ye may learn them, and keep, and do them. The LORD our God made a covenant with us in Horeb. The LORD made not this covenant with our fathers, but with us, even us, who are all of us here alive this day. The LORD talked with you face to face in the mount out of the midst of the fire, (I stood between the LORD and you at that time, to shew you the word of the LORD: for ye were afraid by reason of the fire, and went not up into the mount;) saying,

'"I am the LORD thy God, which brought thee out of the land of Egypt, from the house of bondage.

'"Thou shalt have none other gods before me.

'"Thou shalt not make thee any graven image, or any likeness of any thing that is in heaven above, or that is in the earth beneath, or that is in the waters beneath the earth: Thou shalt not bow down thyself unto them, nor serve them: for I the LORD thy God am a jealous God, visiting the iniquity of the fathers upon the children unto the third and fourth generation of them that hate me, And shewing mercy unto thousands of them that love me and keep my commandments.

'"Thou shalt not take the name of the LORD thy God in vain: for the LORD will not hold him guiltless that taketh his name in vain.

'"Keep the sabbath day to sanctify it, as the LORD thy God hath commanded thee. Six days thou shalt labour, and do all thy work: But the seventh day is the sabbath of the LORD thy God: in it thou shalt not do any work, thou, nor thy son, nor thy daughter, nor thy manservant, nor thy maidservant, nor thine ox, nor thine ass, nor any of thy cattle, nor thy stranger that is within thy gates; that thy manservant and thy maidservant may rest as well as thou. And remember that thou wast a servant in the land of Egypt, and that the LORD thy God brought thee out thence through a mighty hand and by a stretched out arm: therefore the LORD thy God commanded thee to keep the sabbath day.

'"Honour thy father and thy mother, as the LORD thy God hath commanded thee; that thy days may be prolonged, and that it may go well with thee, in the land which the LORD thy God giveth thee.

'"Thou shalt not kill.

'"Neither shalt thou commit adultery.

'"Neither shalt thou steal.

'"Neither shalt thou bear false witness against thy neighbour.

'"Neither shalt thou desire thy neighbour's wife, neither shalt thou covet thy neighbour's house, his field, or his manservant, or his maidservant, his ox, or his ass, or any thing that is thy neighbour's."

'These words the LORD spake unto all your assembly in the mount out of the midst of the fire, of the cloud, and of the thick darkness, with a great voice: and he added no more. And he wrote them in two tables of stone, and delivered them unto me.

'And it came to pass, when ye heard the voice out of the midst of the darkness, (for the mountain did burn with fire,) that ye came near unto me, even all the heads of your tribes, and your elders;

'And ye said, "Behold, the LORD our God hath shewed us his glory and his greatness, and we have heard his voice out of the midst of the fire: we have seen this day that God doth talk with man, and he liveth. Now therefore why should we die? for this great fire will consume us: if we hear the voice of the LORD our God any more, then we shall die. For who is there of all flesh, that hath heard the voice of the living God speaking out of the midst of the fire, as we have, and lived? Go thou near, and hear all that the LORD our God shall say: and speak thou unto us all that the LORD our God shall speak unto thee; and we will hear it, and do it."

'And the LORD heard the voice of your words, when ye spake unto me; and the LORD said unto me, "I have heard the voice of the words of this people, which they have spoken unto thee: they have well said all that they have spoken. O that there were such an heart in them, that they would fear me, and keep all my commandments always, that it might be well with them, and with their children for ever!

'"Go say to them, 'Get you into your tents again.' But as for thee, stand thou here by me, and I will speak unto thee all the commandments, and the statutes, and the judgments, which thou shalt teach them, that they may do them in the land which I give them to possess it.

'"Ye shall observe to do therefore as the LORD your God hath commanded you: ye shall not turn aside to the right hand or to the left. Ye shall walk in all the ways which the LORD your God hath commanded you, that ye may live, and that it may be well with you, and that ye may prolong your days in the land which ye shall possess."'

Deuteronomy 5 (Authorized Version)

Confucius:
Died c. 479 BC

'The danger in teaching ...'

Confucius, a Chinese philosopher and legislator, is rightly celebrated for his great learning, his patriotism and the purity of his morals.

When I enter a country, I can easily tell its type of culture. When the people are gentle and kind and simple-hearted, that shows the teaching of poetry. When people are broad-minded and acquainted with the past, that shows the teaching of history. When the people are generous and show a good disposition, that shows the teaching of music. When the people are quiet and thoughtful, and show a sharp power of observation, that shows the teaching of the philosophy of change. When the people are humble and respectful and frugal in their habits, that shows the teaching of propriety. When the people are cultivated in their speech, ready with expressions and analogies, that shows the teaching of prose, or Spring and Autumn Annals.

The danger in the teaching of poetry is that people remain ignorant, or too simple-hearted. The danger in the teaching of history is that people may be filled with incorrect legends and stories of events. The danger in the teaching of music is that the people grow extravagant. The danger in the teaching of philosophy is that the people become crooked. The danger in the teaching of propriety is that the rituals become too elaborate. And the danger in the teaching of Spring and Autumn Annals is that the people get a sense of the prevailing moral chaos.

When a man is kind and gentle and simple-hearted, and yet not ignorant, we may be sure he is deep in the study of poetry. When a man is broad-minded and acquainted with the past, and yet not filled with incorrect legends or stories of events, we may

which you are now witnessing. Then the reputation of many would not have been imperiled on the eloquence or want of eloquence of one, and their virtues believed or not as he spoke well or ill. For it is difficult to say neither too little nor too much; and even moderation is apt not to give the impression of truthfulness. The friend of the dead who knows the facts is likely to think that the words of the speaker fall short of his knowledge and of his wishes; another who is not so well informed, when he hears of anything which surpasses his own powers, will be envious and will suspect exaggeration. Mankind are tolerant of the praises of others so long as each hearer thinks that he can do as well or nearly as well himself, but, when the speaker rises above him, jealousy is aroused and he begins to be incredulous. However, since our ancestors have set the seal of their approval upon the practice, I must obey, and to the utmost of my power shall endeavour to satisfy the wishes and beliefs of all who hear me.

I will speak first of our ancestors, for it is right and seemly that now, when we are lamenting the dead, a tribute should be paid to their memory. There has never been a time when they did not inhabit this land, which by their valour they will have handed down from generation to generation, and we have received from them a free state. But if they were worthy of praise, still more were our fathers, who added to their inheritance, and after many a struggle transmitted to us their sons this great empire. And we ourselves assembled here today, who are still most of us in the vigour of life, have carried the work of improvement further, and have richly endowed our city with all things, so that she is sufficient for herself both in peace and war. Of the military exploits by which our various possessions were acquired, or of the energy with which we or our fathers drove back the tide of war, Hellenic or Barbarian, I will not speak; for the tale would be long and is familiar to you. But before I praise the dead, I should like to point out by what principles of action we rose to power, and under what institutions and through what manner of life our empire became great. For I conceive that such thoughts are not unsuited to the occasion, and that this numerous assembly of citizens and strangers may profitably listen to them.

Our form of government does not enter into rivalry with the institutions of others. Our government does not copy our neighbours', but is an example to them. It is true that we are called a democracy, for the administration is in the hands of the many and not of the few. But while there exists equal justice to all and alike in their private disputes, the claim of excellence is also recognized; and when a citizen is in any way distinguished, he is preferred to the public service, not as a matter of privilege, but as the reward of merit. Neither is poverty an obstacle, but a man may benefit his country whatever the obscurity of his condition. There is no exclusiveness in our public life, and in our private business we are not suspicious of one another, nor angry with our neighbour if he does what he likes; we do not put on sour looks at him which, though harmless, are not pleasant. While we are thus unconstrained in our private business, a spirit of reverence pervades our public acts; we are prevented from doing wrong by respect for the authorities and for the laws, having a particular regard to those which are ordained for the protection of the injured as well as those unwritten laws which bring upon the transgressor of them the reprobation of the general sentiment.

And we have not forgotten to provide for our weary spirits many relaxations from toil; we have regular games and sacrifices throughout the year; our homes are beautiful and elegant; and the delight which we daily feel in all these things helps to banish sorrow. Because of the greatness of our city the fruits of the whole earth flow in upon us; so that we enjoy the goods of other countries as freely as our own.

Then, again, our military training is in many respects superior to that of our adversaries. Our city is thrown open to the world, though and we never expel a foreigner and prevent him from seeing or learning anything of which the secret if revealed to an enemy might profit him. We rely not upon management or trickery, but upon our own hearts and hands. And in the matter of education, whereas they from early youth are always undergoing laborious exercises which are to make them brave, we live at ease, and yet are equally ready to face the perils which they face. And here is the proof: The Lacedaemonians come into Athenian territory not by themselves, but with their whole confederacy following; we go alone into a neighbour's country; and although our opponents are fighting for their homes and we on a foreign soil, we have seldom any difficulty in overcoming them. Our enemies have never yet felt our united strength, the care of a navy divides our attention, and on land we are obliged to send our own citizens everywhere. But they, if they meet and defeat a part of our army, are as proud as if they had routed us all, and when defeated they pretend to have been vanquished by us all.

If then we prefer to meet danger with a light heart but without laborious training, and with a courage which is gained by habit and not enforced by law, are we not greatly the better for it? Since we do not anticipate the pain, although, when the hour comes, we can be as brave as those who never allow themselves to rest; thus our city is equally admirable in peace and in war. For we are lovers of the beautiful in our tastes and our strength lies, in our opinion, not in deliberation and discussion, but that knowledge which is gained by discussion preparatory to action. For we have a peculiar power of thinking before we act, and of acting, too, whereas other men are courageous from ignorance but hesitate upon reflection. And they are surely to be esteemed the bravest spirits who, having the clearest sense both of the pains and pleasures of life, do not on that account shrink from danger. In doing good, again, we are unlike others; we make our friends by conferring, not by receiving favours. Now he who confers a favour is the firmer friend, because he would rather by kindness keep alive the memory of an obligation; but the recipient is colder in his feelings, because he knows that in requiting another's generosity he will not be winning gratitude but only paying a debt. We alone do good to our neighbours not upon a calculation of interest, but in the confidence of freedom and in a frank and fearless spirit.

To sum up: I say that Athens is the school of Hellas [the Greeks], and that the individual Athenian in his own person seems to have the power of adapting himself to the most varied forms of action with the utmost versatility and grace. This is no passing and idle word, but truth and fact; and the assertion is verified by the position to which these qualities have raised the state. For in the hour of trial Athens alone among her contemporaries is superior to the report of her. No enemy who comes against her is indignant at the reverses which he sustains at the hands of such a city; no subject complains that his masters are unworthy of him. And we shall assuredly not be without witnesses; there are mighty monuments of our power which will make us the wonder of this and of succeeding ages; we shall not need the praises of Homer or of any other panegyrist whose poetry may please for the moment, although his representation of the facts will not bear the light of day. For we have compelled every land and every sea to open a path for our valour, and have everywhere planted eternal memorials of our friendship and of our enmity. Such is the city for whose sake these men nobly fought and died; they could not bear the thought that she might be taken from them; and every one of us who survive should gladly toil on her behalf.

I have dwelt upon the greatness of Athens because I want to show you that we are contending for a higher prize than those who enjoy none of these privileges, and to establish by manifest proof the merit of these men whom I am now commemorating. Their loftiest praise has been already spoken. For in magnifying the city I have magnified them, and men like them whose virtues made her glorious. And of how few Hellenes can it be said as of them, that their deeds when weighed in the balance have been found equal to their fame! I believe that a death such as theirs has been the true measure of a man's worth; it may be the first revelation of his virtues, but is at any rate their final seal. For even those who come short in other ways may justly plead the valour with which they have fought for their country; they have blotted out the evil with the good, and have benefited the state more by their public services than they have injured her by their private actions. None of these men were enervated by wealth or hesitated to resign the pleasures of life; none of them put off the evil day in the hope, natural to poverty, that a man, though poor, may one day become rich. But, deeming that the punishment of their enemies was sweeter than any of these things, and that they could fall in no nobler cause, they determined at the hazard of their lives to be honourably avenged, and to leave the rest. They resigned to hope their unknown chance of happiness; but in the face of death they resolved to rely upon themselves alone. And when the moment came they were minded to resist and suffer, rather than to fly and save their lives; they ran away from the word of dishonour, but on the battlefield their feet stood fast, and in an instant, at the height of their fortune, they passed away from the scene, not of their fear, but of their glory.

Such was the end of these men; they were worthy of Athens, and the living need not desire to have a more heroic spirit, although they may pray for a less fatal issue. The value of such a spirit is not to be expressed in words. Any one can discourse to you for ever about the advantages of a brave defence, which you know already. But instead of listening to him I would have you day by day fix your eyes upon the greatness of Athens, until you become filled with the love of her; and when you are impressed by the spectacle of her glory, reflect that this empire has been acquired by men who knew their duty and had the courage to do it, who in the hour of conflict had the fear of dishonour always present to them, and who, if ever they failed in an enterprise, would not allow their virtues to be lost to their country, but freely gave their lives to her as the fairest offering which they could present at her feast. The sacrifice which they collectively made was individually repaid to them; for they received again each one for himself a praise which grows not old, and the noblest of all tombs. I speak not of that in which their remains are laid, but of that in which their glory survives, and is proclaimed always and on every fitting occasion both in word and deed. For the whole earth is the tomb of famous men; not only are they commemorated by columns and inscriptions in their own country, but in foreign lands there dwells also an unwritten memorial of them, graven not on stone but in the hearts of men. Make them your examples, and, esteeming courage to be freedom and freedom to be happiness, do not weigh too nicely the perils of war. The unfortunate who has no hope of a change for the better has less reason to throw away his life than the prosperous who, if he survive, is always liable to a change for the worse, and to whom any accidental fall makes the most serious difference. To a man of spirit, cowardice and disaster coming together are far more bitter than death striking him unperceived at a time when he is full of courage and animated by the general hope.

Wherefore I do not now pity the parents of the dead who stand here; I would rather comfort them. You know that your dead have passed away amid manifold vicissitudes; and that they may be deemed fortunate who have gained their utmost honour, whether an honourable death like theirs, or an honourable sorrow like yours, and whose share of happiness has been so ordered that the term of their happiness is likewise the term of their life. I know how hard it is to make you feel this, when the good fortune of others will too often remind you of the gladness which once lightened your hearts. And sorrow is felt at the want of those blessings, not which a man never knew, but which were a part of his life before they were taken from him. Some of you are of an age at which they may hope to have other children, and they ought to bear their sorrow better; not only will the children who may hereafter be born make them forget their own lost ones, but the city will be doubly a gainer. She will not be left desolate, and she will be safer. For a man's counsel cannot have equal weight or worth, when he alone has no children to risk in the general danger. To those of you who have passed their prime, I say: 'Congratulate yourselves that you have been happy during the greater part of your days; remember that your life of sorrow will not last long, and be comforted by the glory of those who are gone. For the love of honour alone is ever young, and not riches, as some say, but honour is the delight of men when they are old and useless.'

To you who are the sons and brothers of the departed, I see that the struggle to emulate them will be an arduous one. For all men praise the dead, and, however pre-eminent your virtue may be, I do not say even to approach them, and avoid living their rivals and detractors, but when a man is out of the way, the honour and goodwill which he receives is unalloyed. And, if I am to speak of womanly virtues to those of you who will henceforth

against the later accusations and the later accusers. For many accusers have risen up against me before you, who have been speaking for a long time, many years already, and saying nothing true; and I fear them more than Anytus and the rest, though these also are dangerous; but those others are more dangerous, gentlemen, who persuaded you ... 'There is a certain Socrates, a wise man, a ponderer over the things in the air and one who has investigated the things beneath the earth and who makes the weaker argument the stronger.' These people, men of Athens, who have spread abroad this report, are my dangerous enemies...

Men of Athens ... those who wish to cast a slur upon the state will blame you for having killed Socrates, a wise man; for, you know, those who wish to revile you will say I am wise, even though I am not. Now if you had waited a little while, what you desire would have come to you of its own accord; for you see how old I am, how far advanced in life and how near death. I say this not to all of you, but to those who voted for my death. And to those also I have something else to say. Perhaps you think, gentlemen, that I have been convicted through lack of such words as would have moved you to acquit me, if I had thought it right to do and say everything to gain an acquittal. Far from it. And yet it is through a lack that I have been convicted, not however a lack of words, but of impudence and shamelessness, and of willingness to say to you such things as you would have liked best to hear. You would have liked to hear me wailing and lamenting and doing and saying many things which are, as I maintain, unworthy of me – such things as you frequently hear from others. But I did not think at the time that I ought, on account of the danger I was in, to do anything unworthy of a free man, nor do I now repent of having made my defence as I did, but I much prefer to die after such a defence than to live after a defence of the other sort. For neither in the court nor in war ought I or any other man to plan to escape death by every possible means. In battles it is often plain that a man might avoid death by throwing down his arms and begging mercy of his pursuers; and there are many other means of escaping death in dangers of various kinds if one is willing to do and say anything. But, gentlemen, it is not hard to escape death; it is much harder to escape wickedness, for that runs faster than death.

And now I, since I am slow and old, am caught by the slower runner, and my accusers, who are clever and quick, by the faster, wickedness. And now I shall go away convicted by you and sentenced to death, and they go convicted by truth of villainy and wrong. And I abide by my penalty, and they by theirs. Perhaps these things had to be so, and I think they are well. And now I wish to prophesy to you, O ye who have condemned me; for I am now at the time when men most do prophesy, the time just before death. And I say to you, ye men who have slain me, that punishment will come upon you straight-way after my death, far more grievous in sooth than the punishment of death which you have meted out to me. For now you have done this to me because you hoped that you would be relieved from rendering an account of your lives, but I say that you will find the result far different. Those who will force you to give an account will be more numerous than heretofore; men whom I restrained, though you knew it not; and they will be harsher, inasmuch as they are younger, and you will be more annoyed. For if you think that by putting men to death you will prevent anyone from reproaching you because you do not act as you should, you are mistaken. That mode of escape is neither possible at all nor honourable, but the easiest and most honourable escape is not by suppressing others, but by making yourselves as good as possible. So with this prophecy to you who condemned me I take my leave.

But with those who voted for my acquittal I should like to converse about this which has happened, while the authorities are busy and before I go to the place where I must die. Wait with me so long, my friends; for nothing prevents our chatting with each other while there is time. I feel that you are my friends, and I wish to show you the meaning of this which has now happened to me. For, judges – and in calling you judges I give you your right name – a wonderful thing has happened to me. For hitherto the customary prophetic monitor always spoke to me very frequently and opposed me even in very small matters, if I was going to do anything I should not; but now, as you yourselves see, this thing which might be thought, and is generally considered, the greatest of evils has come upon me; but the divine sign did not oppose me either when I left my home in the morning, or when I came here to the court, or at any point of my speech, when I was going to say anything; and yet on other occasions it stopped me at many points in the midst of a speech; but now, in this affair, it has not opposed me in anything I was doing or saying. What then do I suppose is the reason? I will tell you. This which has happened to me is doubtless a good thing, and those of us who think death is an evil must be mistaken. A convincing proof of this been given me; for the accustomed sign would surely have opposed me if I had not been going to meet with something good.

Let us consider in another way also how good reason there is to hope that it is a good thing. For the state of death is one of two things: either it is virtually nothingness, so that the dead has no consciousness of anything, or it is, as people say, a change and migration of the soul from this to another place. And if it is unconsciousness, like a sleep in which the sleeper does not even dream, death would be a wonderful gain. For I think if any one were to pick out that night in which he slept a dreamless sleep and, comparing with it the other nights and days of his life, were to say, after due consideration, how many days and nights in his life had passed more pleasantly than that night, I believe that not only any private person, but even the great King of Persia himself would find that they were few in comparison with the other days and nights. So if such is the nature of death, I count it a gain; for in that case, all time seems to be no longer than one night. But on the other hand, if death is, as it were, a change of habitation from here to some other place, and if what we are told is true, that all the dead are there, what greater blessing could there be, judges? For if a man when he reaches the other world, after leaving behind these who claim to be judges, shall find those who are really judges who are said to sit in judgement there, Minos and Rhadamanthus, and Aeacus and Triptolemus, and all the other demigods who were just men in their lives, would the change of habitation be undesirable? Or again, what would any of you give to meet with Orpheus and Musaeus and Hesiod and Homer? I am willing to die many times over, if these things are true; for I personally should find the life there wonderful, when I met Palamedes or Ajax, the son of Telamon, or any other men of old who lost their lives through an unjust judgement, and compared my experience with theirs. I think that would not be unpleasant. And the greatest pleasure would be to pass my time in examining and investigating the people there, as I do those here, to find out who among them is wise and who thinks he is when he is not. What price would any of you pay, judges, to examine him who led the great army against Troy, or Odysseus, or Sisyphus, or countless others, both men and women, whom I might mention? To converse and associate with them and examine them would be immeasurable happiness. At any rate, the folk there do not kill people for it; since, if what we are told is true, they are immortal for all future time, besides being happier in other respects than men are here.

But you also, judges, must regard death hopefully and must bear in mind this one truth, that no evil can come to a good man either in life or after death. The gods will not neglect him. So, too, what has come to me has not come by chance, but I see plainly that it was better for me to die now and be freed from troubles. That is the reason why the sign never interfered with me, and I am not at all angry with those who condemned me or with my accusers. And yet it was not with that in view that they condemned and accused me, but because they thought to injure me. They deserve blame for that. However, I make this request of them: when my sons grow up, gentlemen, punish them by troubling them as I have troubled you; if they seem to you to care for money or anything else more than for virtue, and if they think they amount to something when they do not, rebuke them as I have rebuked you because they do not care for what they ought, and think they amount to something when they are worth nothing. If you do this, both I and my sons shall have received just treatment from you.

But now the time has come to go away. I go to die, and you to live; but which of us goes to the better lot, is known to none but God.

Jesus Christ:

c. AD 34

The Beatitudes

The Beatitudes are the most famous sayings of the founder of Christianity.

And seeing the multitudes, he went up into a mountain: and when he was set, his disciples came unto him: And he opened his mouth, and taught them, saying,

'Blessed are the poor in spirit: for theirs is the kingdom of heaven.

'Blessed are they that mourn: for they shall be comforted.

'Blessed are the meek: for they shall inherit the earth.

'Blessed are they which do hunger and thirst after righteousness: for they shall be filled.

'Blessed are the merciful: for they shall obtain mercy.

'Blessed are the pure in heart: for they shall see God.

'Blessed are the peacemakers: for they shall be called the children of God.

'Blessed are they which are persecuted for righteousness' sake: for theirs is the kingdom of heaven.

'Blessed are ye, when men shall revile you, and persecute you, and shall say all manner of evil against you falsely, for my sake.

'Rejoice, and be exceeding glad: for great is your reward in heaven: for so persecuted they the prophets which were before you.

Matthew 5:1–12 (Authorized Version)

Jesus Christ:

c. AD 34

The Sermon on the Mount

The Sermon on the Mount is a collection of the best-known teachings of Christ.

'Ye are the salt of the earth: but if the salt have lost his savour, wherewith shall it be salted? it is thenceforth good for nothing, but to be cast out, and to be trodden under foot of men.

'Ye are the light of the world. A city that is set on an hill cannot be hid. Neither do men light a candle, and put it under a bushel, but on a candlestick; and it giveth light unto all that are in the house. Let your light so shine before men, that they may see your good works, and glorify your Father which is in heaven.

'Think not that I am come to destroy the law, or the prophets: I am not come to destroy, but to fulfil. For verily I say unto you, Till heaven and earth pass, one jot or one tittle shall in no wise pass from the law, till all be fulfilled. Whosoever therefore shall break one of these least commandments, and shall teach men so, he shall be called the least in the kingdom of heaven: but whosoever shall do and teach them, the same shall be called great in the kingdom of heaven. For I say unto you, That except your righteousness shall exceed the righteousness of the scribes and Pharisees, ye shall in no case enter into the kingdom of heaven.

'Ye have heard that it was said by them of old time, "Thou shalt not kill; and whosoever shall kill shall be in danger of the judgment": But I say unto you, That whosoever is angry with his brother without a cause shall be in danger of the judgment: and whosoever shall say to his brother, "Raca," shall be in danger of the council: but whosoever shall say, "Thou fool," shall be in danger of hell fire.

'Therefore if thou bring thy gift to the altar, and there rememberest that thy brother hath ought against thee; Leave there thy gift before the altar, and go thy way; first be reconciled to thy brother, and then come and offer thy gift.

'Agree with thine adversary quickly, whiles thou art in the way with him; lest at any time the adversary deliver thee to the judge, and the judge deliver thee to the officer, and thou be cast into prison. Verily I say unto thee, Thou shalt by no means come out thence, till thou hast paid the uttermost farthing.

'Ye have heard that it was said by them of old time, "Thou shalt not commit adultery": But I say unto you, That whosoever looketh on a woman to lust after her hath committed adultery with her already in his heart. And if thy right eye offend thee, pluck it out, and cast it from thee: for it is profitable for thee that one of thy members should perish, and not that thy whole body should be cast into hell. And if thy right hand offend thee, cut if off, and cast it from thee: for it is profitable for thee that one of thy members should perish, and not that thy whole body should be cast into hell.

'It hath been said, "Whosoever shall put away his wife, let him give her a writing of divorcement": But I say unto you, That whosoever shall put away his wife, saving for the cause of fornication, causeth her to commit adultery: and whosoever shall marry her that is divorced committeth adultery.

'Again, ye have heard that it hath been said by them of old time, "Thou shalt not forswear thyself, but shalt perform unto the Lord thine oaths": But I say unto you, Swear not at all; neither by heaven; for it is God's throne: Nor by the earth; for it is his footstool: neither by Jerusalem; for it is the city of the great King. Neither shalt thou swear by thy head, because thou canst not make one hair white or black. But let your communication be, "Yea, yea"; "Nay, nay": for whatsoever is more than these cometh of evil.

'Ye have heard that it hath been said, "An eye for an eye, and a tooth for a tooth": But I say unto you, That ye resist not evil: but whosoever shall smite thee on thy right cheek, turn to him the other also. And if any man will sue thee at the law, and take away thy coat, let him have thy cloke also. And whosoever shall compel thee to go a mile, go with him twain. Give to him that asketh thee, and from him that would borrow of thee turn not thou away.

'Ye have heard that it hath been said, "Thou shalt love thy neighbour, and hate thine enemy." But I say unto you, Love your enemies, bless them that curse you, do good to them that hate you, and pray for them which despitefully use you, and persecute you; That ye may be the children of your Father which is in heaven: for he maketh his sun to rise on the evil and on the good, and sendeth rain on the just and on the unjust. For if ye love them which love you, what reward have ye? do not even the publicans the same? And if ye salute your brethren only, what do ye more than others? do not even the publicans so? Be ye therefore perfect, even as your Father which is in heaven is perfect.

'Take heed that ye do not your alms before men, to be seen of them: otherwise ye have no reward of your Father which is in heaven.

'Therefore when thou doest thine alms, do not sound a trumpet before thee, as the hypocrites do in the synagogues and in the streets, that they may have glory of men. Verily I say unto you, They have their reward. But when thou doest alms, let not thy left hand know what thy right hand doeth: That thine alms may be in secret: and thy Father which seeth in secret himself shall reward thee openly.

'And when thou prayest, thou shalt not be as the hypocrites are: for they love to pray standing in the synagogues and in the corners of the streets, that they may be seen of men. Verily I say unto you, They have their reward. But thou, when thou prayest, enter into thy closet, and when thou hast shut thy door, pray to thy Father which is in secret; and thy Father which seeth in secret shall reward thee openly. But when ye pray, use not vain repetitions, as the heathen do: for they think that they shall be heard for their much speaking. Be not ye therefore like unto them: for your Father knoweth what things ye have need of, before ye ask him. After this manner therefore pray ye:

> Our Father which art in heaven,
> Hallowed be thy name.
> Thy kingdom come.
> Thy will be done in earth, as it is in heaven.
> Give us this day our daily bread.
> And forgive us our debts, as we forgive our debtors.
> And lead us not into temptation, but deliver us from evil:
> For thine is the kingdom, and the power, and the glory, for ever. Amen.

'For if ye forgive men their trespasses, your heavenly Father will also forgive you: But if ye forgive not men their trespasses, neither will your Father forgive your trespasses. Moreover when ye fast, be not, as the hypocrites, of a sad countenance: for they disfigure their faces, that they may appear unto men to fast. Verily I say unto you, They have their reward. But thou, when thou fastest, anoint thine head, and wash thy face; That thou appear not unto men to fast, but unto thy Father which is in secret: and thy Father, which seeth in secret, shall reward thee openly.

'Lay not up for yourselves treasures upon earth, where moth and rust doth corrupt, and where thieves break through and steal: But lay up for yourselves treasures in heaven, where neither moth nor rust doth corrupt, and where thieves do not break through nor steal: For where your treasure is, there will your heart be also.

'The light of the body is the eye: if therefore thine eye be single, thy whole body shall be full of light. But if thine eye be evil, thy whole body shall be full of darkness. If therefore the light that is in thee be darkness, how great is that darkness!

'No man can serve two masters: for either he will hate the one, and love the other; or else he will hold to the one, and despise the other. Ye cannot serve God and mammon.

'Therefore I say unto you, Take no thought for your life, what ye shall eat, or what ye shall drink; nor yet for your body, what ye shall put on. Is not the life more than meat, and the body than raiment? Behold the fowls of the air: for they sow not, neither do they reap, nor gather into barns; yet your heavenly Father feedeth them. Are ye not much better than they? Which of you by taking thought can add one cubit unto his stature?

'And why take ye thought for raiment? Consider the lilies of the field, how they grow; they toil not, neither do they spin: And yet I say unto you, That even Solomon in all his glory was not arrayed like one of these. Wherefore, if God so clothe the grass of the field, which to day is, and to morrow is cast into the oven, shall he not much more clothe you, O ye of little faith? Therefore take no thought, saying, "What shall we eat?" or, "What shall we drink?" or, "Wherewithal shall we be clothed?" (For after all these things do the Gentiles seek:) for your heavenly Father knoweth that ye have need of all these things. But seek ye first the kingdom of God, and his righteousness; and all these things shall be added unto you. Take therefore no thought for the morrow: for the morrow shall take thought for the things of itself. Sufficient unto the day is the evil thereof.

'Judge not, that ye be not judged. For with what judgment ye judge, ye shall be judged: and with what measure ye mete, it shall be measured to you again.

'And why beholdest thou the mote that is in thy brother's eye, but considerest not the beam that is in thine own eye? Or how wilt thou say to thy brother, "Let me pull out the mote out of thine eye"; and, behold, a beam is in thine own eye? Thou hypocrite, first cast out the beam out of thine own eye; and then shalt thou see clearly to cast out the mote out of thy brother's eye.

'Give not that which is holy unto the dogs, neither cast ye your pearls before swine, lest they trample them under their feet, and turn again and rend you.

'Ask, and it shall be given you; seek, and ye shall find; knock, and it shall be opened unto you: For every one that asketh receiveth; and he that seeketh findeth; and to him that knocketh it shall be opened.

'Or what man is there of you, whom if his son ask bread, will he give him a stone? Or if he ask a fish, will he give him a serpent? If ye then, being evil, know how to give good gifts unto your children, how much more shall your Father which is in heaven give good things to them that ask him? Therefore all things whatsoever ye would that men should do to you, do ye even so to them: for this is the law and the prophets.

'Enter ye in at the strait gate: for wide is the gate, and broad is the way, that leadeth to destruction, and many there be which go in thereat: Because strait is the gate, and narrow is the way, which leadeth unto life, and few there be that find it.

'Beware of false prophets, which come to you in sheep's clothing, but inwardly they are ravening wolves. Ye shall know them by their fruits. Do men gather grapes of thorns, or figs of thistles? Even so every good tree bringeth forth good fruit; but a corrupt tree bringeth forth evil fruit. A good tree cannot bring forth evil fruit, neither can a corrupt tree bring forth good fruit. Every tree that bringeth not forth good fruit is hewn down, and cast into the fire. Wherefore by their fruits ye shall know them.

'Not every one that saith unto me, "Lord, Lord," shall enter into the kingdom of heaven; but he that doeth the will of my Father which is in heaven. Many will say to me in that day, "Lord, Lord, have we not prophesied in thy name? and in thy name have cast out devils? and in thy name done many wonderful works?" And then will I profess unto them, "I never knew you: depart from me, ye that work iniquity."

'Therefore whosoever heareth these sayings of mine, and doeth them, I will liken him unto a wise man, which built his house upon a rock: And the rain descended, and the floods came, and the winds blew, and beat upon that house; and it fell not: for it was founded upon a rock. And every one that heareth these sayings of mine, and doeth them not, shall be likened unto a foolish man, which built his house upon the sand: And the rain descended, and the floods came, and the winds blew, and beat upon that house; and it fell: and great was the fall of it.'

And it came to pass, when Jesus had ended these sayings, the people were astonished at his doctrine: For he taught them as one having authority, and not as the scribes.

Matthew 5:13 – 7:29 (Authorized Version)

Paul:

AD 50s

'I made my journey ... unto Damascus'

Paul, the greatest theologian and pioneer missionary of the Early Church, makes a spirited defence in front of a hostile crowd.

And as Paul was to be led into the castle, he said unto the chief captain, 'May I speak unto thee?'

Who said, 'Canst thou speak Greek? Art not thou that Egyptian, which before these days madest an uproar, and leddest out into the wilderness four thousand men that were murderers?'

But Paul said, 'I am a man which am a Jew of Tarsus, a city in Cilicia, a citizen of no mean city: and, I beseech thee, suffer me to speak unto the people.'

And when he had given him licence, Paul stood on the stairs, and beckoned with the hand unto the people. And when there was made a great silence, he spake unto them in the Hebrew tongue, saying,

'Men, brethren, and fathers, hear ye my defence which I make now unto you.' (And when they heard that he spake in the Hebrew tongue to them, they kept the more silence: and he saith,) 'I am verily a man which am a Jew, born in Tarsus, a city in Cilicia, yet brought up in this city at the feet of Gamaliel, and taught according to the perfect manner of the law of the fathers, and was zealous toward God, as ye all are this day. And I persecuted this way unto the death, binding and delivering into prisons both men and women. As also the high priest doth bear me witness, and all the estate of the elders: from whom also I received letters unto the brethren, and went to Damascus, to bring them which were there bound unto Jerusalem, for to be punished.

'And it came to pass, that, as I made my journey, and was come nigh unto Damascus about noon, suddenly there shone from heaven a great light round about me. And I fell unto the ground, and heard a voice saying unto me, "Saul, Saul, why persecutest thou me?"

'And I answered, "Who art thou, Lord?" And he said unto me, "I am Jesus of Nazareth, whom thou persecutest." And they that were with me saw indeed the light, and were afraid; but they heard not the voice of him that spake to me.

'And I said, "What shall I do, Lord?" And the Lord said unto me, "Arise, and go into Damascus; and there it shall be told thee of all things which are appointed for thee to do." And when I could not see for the glory of that light, being led by the hand of them that were with me, I came into Damascus.

'And one Ananias, a devout man according to the law, having a good report of all the Jews which dwelt there, came unto me, and stood, and said unto me, "Brother Saul, receive thy sight." And the same hour I looked up upon him.

'And he said, "The God of our fathers hath chosen thee, that thou shouldest know his will, and see that Just One, and shouldest hear the voice of his mouth. For thou shalt be his witness unto all men of what thou hast seen and heard. And now why tarriest thou? arise, and be baptized, and wash away thy sins, calling on the name of the Lord."

'And it came to pass, that, when I was come again to Jerusalem, even while I prayed in the temple, I was in a trance; And saw him saying unto me, "Make haste, and get thee quickly out of Jerusalem: for they will not receive thy testimony concerning me."

'And I said, "Lord, they know that I imprisoned and beat in every synagogue them that believed on thee: And when the blood of thy martyr Stephen was shed, I also was standing by, and consenting unto his death, and kept the raiment of them that slew him."

'And he said unto me, "Depart: for I will send thee far hence unto the Gentiles."'

And they gave him audience unto this word, and then lifted up their voices, and said, 'Away with such a fellow from the earth: for it is not fit that he should live.'

Acts 21:37 – 22:22 (Authorized Version)

Augustine:

c. AD 408

'Dig this foundation of lowliness deep in thee'

Augustine was one of the greatest Christian theologians and is admired by both Protestants and Catholics. Below is his sermon on Jesus' words, 'Come unto me, all ye that labour and are heavy laden' (Matthew 11:28).

We heard in the Gospel that the Lord, rejoicing greatly in Spirit, said unto God the Father, 'I confess to Thee, O Father, Lord of heaven and earth, because Thou hast hid these things from the wise and prudent, and hast revealed them unto babes. Even so, Father: for so it seemed good in Thy sight. All things are delivered unto Me of My Father: and no man knoweth the Son, but the Father; neither knoweth any man the Father, save the Son, and he to whomsoever the Son will reveal Him.' I have labour in talking, you in hearing: let us then both give ear to Him who goes on to say, 'Come unto Me, all ye that labour.' For why do we labour all, except that we are mortal men, frail creatures and infirm, bearing about vessels of clay which crowd and straiten one another. But if these vessels of flesh are straitened, let the open expanse of charity be enlarged. What then does He mean by, 'Come unto Me, all ye that labour,' but that ye may labour no more? In a word, His promise is clear enough; forasmuch as He called those who were in labour, they might perchance enquire, for what profit they were called: 'and,' saith He, 'I will refresh you.'

'Take My yoke upon you, and learn of Me;' not to raise the fabric of the world, not to create all things visible and invisible, not in the world so created to work miracles and raise the dead; but, 'that I am meek and lowly in heart.' Thou wishest to be great, begin from the least. Thou art thinking to construct some mighty fabric in height; first think of the foundation of humility. And how great soever a mass of building one may wish and design to place above it, the greater the building is to be, the deeper does he dig his foundation. The building in the course of its erection, rises up on high, but he who digs its foundation, must first go down very low. So then you see even a building is low before it is high, and the top is raised only after humiliation.

What is the top of that building which we are constructing? Whither will the highest point of this building reach? I say at once, even to the vision of God. Ye see how high, how great a thing it is to see God. Whoever longs after it, understands both what I say and what he hears. The Vision of God is promised to us, of the very God, the Supreme God. For this is good, to see Him who seeth. For they who worship false gods, see them easily; but they see them 'who have eyes and see not.' But to us is promised the Vision of the Living and the Seeing God, that we may desire eagerly to see that God of whom Scripture saith, 'He that planted the ear, shall he not hear? He that formed the eye, doth he not consider?' Doth He then not hear, who hath made for thee that whereby thou hearest? and doth not He see, who hath created that whereby thou seest? Well therefore in the foregoing words of this very Psalm doth He say, 'Understand therefore ye unwise among the people, and ye fools at length be wise.' For many men commit evil deeds whilst they think they are not seen by God. And it is difficult indeed for them to believe that He cannot see them; but they think that He will not. Few are found of such great impiety, that that should be fulfilled in them which is written, 'The fool hath said in his heart, There is no God.' This is but the madness of a few. For as great piety belongs but to the few, no less also does great impiety.

But the multitude of men speak thus: What! is God thinking now upon this, that He should know what I am doing in my house, and does God care for what I may choose to do upon my bed? Who says this? 'Understand, ye unwise among the people, and ye fools at length be wise.' Because as being a man, it is a labour for thee to know all that takes place in thy house, and for all the doings and words of thy servants to reach thee; thinkest thou that it is a like labour for God to observe thee, who did not labour to create thee? Doth not He fix His eye upon thee, who made thine eye? Thou wast not, and He created thee and gave thee being; and doth not He care for thee now that thou art, who 'calleth those things which be not as though they were'? Do not then promise thyself this. Whether thou wilt or no, He seeth thee, and there is no place whither thou canst hide thyself from His eyes. 'For if thou goest up into heaven, He is there; if thou goest down into hell, He is there also.' Great is thy labour, whilst unwilling to depart from evil deeds: yet wishest not to be seen by God. Hard labour truly! Daily art thou wishing to do evil, and dost thou suspect that thou art not seen? Hear the Scripture which saith, 'He that planted the ear, shall He not hear? He that formed the eye, doth not He consider?' Where canst thou hide thy evil deeds from the eyes of God? If thou wilt not depart from them, thy labour is great indeed.

Hear Him then who saith, 'Come unto Me, all ye that labour.' Thou canst not end thy labour by flying. Dost thou choose to fly from Him, and not rather to Him? Find out then whither thou canst escape, and so flee. But if thou canst not flee from Him, for that He is everywhere present; flee to God, who is present where thou art standing. Flee. Lo in thy flight thou hast passed the heavens, He is there; thou hast descended into hell, He is there; whatever deserts of the earth thou shalt choose, there is He, who hath said, 'I fill heaven and earth.' If then He fills heaven and earth, and there is no place whither thou canst fly from Him; cease this thy labour, and fly to His presence, lest thou feel His coming. Take courage from the hope that thou shalt by well-living see Him, by whom even in thy evil living thou art seen. For in evil living thou canst be seen, thou canst not see; but by well-living thou art both seen and seest. For with how much more tenderness is He who crowneth the worthy look on thee, who in His pity saw thee that He might call thee when unworthy?

Nathanael said to the Lord whom as yet he did not know, 'Whence knewest thou me?' The Lord said unto him, 'When thou wast under the fig-tree I saw thee.' Christ saw thee in thine own shade; and will He not see thee in His Light? For what is, 'When thou wast under the fig-tree I saw thee'? What does it mean? Call to mind the original sin of Adam, in whom we all die. When he first sinned, he made himself aprons of fig-leaves, signifying by these leaves the irritations of lust to which he had been reduced by sinning. Hence are we born; in this condition are we born; born in sinful flesh, which 'the likeness of sinful flesh' alone can cure. Therefore 'God sent His own Son in the likeness of sinful flesh.' He came of this flesh, but He came not as other men. For the Virgin conceived Him not by lust, but by faith. He came into the Virgin, who was before the Virgin. He made choice of her whom He created, He created her whom He designed to choose. He brought to the Virgin fruitfulness: He took not away her unimpaired purity. He then who came to thee without the irritation of the leaves of the fig-tree, 'when thou wast under the fig-tree,' saw thee. Make ready then to see Him in His height of glory, by whom in His pity thou wast seen. But because the top is high, think of the foundation. What foundation? dost thou say? 'Learn of Him, for He is meek and lowly in heart.' Dig this foundation of lowliness deep in thee, and so wilt thou attain to the crowning top of charity.

Sermons

PART II

The Fifteenth, Sixteenth and Seventeenth Centuries

Joan of Arc:
1431

'I had a voice from God to help me'

When she was 13 years old Joan heard 'voices' telling her that she should lead France in war. Her trial began on 9 January 1431. Her only judges were bishop Pierre Cauchon, who had always favoured the English cause, and Inquisitor Jean Lemaitre. She was charged with a variety of crimes, including being a witch. Eventually she was convicted for wearing men's clothing, which implied a lack of submission to the Church. On 30 May 1431 she was burned at the stake.

Joan: When I was thirteen years old, I had a voice from God to help me govern my conduct. And the first time I was very fearful. And came this voice, about the hour of noon, in the summer-time, in my father's garden; I had not fasted on the eve preceding that day. I heard the voice on the right-hand side, towards the church; and rarely do I hear it without a brightness. This brightness comes from the same side as the voice is heard. It is usually a great light. When I came to France, often I heard this voice.

The voice was sent to me by God and, after I had thrice heard this voice, I knew that it was the voice of an angel. This voice has always guarded me well and I have always understood it clearly.

I act by their advice, that they were bidden to lead me in what I had to do and that I should believe in what they would say to me and that it was by God's order.

La Fontaine: What say you of that woman's clothing which is offered you that you may go and hear mass?

Joan: As for women's clothing, I shall not put it on until it please God; and if it should be that I must be brought even to judgment, I trust in the lords of the Church that they will grant me the mercy of having a woman's shift and a covering for my head. And I would rather die than revoke what God has made me do, for I believe firmly that God will not let it happen that I be brought so low without I have immediate succour, and by miracle.

La Fontaine: Since you say that you wear (a man's) habit by God's commandment, why do you ask for a woman's shift when it comes to dying?

Joan: It will suffice if it be long.

La Fontaine: Since you have said that you would wear woman's clothes if you were allowed to go away, would that please God?

Joan: If permission were given me to withdraw in woman's clothes, immediately (thereafter) I should dress myself in man's clothes and do what is commanded me by God; and I have answered elsewhere that not for anything whatsoever would I take oath not to put on armour and not to wear man's clothes to do the Lord's commandment.

Martin Luther:

18 April 1521

'I neither can nor will recant anything'

Few moments in history have been at once so dramatic and so decisive as that day when Luther appeared before Emperor Charles V at the Diet of Worms. Luther had expected that he would be called on to defend certain articles of faith and that he would be given the opportunity to debate them. He did not expect that he would be given no opportunity to present his case, but would be called upon to recant. Eck asked him, 'Do you wish to defend all your books or to retract part of them?' Luther made the following great oration, first in German and then in Latin. After the Diet of Worms the die was cast for the Reformation in Germany.

Most Serene Emperor, Most Illustrious Princes, Most Clement Lords! At the time fixed yesterday I obediently appear, begging for the mercy of God, that your Most Serene Majesty and your Illustrious Lordships may deign to hear this cause, which I hope may be called the cause of justice and truth, with clemency; and if, by my inexperience, I should fail to give anyone the titles due to him, or should sin against the etiquette of the court, please forgive me, as a man who has not lived in courts but in monastic nooks, one who can say nothing for himself but that he has hitherto tried to teach and to write with a sincere mind and single eye to the glory of God and the edification of Christians.

Most Serene Emperor, Most Illustrious Princes! Two questions were asked me yesterday. To the first, whether I would recognize that the books published under my name were mine, I gave a plain answer, to which I hold and will hold for ever, namely, that the books are mine, as I published them, unless perchance it may have happened that the guile or meddlesome wisdom of my opponents has changed something in them. For I only recognize what has been written by myself alone, and not the interpretation added by another.

In reply to the second question I beg your Most Sacred Majesty and your lordships to be pleased to consider that all my books are not of the same kind. In some I have treated piety, faith, and morals so simply and evangelically that my adversaries themselves are forced to confess that these books are useful, innocent, and worthy to be read by Christians. Even the bull, though fierce and cruel, states that some things in my books are harmless, although it condemns them by a judgement simply monstrous. If, therefore, I should undertake to recant these, would it not happen that I alone of all men should damn the truth which all, friends and enemies alike, confess?

The second class of my works inveighs against the papacy as against that which both by precept and example has laid waste all Christendom, body and soul. No one can deny or dissemble this fact, since general complaints witness that the consciences of all believers are snared, harassed, and tormented by the laws of the Pope and the doctrines of men, and especially that the goods of this famous German nation have been and are devoured in numerous and ignoble ways. Yet the Canon Law provides that the laws and doctrines of the Pope contrary to the gospel and the Fathers are to be held erroneous and rejected. If, therefore, I should withdraw these books, I would add strength to tyranny and open windows and doors to their impiety, which would then flourish and burgeon more freely than it ever dared before. It would come to pass that their wickedness would go unpunished, and therefore would become more licentious on account of my recantation, and their government of the people, thus confirmed and established, would become intolerable, especially if they could boast that I had recanted with the full authority of your Sacred and Most Serene Majesty and of the whole Roman Empire. Good God! In that case I would be the tool of iniquity and tyranny.

In a third sort of books I have written against some private individuals who tried to defend the Roman tyranny and tear down my pious doctrine. In these I confess I was more bitter than is becoming to a minister of religion. For I do not pose as a saint, nor do I discuss my life but the doctrine of Christ. Yet neither is it right for me to recant what I have said in these, for then tyranny and impiety would rage and reign against the people of God more violently than ever by reason of my acquiescence.

As I am a man and not God, I wish to claim no other defence for my doctrine than that which the Lord Jesus put forward when he was questioned before Annas and smitten by a servant: he then said: 'If I have spoken evil, bear witness of the evil.' If the Lord himself, who knew that he could not err, did not scorn to hear testimony against his doctrine from a miserable servant, how much more should I, the dregs of men, who can do nothing but err, seek and hope that someone should bear witness against my doctrine. I therefore beg by God's mercy that if your Majesty or your illustrious Lordships, from the highest to the lowest, can do it, you should bear witness and convict me of error and conquer me by proofs drawn from the gospels or the prophets, for I am most ready to be instructed and when convinced will be the first to throw my books into the fire.

From this I think it is sufficiently clear that I have carefully considered and weighed the discords, perils, emulation, and dissension excited by my teaching, concerning which I was gravely and urgently admonished yesterday. To me the happiest side of the whole affair is that the Word of God is made the object of emulation and dissent. For this is the course, the fate, and the result of the Word of God, as Christ says: 'I am come not to send peace but a sword, to set a man against his father and a daughter against her mother.' We must consider that our God is wonderful and terrible in his counsels. If we should begin to heal our dissensions by damning the Word of God, we should only turn loose an intolerable deluge of woes. Let us take care that the rule of this excellent youth, Prince Charles (in whom, next to God, there is much hope), does not begin inauspiciously. For I could show by many examples drawn from scripture that when Pharaoh and the king of Babylon and the kings of Israel thought to pacify and strengthen their kingdoms by their own wisdom, they really only ruined themselves. For he taketh the wise in their own craftiness and removeth mountains and they know it not. We must fear God. I do not say this as though your lordships needed either my teaching or my admonition, but because I could not shirk the duty I owed Germany. With these words I commend myself to your Majesty and your Lordships, humbly begging that you will not let my enemies make me hateful to you without cause. I have spoken.

*Eck replied: 'Luther, you have not answered the point. You ought not to call in question what has been decided and condemned by councils. Therefore I beg you to give a simple, unsophisticated answer without horns [*non cornutum*]. Will you recant or not?' Luther replied:*

Since your Majesty and your Lordships ask for a plain answer, I will give you one without either horns or teeth. Unless I am convicted by scripture or by right reason (for I trust neither in popes nor in councils, since they have often erred and contradicted themselves) – unless I am thus convinced, I am bound by the texts of the Bible, my conscience is captive to the Word of God, I neither can nor will recant anything, since it is neither safe nor right to act against conscience. God help me. Amen.

John Dudley:
23 August 1553

'I dye in the true catholyke fayth'

John Dudley, Duke of Northumberland, gained control over the young King Edward VI as he lay dying of tuberculosis, and persuaded him to settle the crown on Dudley's own daughter-in-law, Lady Jane. The ensuing struggle ended with the victory of Mary. This is Dudley's 'dying speech', before he was executed on Tower Hill, London, in 1553.

'Good people, all you that be here present to see me dye. Though my death be odyouse and horrible to the flesh, yet I pray you judge the beste in God's workes, for he doth all for the best. And as for me, I am a wretched synner, & have deserved to dye, and most justly am condemned to dye by a law. And yet this acte wherefore I dye, was not altogither of me (as it is thoughte) but I was procured and induced thereunto by other. I was I saye induced thereunto by other, howbeit, God forbyd that I shoulde name any man unto you, I wyll name no man unto you, & therfore I beseche you look not for it.

'I for my parte forgive all men, and praye God also to forgive them. And if I have offended any of you here, I praye you and all the Worlde to forgive me: and most chiefly I desire fogiveness of the Queen's highness, whom I have most grievously offended.'

'Amen,' sayde the people.

'And I pray you all to witness with me, that I depart in perfyt love and charitie with all the worlde, & that you wyll assiste me with youre prayers at the houre of death.

'And one thinge more good people I have to saye unto you, whiche I am chiefly moved to do for discharge of my conscience, & that is to warne you and exhorte you to beware of these seditiouse preachers, and teachers of newe doctryne, which pretende to preache God's worde, but in very deede they preache theyr owne phansies, who were never able to explicate themselves, they know not to day what they wold have to morowe, there is no stay in theyr teaching & doctryne, they open the book, but they cannot shut it agayne. Take heed how you enter into strange opinions or newe doctryne, whiche hath done no smal hurt in this realme, and hath justly procured the ire and wrath of God upon us, as well maye appeare who so lyst to call to remembraunce the manyfold plagues that this realme hath been touched with all synce we dissevered oure selves from the catholyke church of Christ, and from the doctryne whiche hath been received by the holy apostles, martyrs, and all sayntes, and used throughe all realmes christened since Christ.

'And I verily believe, that all the plagues that have chanced to this realme of late yeares synce afore the death of Kynge Henrye the eight, hath justly fallen upon us, for that we have divided ourselfe from the rest of Christendome wherof we be but as a sparke in comparison: Have we not had warre, famyne, pestylence, the death of our kinge, rebellion, sedition amonge ourselves, conspiracies? Have we not had sondrye erronious opinions spronge up amonge us in this realme, synce we have forsaken the unitie of the catholyke Churche? and what other plagues be there that we have not felt?

'And if this be not able to move you, then look upon Germanye, whiche synce it is fallen into this schism and division from the unitie of the catholike church, is by continuall dissention and discorde, broughte almost to utter ruine & decaye. Therfore, leste an utter ruine come amonge you, by provokynge to muche the juste vengeaunce of God, take up betymes these contentions, & be not ashamed to returne home agayne, and joyne youre selves to the rest of Christen realmes, and so shall you brynge your selves againe to be membres of Christes body, for he cannot be head of a dyfformed or monstruous body.

'Look upon your crede, have you not there these wordes: I believe in the holy ghost, the holy catholik churche, the communion of sayntes, which is the universal number of all faythfull people, professynge Christe, dispersed throughe the universal worlde: of whiche number I trust to be one. I could bryng many more thinges for this pupose, albeit I am unlearned, as all you knowe, but this shall suffice.

'And heare I do protest unto you good people, most earnestly, even from the bottome of my harte, that this which I have spoken is of my selfe, not beinge required nor moved therunto by any man, nor for any flattery, or hope of life, and I take witness of my lord of Worcestre here, myne olde frende and gostely father, that he founde me in this mynde and opinion when he came to me: but I have declared this onely upon myne owne mynde and affection, for discharge of my conscience, & for the zeale and love that I beare to my naturall countreye. I coulde good people reherse muche more even by experience that I have of this evil that is happened to this realme by these occasions, but you knowe I have an other thyng to do, wherunto I must prepare me, for the tyme draweth awaye.

'And nowe I beseeche the Queen's highness to forgive me myne offences agaynst her majestie, wherof I have a singular hope, forasmuch as she hath already extended her goodnes & clemency so farre upon me that where as she myghte forthwith without judgement or any further tryall, have put me to moste vile & cruell death, by hanging drawing, and quartering, forasmuch as I was in the field in armes agaynst her highnesse, her majestie nevertheless of her most mercyfull goodness suffered me to be brought to my judgement, and to have my tryall by the lawe, where I was most justly & worthily condemned. And her highness hath now also extended her mercye and clemencye upon me for the manner and kynde of my death. And therefore my hope is, that her grace of her goodness will remit all the rest of her indignation and displeasure towardes me, whiche I beseche you all most hartily to praye for, and that it maye please God longe to preserve her majestie to reigne over you in muche honour and felicitie.'

'Amen,' sayd the people.

And after he hadde thus spoken he kneeled downe, sayinge to them that were about: 'I beseche you all to beare me witness that I dye in the true catholyke fayth,' and then sayde the Psalmes of *Miserere*, and *De profundis*, and his *Pater nostre* in Latin, and sixe of the first verses of the psalme, *In te domine sperant*, endynge with this verse, 'Into thy handes O lorde I commend my spirite.' And when he had thus finished his prayers, the executioner asked him forgiveness, to whom he sayde: 'I forgive you with all my harte, and do thy parte without feare.' And bowing towarde the block he sayd, 'I have deserved a thousand deaths,' and therupon he made a crosse upon the strawe, and kyssed it, and layde his head upon the blocke, and so dyed.

Johann Bugenhagen Pomeranus:
1546

The Sermon at Martin Luther's Funeral

Paul, the holy apostle, says in 1 Thessalonians 4: 'We do not want to hold back, dear brothers, concerning those who are asleep so that you may not be sorrowful as the others who have no hope. For since we believe that Jesus has died and risen, even so, God will bring those with Him who have fallen asleep through Jesus.'

Dear friends, I am now supposed to preach a sermon at the funeral of our dearly beloved father, blessed Dr Martin, and gladly do so. But what shall I say and how shall I speak, since I probably will not be able to utter a word because of my tears? And who shall comfort you if I, your pastor and preacher, cannot speak? Where can I turn from you? I will, no doubt, cause more crying and mourning with my sermon. For how should we not all mourn heartily, since God has sent us this sorrow and has taken from us the noble and dear man, the venerable Dr Martin Luther?

Through him God has rendered inexpressible gifts and grace to all of us and to all the churches of Christ in Germany, as well as to many in foreign countries. Through him God has also triumphed gloriously over the kingdom of Satan and against so much shameful idolatry and human ordinance, indeed, as Paul says, against the devil's teachings throughout the world, and has revealed to us in the Gospel the sublime, great heavenly secret, his dear Son Jesus Christ (as Paul also says in Ephesians and Colossians). Through him, our dear father, Christ has defended his Gospel against the grievous pope and various rabble and tyrants, indeed, against all the portals of hell.

He gave to this dear man the spirit of power and strength so that he is afraid of no one, however great and mighty he may be. He held so boldly to the Gospel and to pure doctrine that the world often believed that he was too sharp and too excessive with his rebuking and scolding, just as the Jews and Pharisees, the bitter and poisonous vipers, accused Christ, for it hurt them severely and caused them pain that they were chastised by means of the pure truth. However, they did not accept the salutary teaching.

God has taken away from us this great teacher, prophet, and

divinely sent reformer of the church. Oh, how can we cease mourning and crying? How can we, after all, obey the dear Paul here when he says: 'You should not grieve because of those who are asleep'? But he adds immediately: 'Like the others who have no hope.' We who believe know that those who have fallen asleep in Christ will be awakened again to a better life where we will meet them again and be together with them eternally.

However, the world was not worthy to have this dear man of God any longer, to continue to slander and persecute him. Albeit, that same, ungrateful world received much good through this great man, especially that it has been freed from a variety of oppression and tyranny of the loathsome papacy. Therefore, many of the adversaries (who still have some wisdom and understanding) would have preferred that the dear man had continued to live for a long time.

This I have said initially, that we truly have great cause to mourn heartily since we have lost such a great and dear man. And truly (since this may help a bit) Christian kings, princes, and cities and all who have recognized the Gospel of truth mourn with us. Therefore, we do not mourn alone, but many thousands in Christendom mourn with us from time to time. It was not fitting that the current, grievous pope, the Cardinal of Mainz, or Duke Henry (all of whom he enraged mightily with the truth) should ever delight in the death of this man. And I hope that the adversaries will not delight in his death for long. For the person has indeed died in Christ, but the mighty, blessed, godly doctrine of this precious man still lives most powerfully.

For he was without doubt the angel concerning whom it is written in Revelation 14, who flew through the midst of heaven and had an eternal Gospel, etc., as the text says: 'And I saw an angel flying through the midst of heaven. He had an eternal Gospel to proclaim to those who sit and dwell on earth, to all heathen and races and languages and nations. And he said with a loud voice: "Fear God and give him honour, for the time of his judgment has come. Worship the one who has made heaven and earth, the seas and the springs of water." And another angel followed and said: "She has fallen, she has fallen, Babylon, the great city, for she has made drunk all the heathen with the wine of her harlotry."' This angel who says, 'Fear God and give him the honour,' was Dr Martin Luther. And what is written here, 'Fear God and give him the honour,' are the two parts of Dr Martin Luther's doctrine, the Law and the Gospel, through which all of Scripture is unlocked and Christ, our righteousness and eternal life, is recognized. To these two he has also added this passage ('the time of his judgment has come') and has taught regarding proper prayer and invocation of God the heavenly Father in Spirit and in truth. As the angel also says in Revelation 14: 'Worship the one who has made heaven and earth, etc.'

For after the teaching of this angel, another angel will follow, who will proclaim comfort to the sorrowful and persecuted church and the lightning and thunder of eternal judgment and condemnation against the adversaries, as, after all, the other angel said: 'She has fallen; she has fallen, Babylon, the great city.' Therefore, the adversaries will not rejoice long over our sorrow, as Christ also says in John 16: 'Your sorrow shall turn to joy.' For according to Revelation, the aforementioned fourteenth chapter, we see that this has happened before and still happens. If Revelation has some validity, then the other will, without doubt, follow.

But, oh, how do I ramble on so with my sermon in this time of our crying and sorrow? This is enough said about our rightful mourning, for we mourn justly that such a dear man, a proper bishop and shepherd of souls, has departed from us. But in this sorrow we should also rightly recognize God's grace and mercy to us and thank God that he has awakened for us through his Spirit this dear Dr Martin Luther against the antichristian doctrines of the abominable, satanic pope and against the devil's doctrines only one hundred years after the death of the holy John Hus (who was killed for the sake of the truth in the year 1415), just as John Hus himself prophesied before his death about a future swan. Hus means 'goose' in the Bohemian language. 'You are now roasting a goose,' (says John Hus), 'but God will awaken a swan whom you will not burn or roast.' And as they shouted much against him, which he could not answer, he supposedly said: 'After one hundred years I will answer you.' He has done that uprightly through our dear father, Dr Luther, and has begun it precisely in the one-hundred-and-first year. Yes, we should thank God that he preserved this dear man for us and his churches in the violent disputes, in so many difficult conflicts, and that through him Christ has triumphed so often now for almost thirty years. To the Lord Christ be praise and honour in eternity. Amen.

But we should also rejoice with our dear father Luther that he left and departed from us to the Lord Christ in the highest apostolic and prophetic office in which he faithfully accomplished what he was commanded. For with Christ are the holy patriarchs, prophets, apostles, and many to whom he preached the Gospel, all the holy angels, Lazarus in the bosom of Abraham, that is, in the eternal joy of all believers. We will experience what this interim period until the Day of Judgment is like, as Paul says in Philippians 1: 'I desire to depart and to be with Christ'; and as Stephen also says in Acts: 'Lord Jesus, receive my spirit'; and Jesus to the thief: 'Today you will be with me in paradise.'

For there is no doubt, just as the spirit of Christ was in the hands of the Father until the resurrection on Easter, since he said: 'Father, into your hands I commend my spirit, etc.,' so will our spirits be in the hands of Christ until our resurrection. For that is the meaning of the words of Lazarus: 'But now he is comforted while you are tormented.'

What kind of peace or comfort the believers have and what kind of anxiety or torment the unbelievers have in the meantime, until the day of judgment, we cannot say so precisely on the basis of Scripture. Scripture says that they are asleep, as Paul says in Thessalonians, 'concerning those who are asleep.' However, just as in natural sleep the healthy rest in a sweet sleep and are thereby refreshed and become stronger and healthier, while the sick or the sorrowing and especially those who are in the terror or fear of death sleep with difficulty, with horrible dreams, and restlessly so that sleep is not rest for them but a more frightful, more desolate unrest than being awake, in the same way there is a difference between the sleep of the believers and the godless. But about this we cannot speak further or infer other than what the words of Scripture say.

Our dear father Dr Martin Luther has now attained what he often desired. And if he were to return to us again now, he would reprimand our mourning and faint-heartedness with the word of Christ from John 16: 'If you loved me you would rejoice because I go to the Father, and you would not begrudge me this eternal rest and joy.' Christ has conquered death for us. Why, then, are we afraid? The death of the body is for us a beginning of life eternal through Jesus Christ our Lord, who has become for us a noble, precious sacrifice.

I still remember that when our honourable, dear father, Dr Martin Luther, saw several depart sweetly in the confession of Christ, he said: 'May God grant me that I may also depart so sweetly in the bosom of Christ and that the body may not be tormented with lengthy pains of death. But may God's will be done.'

Master Ambrosius Bernardus von Goterboch, my dear

brother and a truly pious man who loved Christ, was here with us in Wittenberg at the university. For several days before his end he lay very weak and sick unto death, and yet God took from him the feeling of his sickness as if he were already in another life. He spoke with us how he wanted to come to us and be joyous with us. He did not know at all that he was so ill and had to die. He certainly did not see death. Therefore, he could not be afraid of death. Indeed, he was no longer in this life except when one spoke of Christ. Then he confessed freely from his heart the great grace and bliss that has been given to us by the heavenly Father in Christ, for he loved Christ and was in the habit of praying gladly and of calling on God the Father in Spirit and truth. If one then wanted to tell him soon thereafter (as one who had come to his senses) about his beloved wife, children, house, money, debt, etc., he was soon out of his senses again and as if in another world, (although he recognized us all and called us by name), spoke joyously, with laughter and charming jest, concerning other matters in such a manner that one, who was unaware of his delirium, might think that he was wholly well and had to lie in bed because of boredom, etc. But our dear Lord Jesus Christ took him out of this life to himself in this state of delirium and yet in the good confession of the Christian faith. Thus he was already dead to this world for several days before he died, for he knew nothing on this earth of which he needed to be concerned. Indeed, he was relieved of everything so that he also did not experience his sickness and was not concerned about his death. Indeed, he also did not see death. How, then, could he be afraid of sin and death?

Thus we saw in him plainly the word of Christ from John 8 which every believer experiences: 'If someone keeps my word, that person will never see death.' For even if they do not all die so easily as this Ambrosius, but with great pain, as the Son of

God himself died on the cross, yet when the dear hour comes, they see life and not death and all of them say: 'Father, into your hands I commend my spirit.' In this way our Lord Jesus Christ took our dearly beloved father, Dr Martin, to himself with such a blessed parting from this vale of tears. To God be praise and thanks eternally.

During the illness of Master Ambrosius, when I saw that he also did not sleep, I asked two medical doctors that they prepare a strong drink to help him sleep. They responded that this would be dangerous and that they might be given blame if something went wrong. I said: 'I will be responsible even if he were to die. Give it to him in God's name as a desperate act. Who knows, it might help.' The doctors gave him such a drink, but not as strong as I desired, for they were somewhat concerned. Then he fell into a mighty sleep so that he slept almost two hours. However, when he awoke he felt his pain and complained about it and spoke intelligibly to his wife about all sorts of urgent matters. But soon thereafter, after about an hour-and-a-half, he was again in his happy condition, as before. He was no longer aware of this world until he gave up his spirit to Christ a few days later.

I have now gladly recounted this blessed and joyous story about Master Ambrosius, our dear brother, for two reasons. First of all, that I might stop you dear ones a bit from your howling and crying, which have now rightly overtaken us. God has made us sad. May his grace comfort us again.

Secondly, so that this story may be of help to us in the matter concerning which we are now speaking. For this Master Ambrosius was Dr Martin's brother-in-law. Therefore, Dr Martin visited him so much in his illness, and when he spoke with him about Christ, then Ambrosius also spoke about Christ according to the dear Gospel, as we have said. But when he wanted to speak to him about his wife, children, and goods, etc., Ambrosius knew nothing about such things but soon fantasized happily with unrelated words, as we have said before. He especially said to the Doctor with laughter and thanksgiving: 'Sir Doctor, thank you for visiting me. I will visit you again some evening. At that time we will have a good supper together, and I will then speak with you about many joyous matters.' Indeed, they may both be accomplishing this in the life eternal to which they have both travelled. In this life they were unable to meet in this way.

After Dr Martin left him, the Doctor said to me: 'He is gone and does not recognize death. When we want to counsel him how he should put his things in order, he no longer knows anything about this world and this life. Rather, he is happy, laughs, and proposes other things in his joyous delirium. He even mocks us with such words, as if he wanted to say: "I no longer know what to set in order or attend to on earth." May God also give me soon such a peaceful and blessed hour of death. What more should I accomplish on earth?'

After Master Ambrosius was buried in the harsh winter of January 1542, Dr Martin went to the grave with me not long thereafter. Then he pointed to the grave with his hand and said: 'He did not know that he was sick. He also did not know that he was dying and yet was not without a confession of Christ. Here he lies and still does not know that he is dead. Dear Lord Jesus Christ, take me also in similar fashion out of this vale of tears to you, etc.'

I often had to hear such things from my dear father, and when he noticed my annoyance, at times probably also from my words, he said to me: 'Implore our dear Lord God that He may soon take me to Himself from here. I can do nothing more on earth. I am no longer of use to you. Help me with your prayer. Do not ask that I live longer.' Now, everyone can, no doubt, imagine how I responded to such words of my dear father, our dearly beloved Doctor. All of this indicates how eagerly he desired, in his last days, to be rid of this miserable life and to be with Christ. Thereby he also sang his *consummatum est* and commended his spirit into the heavenly Father's hands.

There were also advance indications that our dear father, Dr Martin, would wander into a better life, for throughout this whole year he often said to us that he desired to go to another place. He also travelled more in this year before his death than he had done in many years, namely to his homeland in Mansfeld, to the Bishop of Zeitz, to Merseburg, to Halle. These were an indication and prophecy that he would undertake this blessed journey into a better life. Therefore, it also happened that he departed and left this life while he was with the noble and honourable Counts of Mansfeld in the city of Eisleben, where he was born and baptized. This was as he had desired, except that he would have preferred to be with us at that time, with his wife and children. But God ordained it otherwise.

Dear friends, so that you might also have a short report about our dearly beloved father, Dr Martin's, blessed parting, I will give it. When he noticed that his hour had come, he prayed thus: 'O my heavenly Father, one God and Father of our Lord Jesus Christ, God of all comfort, I thank you that you have revealed to me your dear Son, Jesus Christ, in whom I believe, whom I have preached and confessed, whom I have loved and praised, whom the loathsome pope and all the godless revile, persecute, and blaspheme. I implore you, my Lord Jesus Christ, let my little soul be commended to you. O heavenly Father, although I must leave this body and be snatched away from this life, I am, nevertheless, certain that I will remain with you eternally and that no one can tear me out of your hands.'

And then he said three times: 'Into your hands I commend

my spirit. You have redeemed me, you faithful God.' Also John 3: 'For God so loved the world that he gave his only-begotten Son so that all who believe in him will not be lost but have eternal life.'

Then he folded his hands and gave up his spirit to Christ in grand silence. Therefore we should also justly rejoice with him, as much as we are able to do so in our grief.

Here I must remember the holy Bishop, St Martin, concerning whom history says that all heretics turned pale and faded at the mention of his name. Furthermore, there was a great crying and mourning on the part of all believing and true Christians at the death of St Martin. Furthermore, a dispute and quarrel arose among several cities and territories about who should retain the body of St Martin and where he should be buried. All of this happened in similar fashion with this holy apostle and prophet of Christ, our preacher and evangelist in the German territories, Dr Martin. But about this I do not want to speak at length. God himself now holds him precious and beloved and sustains him in his bosom who in this life dearly loved us and the churches of Christ. May God requite it to our dearly beloved father in the life to come, where we all also hope to join him.

May God grant that the Spirit of God may also be spoken of doubly with regard to the descendants and in the churches planted by the dear father than was spoken of by the lofty, dear man, as the prophet Elisha petitioned from Elijah, who was taken from Elisha in a storm.

But if we fear or imagine that God has taken away the precious man because of our sin and ingratitude, then we should improve our life, petition God our heavenly Father through Christ that we remain in the blessed, pure teaching concerning faith and be protected through Christ from the rabble and tyrants and against all the portals of hell. Protect your poor Christendom, Lord Christ, that it may praise you eternally. Help us God our Saviour and rescue us for the honour of your name and have mercy on our sins for the sake of your holy name. Preserve in your church faithful and good preachers. Give them power and strength through the Holy Spirit, as Psalm 68 says: 'The Lord gives the Word with large numbers of evangelists.'

The impudent, atrocious, great blasphemies of the adversaries and the obdurate priests and monks and, in addition, our ingratitude may now well be the cause of great misfortune and God's punishment in the world. But we should petition God the Father in the name of the Son, our Lord Jesus Christ, that for his name's sake he may accomplish, fulfil, and bring about the epitaph and prophecy that our dear father, Dr Martin, himself made to him: *Pestis eram vivus, moriens tua mors ero Papa*. That is in German: 'Pope, pope, when I lived I was your pestilence. When I die I will be your bitter death.' God be praised eternally through Jesus Christ our Lord. Amen. Let us pray, etc.

Thomas Cranmer:
21 March 1556

Cranmer's Last Words

Thomas Cranmer was Archbishop of Canterbury and the compiler of the Book of Common Prayer. In Queen Mary's reign he was tried and condemned as a heretic. Before his execution, he signed recantations of the beliefs which were really his. He later insisted, prior to his matrydom: 'I recant of my recantations.'

'Good people – my dearly beloved brethren in Christ, I beseech you most heartily to pray for me to Almighty God, that he will forgive me all my sins and offences, which are without number, and great above measure. But yet one thing grieveth my conscience more than all the rest, whereof, God willing, I intend to speak more hereafter. But how great and how many soever my sins be, I beseech you to pray to God of his mercy to pardon and forgive them all.'

And here, kneeling down, he said the following prayer:

'O Father of heaven, O Son of God, Redeemer of the world, O Holy Ghost, three persons and one God, have mercy upon me, most wretched caitiff and miserable sinner. I have offended both against heaven and earth more than my tongue can express. Whither, then, may I go, or whither shall I flee? To heaven I may be ashamed to lift up mine eyes, and in earth I find no place of refuge or succour. To thee, therefore, O Lord, do I run; to thee do I humble myself, saying, O Lord my God, my sins be great, but yet have mercy upon me for thy great mercy. The great mystery that God became man was not wrought for little or few offences. Thou didst not give thy Son, O heavenly Father, unto death for small sins only, but for all the greatest sins of the world, so that the sinner return to thee with his whole heart, as I do at this present. Wherefore have mercy on me, O God, whose property is always to have mercy; have mercy upon me, O Lord, for thy great mercy. I crave nothing for mine own merits, but for thy name's sake. And now, O Father of heaven, hallowed be thy name.'

And after repeating the Lord's Prayer, he continued:

'Every man, good people, desireth at the time of his death to give some good exhortation, that others may remember the same before their death, and be the better thereby; so I beseech God grant me that I may speak something at this my departing, whereby God may be glorified, and you edified.

'First, it is a heavy cause to see that so many folk so much dote upon the love of this false world, and be so careful for it, that of the love of God, or the world to come, they seem to care very little or nothing. Therefore, this shall be my first exhortation: That you set not your minds over much upon this deceitful world, but upon God, and upon the world to come, and to learn to know what this lesson meaneth which St John teacheth, that the love of this world is hatred against God.

'The second exhortation is, That next unto God you obey your King and Queen, willingly and gladly.

'The third exhortation is, That you love altogether like brethren and sisters.

'The fourth exhortation shall be to them that have great substance and riches of this world, That they will well consider and weigh Luke 18:24, 1 John 3:17 and James 5:1–3. Let them that be rich ponder well these three sentences; for if they ever had occasion to show their charity, they have it now at this present, the poor people being so many, and victuals so dear.

'And now, forasmuch as I am come to the last end of my life, whereupon hangeth all my life past and all my life to come, either to live with my master Christ for ever in joy, or else to be in pain for ever with wicked devils in hell, and I see before my eyes presently either heaven ready to receive me, or else hell ready to swallow me up; I shall therefore declare to you my very faith – how I believe, without any colour of dissimulation, for now is no time to dissemble, whatsoever I have said or written in times past.

'First, I believe in God the Father Almighty, maker of heaven and earth etc. And I believe every article of the catholic faith, every word and sentence taught by our Saviour Jesus Christ, his apostles and prophets, in the New and Old Testament.

'And now I come to the great thing, that so much troubleth

my conscience, more than any thing that ever I did or said in my whole life; and this is the setting abroad of a writing contrary to the Truth; which now here I renounce and refuse, as things written with my hand, contrary to the truth which I thought in my heart, and written for fear of death, and to save my life, if it might be; and that is, all such bills and papers which I have written or signed with my hand since my degradation, wherein I have written many things untrue. And forasmuch as my hand offended, writing contrary to my heart, my hand shall first be punished therefore; for, may I come to the fire it shall be first burned.'

John Foxe, The Book of Martyrs, *pp. 401–15*

Elizabeth I:
1588

'I have the heart of a king'

One of the most powerful women who ever lived was Queen Elizabeth I of England (1533–1603). The daughter of King Henry VIII and Anne Boleyn, she was known as the Virgin Queen or Good Queen Bess. She spoke these words when she visited her troops in the field as they prepared to fight King Philip II of Spain's Armada.

My loving people, we have been persuaded by some, that are careful of our safety, to take heed how we commit ourselves to armed multitudes, for fear of treachery; but I assure you, I do not desire to live to distrust my faithful and loving people. Let tyrants fear; I have always so behaved myself that, under God, I have placed my chiefest strength and safeguard in the loyal hearts and good will of my subjects. And therefore I am come amongst you at this time, not as for my recreation or sport, but being resolved, in the midst and heat of the battle, to live or die amongst you all; to lay down, for my God, and for my kingdom, and for my people, my honour and my blood, even in the dust. I know I have but the body of a weak and feeble woman; but I have the heart of a king, and of a king of England, too; and think foul scorn that Parma or Spain, or any prince of Europe, should dare to invade the borders of my realms: to which, rather than any dishonour should grow by me, I myself will take up arms; I myself will be your general, judge, and rewarder of every one of your virtues in the field. I know already, by your forwardness, that you have deserved rewards and crowns; and we do assure you, on the word of a prince, they shall be duly paid you. In the mean my lieutenant general shall be in my stead, than whom never prince commanded a more noble and worthy subject; not doubting by your obedience to my general, by your concord in the camp, and by your valour in the field, we shall shortly have a famous victory over the enemies of my God, of my kingdom, and of my people.

John Winthrop:
1630

'We shall be as a city upon a hill'

Winthrop, known as 'the first great American', fled from the persecutions which Puritans had endured in England. The following extract is from a sermon (preached on board the *Arbella*) in which he outlined his ideals for government in the New World. American presidents such as Reagan and Kennedy have used extracts from this sermon in their own addresses. The section containing the words 'We shall be as a city upon a hill' is carved into a stone monument on Boston Common.

Thus stands the case between God and us. We are entered into a covenant with him for this work. We have taken out a commission. The Lord hath given us leave to draw our own articles. We have professed to enterprise these and those ends, upon these and those accounts. We have hereupon besought of him favor and blessing. Now if the Lord shall please to hear us, and bring us in peace to the place we desire, then hath he ratified this covenant and sealed our commission, and will expect a strict performance of the articles contained in it; but if we shall neglect the observation of these articles which are the ends we have propounded, and, dissembling with our God, shall fall to embrace this present world and prosecute our carnal intentions, seeking great things for ourselves and our prosperity, the Lord will surely break out in wrath against us; be revenged of such a people, and make us know the price of the breach of such a covenant.

Now the only way to avoid this shipwreck, and to provide for our posterity, is to follow the counsel of Micah, to do justly, to love mercy, to walk humbly with our God. For this end, we must be knit together, in this work, as one man. We must entertain each other in brotherly affection. We must be willing to abridge ourselves of our superfluities, for the supply of others' necessities. We must uphold a familiar commerce together in all meekness, gentleness, patience, and liberality. We must delight in each other; make others' conditions our own; rejoice together, always having before our eyes our commission and community in the work, as members of the same body. So shall we keep the unity of the spirit in the bond of peace. The Lord will be our God, and delight to dwell among us, as his own people, and will command a blessing upon us in all our ways. So that we shall see much more of his wisdom, power, goodness and truth, than formerly we have been acquainted with. We shall find that the God of Israel is among us, when ten of us shall be able to resist a thousand of our enemies; when he shall make us a praise and a glory, that men shall say of succeeding plantations, 'The Lord make it like that of New England.' For we must consider that we shall be as a city upon a hill. The eyes of all people are upon us.

So that if we shall deal falsely with our God in this work we have undertaken, and so cause him to withdraw his present help from us, we shall be made a story and a by-word throughout the world. We shall open the mouths of enemies to speak evil of the ways of God, and all professors for God's sake. We shall shame the face of many of God's worthy servants, and cause their prayers to be turned into curses upon us till we be consumed out of the good land whither we are a-going.

I shall shut up this discourse with that exhortation of Moses, that faithful servant of the Lord, in his last farewell to Israel in Deuteronomy chapter 30. Beloved, there is now set before us life and good, death and evil, in that we are commanded this day to love the Lord our God, and to love one another, to walk in his ways and to keep his commandments and his ordinance and his laws, and the articles of our covenant with him, that we may live and be multiplied, and that the Lord our God may bless us in the land whither we go to possess it. But if our hearts shall turn away, so that we will not obey, but shall be seduced, and worship and serve other gods, our pleasure and profits, and serve them; it is propounded to us this day, we shall surely perish out of the good land whither we pass over this vast sea to possess it; therefore let us choose life that we, and our seed may live, by obeying his voice and cleaving to him, for he is our life and our prosperity.

John Winthrop:

1645

On Liberty

Because of the principles espoused within it, Winthrop's acquittal speech before the General Court of the Massachusetts Bay Colony has become more important than the particular grievances against him.

I suppose something may be expected from me upon this charge that is befallen me, which moves me to speak now to you; yet I intend not to intermeddle in the proceedings of the court, or with any of the persons concerned therein. Only I bless God that I see an issue of this troublesome business. I also acknowledge the justice of the court, and, for mine own part, I am well satisfied, I was publicly charged, and I am publicly and legally acquitted, which is all I did expect or desire. And though this be sufficient for my justification before men, yet not so before the God who hath seen so much amiss in my dispensations (and even in this affair) as calls me to be humble. For to be publicly and criminally charged in this court is matter of humiliation (and I desire to make a right use of it), notwithstanding I be thus acquitted. 'If her father had spit in her face,' saith the Lord concerning Miriam, 'should she not have been ashamed seven days?' Shame had lien upon her, whatever the occasion had been. I am unwilling to stay you from your urgent affairs, yet give me leave (upon this special occasion) to speak a little more to this assembly. It may be of some good use to inform and rectify the judgments of some of the people, and may prevent such distempers as have arisen amongst us.

The great questions that have troubled the country are about the authority of the magistrates and the liberty of the people. It is yourselves who have called us to this office, and, being called by you, we have our authority from God, in way of an ordinance, such as hath the image of God eminently stamped upon it, the contempt and violation whereof hath been vindicated with examples of divine vengeance. I entreat you to consider that, when you choose magistrates, you take them from among yourselves, men subject to like passions as you are. Therefore, when you see infirmities in us, you should reflect upon your own, and that would make you bear the more with us, and not be severe censurers of the failings of your magistrates, when you have continual experience of the like infirmities in yourselves and others. We account him a good servant who breaks not his covenant. The covenant between you and us is the oath you have taken of us, which is to this purpose, that we shall govern you and judge your causes by the rules of God's laws and our own, according to our best skill. When you agree with a workman to build you a ship or house, etc., he undertakes as well for his skill as for his faithfulness; for it is his profession, and you pay him for both. But, when you call one to be a magistrate, he doth not profess nor undertake to have sufficient skill for that office, nor can you furnish him with gifts, etc., therefore you must run the hazard of his skill and ability. But if he fail in faithfulness, which by his oath he is bound unto, that he must answer for. If it fall out that the case be clear to common apprehension, and the rule clear also, if he transgress here, the error is not in the skill, but in the evil of the will: it must be required of him. But if the case be doubtful, or the rule doubtful, to men of such understanding and parts as your magistrates are, if your magistrates should err here, yourselves must bear it. If you stand for your natural corrupt liberties ... you will not endure the least weight of authority.

For the other point concerning liberty, I observe a great mistake in the country about that. There is a twofold liberty, natural (I mean as our nature is now corrupt) and civil or

love in all, and is refreshed, supported, and instructed by every such dispensation of his authority over her.

On the other side, ye know who they are that complain of this yoke and say, let us break their bands, etc., we will not have this man to rule over us. Even so, brethren, it will be between you and your magistrates. If you stand for your natural corrupt liberties, and will do what is good in your own eyes, you will not endure the least weight of authority, but will murmur, and oppose, and be always striving to shake off that yoke; but if you will be satisfied to enjoy such civil and lawful liberties, such as Christ allows you, then will you quietly and cheerfully submit unto that authority which is set over you, in all the administrations of it, for your good. Wherein, if we fail at any time, we hope we shall be willing (by God's assistance) to hearken to good advice from any of you, or in any other way of God; so shall your liberties be preserved, in upholding the honor and power of authority amongst you.

PART III

The Eighteenth Century

King William III:
31 December 1701

'The quiet enjoyment of your Religion and Liberties'

King William III of England made the following address to Parliament on the 'French Question'.

My Lords and Gentlemen; I promise myself you are met together full of that just sense of the common danger of Europe, and the resentment of the late proceedings of the French king, which has been so fully and universally expressed in the loyal and seasonable Addresses of my people. The owning and setting up the pretended Prince of Wales for king of England, is not only the highest indignity offered to me and the nation, but does so nearly concern every man, who has a regard for the Protestant Religion, or the present and future quiet and happiness of his country, that I need not press you to lay it seriously to heart, and to consider what further effectual means may be used, for securing the Succession of the Crown in the Protestant line, and extinguishing the hopes of all Pretenders, and their open and secret abettors. By the French king's placing his Grandson on the throne of Spain, he is in a condition to oppress the rest of Europe, unless speedy and effectual measures be taken. Under this pretence, he is become the real Master of the whole Spanish Monarchy; he has made it to be entirely depending on France, and disposes of it, as of his own dominions, and by that means he has surrounded his neighbours in such a manner, that, though the name of peace may be said to continue, yet they are put to the expence and inconveniencies of war. This must affect England in the nearest and most sensible manner, in respect to our trade, which will soon become precarious in all the variable branches of it; in respect to our peace and safety at home, which we cannot hope should long continue; and in respect to that part, which England ought to take in the preservation of the liberty of Europe.

In order to obviate the general calamity, with which the rest of Christendom is threatened by this exorbitant power of France, I have concluded several Alliances, according to the encouragement given me by both houses of Parliament, which I will direct shall be laid before you, and which, I doubt not, you will enable me to make good. There are some other Treaties still depending, that shall be likewise communicated to you as soon as they are perfected. It is fit I should tell you, the eyes of all Europe are upon this Parliament; all matters are at a stand, till your resolutions are known; and therefore no time ought to be lost. You have yet an opportunity, by God's blessing, to secure to you and your posterity the quiet enjoyment of your Religion and Liberties, if you are not wanting to yourselves, but will exert the ancient vigour of the English nation; but I tell you plainly, my opinion is, if you do not lay hold on this occasion, you have no reason to hope for another. In order to do your part, it will be necessary to have a great strength at sea, and to provide for the security of our ships in harbour; and also that there be such a force at land, as is expected in proportion to the forces of our Allies.

Gentlemen of the House of Commons; I do recommend these matters to you with that concern and earnestness, which their importance requires. At the same time I cannot but press you to take care of the public credit, which cannot be preserved but by keeping sacred that maxim, that they shall never be losers, who trust to a Parliamentary security. It is always with regret, when I do ask aids of my people; but you will observe, that I desire nothing, which relates to any personal expence of mine; I am only pressing you to do all you can for your own safety and honour, at so critical and dangerous a time; and am willing, that what is given, should be wholly appropriated to the purposes for which it is intended ...

I should think it as great a blessing as could befall England, if I could observe you as much inclined to lay aside those unhappy fatal animosities, which divide and weaken you, as I am disposed to make all my subjects safe and easy as to any, even the highest offences, committed against me. Let me conjure you to disappoint the only hopes of our enemies by your unanimity. I have shewn, and will always shew, how desirous I am to be the common father of all my people. Do you, in like manner, lay aside parties and divisions. Let there be no other distinction heard of amongst us for the future, but of those, who are for the Protestant Religion, and the present establishment, and of those, who mean a Popish Prince, and a French government. I will only add this; if you do in good earnest desire to see England hold the balance of Europe, and to be indeed at the head of the Protestant interest, it will appear by your right improving the present opportunity.

Jonathan Edwards:

8 July 1741

Sinners in the Hands of an Angry God

Jonathan Edwards (1703–58), American theologian and metaphysician, gained a wide following by his forceful preaching and powerful logic in support of Calvinist doctrine. The revival meetings that he held in 1734 and 1735 effectively brought the 'Great Awakening' to New England. He is often regarded as the last great New England Calvinist, and his sermon

'Sinners in the Hands of an Angry God', originally preached at Enfield, Massachusetts, is still read today.

'Their foot shall slide in due time' (Deuteronomy 32:35). In this verse is threatened the vengeance of God on the wicked unbelieving Israelites, who were God's visible people, and who lived under the means of grace; but who, notwithstanding all God's wonderful works towards them, remained (as verse 28) void of counsel, having no understanding in them. Under all the cultivations of heaven, they brought forth bitter and poisonous fruit; as in the two verses next preceding the text.

The expression I have chosen for my text, 'Their foot shall slide in due time', seems to imply the following things, relating to the punishment and destruction to which these wicked Israelites were exposed.

1. That they were always exposed to destruction; as one that stands or walks in slippery places is always exposed to fall. This is implied in the manner of their destruction coming upon them, being represented by their foot sliding. The same is expressed, Psalm 72:18: 'Surely thou didst set them in slippery places; thou castedst them down into destruction.'

2. It implies, that they were always exposed to sudden unexpected destruction. As he that walks in slippery places is every moment liable to fall, he cannot foresee one moment whether he shall stand or fall the next; and when he does fall, he falls at once without warning: Which is also expressed in Psalm 73:18–19: 'Surely thou didst set them in slippery places; thou castedst them down into destruction: How are they brought into desolation as in a moment!'

3. Another thing implied is, that they are liable to fall of themselves, without being thrown down by the hand of another; as he that stands or walks on slippery ground needs nothing but his own weight to throw him down.

4. That the reason why they are not fallen already and do not fall now is only that God's appointed time is not come. For it is said, that when that due time, or appointed time comes, their foot shall slide. Then they shall be left to fall, as they are inclined by their own weight. God will not hold them up in these slippery places any longer, but will let them go; and then, at that very instant, they shall fall into destruction; as he that stands on such slippery declining ground, on the edge of a pit, he cannot stand alone, when he is let go he immediately falls and is lost.

The observation from the words that I would now insist upon is this. – 'There is nothing that keeps wicked men at any one moment out of hell, but the mere pleasure of God.' – By the mere pleasure of God, I mean his sovereign pleasure, his arbitrary will, restrained by no obligation, hindered by no manner of difficulty, any more than if nothing else but God's mere will had in the least degree, or in any respect whatsoever, any hand in the preservation of wicked men one moment. – The truth of this observation may appear by the following considerations.

1. There is no want of power in God to cast wicked men into hell at any moment. Men's hands cannot be strong when God rises up. The strongest have no power to resist him, nor can any deliver out of his hands. – He is not only able to cast wicked men into hell, but he can most easily do it. Sometimes an earthly prince meets with a great deal of difficulty to subdue a rebel, who has found means to fortify himself, and has made himself strong by the numbers of his followers. But it is not so with God. There is no fortress that is any defence from the power of God. Though hand join in hand, and vast multitudes of God's enemies combine and associate themselves, they are easily broken in pieces. They are as great heaps of light chaff before the whirlwind; or large quantities of dry stubble before devouring

flames. We find it easy to tread on and crush a worm that we see crawling on the earth; so it is easy for us to cut or singe a slender thread that any thing hangs by: thus easy is it for God, when he pleases, to cast his enemies down to hell. What are we, that we should think to stand before him, at whose rebuke the earth trembles, and before whom the rocks are thrown down?

2. They deserve to be cast into hell; so that divine justice never stands in the way, it makes no objection against God's using his power at any moment to destroy them. Yea, on the contrary, justice calls aloud for an infinite punishment of their sins. Divine justice says of the tree that brings forth such grapes of Sodom, 'Cut it down, why cumbereth it the ground?' (Luke 13:7). The sword of divine justice is every moment brandished over their heads, and it is nothing but the hand of arbitrary mercy, and God's mere will, that holds it back.

3. They are already under a sentence of condemnation to hell. They do not only justly deserve to be cast down thither, but the sentence of the law of God, that eternal and immutable rule of righteousness that God has fixed between him and mankind, is gone out against them, and stands against them; so that they are bound over already to hell. John 3:18: 'He that believeth not is condemned already.' So that every unconverted man properly belongs to hell; that is his place; from thence he is, John 8:23: 'Ye are from beneath'. And thither he is bound; it is the place that justice, and God's word, and the sentence of his unchangeable law assign to him.

4. They are now the objects of that very same anger and wrath of God, that is expressed in the torments of hell. And the reason why they do not go down to hell at each moment, is not because God, in whose power they are, is not then very angry with them; as he is with many miserable creatures now tormented in hell, who there feel and bear the fierceness of his

wrath. Yea, God is a great deal more angry with great numbers that are now on earth: yea, doubtless, with many that are now in this congregation, who it may be are at ease, than he is with many of those who are now in the flames of hell.

So that it is not because God is unmindful of their wickedness, and does not resent it, that he does not let loose his hand and cut them off. God is not altogether such an one as themselves, though they may imagine him to be so. The wrath of God burns against them, their damnation does not slumber; the pit is prepared, the fire is made ready, the furnace is now hot, ready to receive them; the flames do now rage and glow. The glittering sword is whet, and held over them, and the pit hath opened its mouth under them.

5. The devil stands ready to fall upon them, and seize them as his own, at what moment God shall permit him. They belong to him; he has their souls in his possession, and under his dominion. The scripture represents them as his goods (Luke 11:12). The devils watch them; they are ever by them at their right hand; they stand waiting for them, like greedy hungry lions that see their prey, and expect to have it, but are for the present kept back. If God should withdraw his hand, by which they are restrained, they would in one moment fly upon their poor souls. The old serpent is gaping for them; hell opens its mouth wide to receive them; and if God should permit it, they would be hastily swallowed up and lost.

6. There are in the souls of wicked men those hellish principles reigning, that would presently kindle and flame out into hell fire, if it were not for God's restraints. There is laid in the very nature of carnal men, a foundation for the torments of hell. There are those corrupt principles, in reigning power in them, and in full possession of them, that are seeds of hell fire. These principles are active and powerful, exceeding violent in their

nature, and if it were not for the restraining hand of God upon them, they would soon break out, they would flame out after the same manner as the same corruptions, the same enmity does in the hearts of damned souls, and would beget the same torments as they do in them. The souls of the wicked are in scripture compared to the troubled sea (Isaiah 57:20). For the present, God restrains their wickedness by his mighty power, as he does the raging waves of the troubled sea, saying, 'Hitherto shalt thou come, but no further;' but if God should withdraw that restraining power, it would soon carry all before it. Sin is the ruin and misery of the soul; it is destructive in its nature; and if God should leave it without restraint, there would need nothing else to make the soul perfectly miserable. The corruption of the heart of man is immoderate and boundless in its fury; and while wicked men live here, it is like fire pent up by God's restraints, whereas if it were let loose, it would set on fire the course of nature; and as the heart is now a sink of sin, so if sin was not restrained, it would immediately turn the soul into fiery oven, or a furnace of fire and brimstone.

7. It is no security to wicked men for one moment, that there are no visible means of death at hand. It is no security to a natural man, that he is now in health, and that he does not see which way he should now immediately go out of the world by any accident, and that there is no visible danger in any respect in his circumstances. The manifold and continual experience of the world in all ages, shows this is no evidence, that a man is not on the very brink of eternity, and that the next step will not be into another world. The unseen, unthought-of ways and means of persons going suddenly out of the world are innumerable and inconceivable. Unconverted men walk over the pit of hell on a rotten covering, and there are innumerable places in this covering so weak that they will not bear their weight, and these

places are not seen. The arrows of death fly unseen at noon-day; the sharpest sight cannot discern them. God has so many different unsearchable ways of taking wicked men out of the world and sending them to hell, that there is nothing to make it appear, that God had need to be at the expense of a miracle, or go out of the ordinary course of his providence, to destroy any wicked man, at any moment. All the means that there are of sinners going out of the world, are so in God's hands, and so universally and absolutely subject to his power and determination, that it does not depend at all the less on the mere will of God, whether sinners shall at any moment go to hell, than if means were never made use of, or at all concerned in the case.

8. Natural men's prudence and care to preserve their own lives, or the care of others to preserve them, do not secure them a moment. To this, divine providence and universal experience do also bear testimony. There is this clear evidence that men's own wisdom is no security to them from death; that if it were otherwise we should see some difference between the wise and politic men of the world, and others, with regard to their liableness to early and unexpected death: but how is it in fact? Eccles. 2:16: 'How dieth the wise man? even as the fool.'

9. All wicked men's pains and contrivance which they use to escape hell, while they continue to reject Christ, and so remain wicked men, do not secure them from hell one moment. Almost every natural man that hears of hell, flatters himself that he shall escape it; he depends upon himself for his own security; he flatters himself in what he has done, in what he is now doing, or what he intends to do. Every one lays out matters in his own mind how he shall avoid damnation, and flatters himself that he contrives well for himself, and that his schemes will not fail. They hear indeed that there are but few saved, and that the greater part of men that have died heretofore are gone to hell;

but each one imagines that he lays out matters better for his own escape than others have done. He does not intend to come to that place of torment; he says within himself, that he intends to take effectual care, and to order matters so for himself as not to fail.

But the foolish children of men miserably delude themselves in their own schemes, and in confidence in their own strength and wisdom; they trust to nothing but a shadow. The greater part of those who heretofore have lived under the same means of grace, and are now dead, are undoubtedly gone to hell; and it was not because they were not as wise as those who are now alive: it was not because they did not lay out matters as well for themselves to secure their own escape. If we could speak with them, and inquire of them, one by one, whether they expected, when alive, and when they used to hear about hell, ever to be the subjects of misery: we doubtless, should hear one and another reply, 'No, I never intended to come here: I had laid out matters otherwise in my mind; I thought I should contrive well for myself – I thought my scheme good. I intended to take effectual care; but it came upon me unexpected; I did not look for it at that time, and in that manner; it came as a thief – Death outwitted me: God's wrath was too quick for me. Oh, my cursed foolishness! I was flattering myself, and pleasing myself with vain dreams of what I would do hereafter; and when I was saying, Peace and safety, then sudden destruction came upon me.'

10. God has laid himself under no obligation, by any promise to keep any natural man out of hell one moment. God certainly has made no promises either of eternal life, or of any deliverance or preservation from eternal death, but what are contained in the covenant of grace, the promises that are given in Christ, in whom all the promises are yea and amen. But surely they have no interest in the promises of the covenant of grace

who are not the children of the covenant, who do not believe in any of the promises, and have no interest in the Mediator of the covenant.

So that, whatever some have imagined and pretended about promises made to natural men's earnest seeking and knocking, it is plain and manifest, that whatever pains a natural man takes in religion, whatever prayers he makes, till he believes in Christ, God is under no manner of obligation to keep him a moment from eternal destruction.

So that, thus it is that natural men are held in the hand of God, over the pit of hell; they have deserved the fiery pit, and are already sentenced to it; and God is dreadfully provoked, his anger is as great towards them as to those that are actually suffering the executions of the fierceness of his wrath in hell, and they have done nothing in the least to appease or abate that anger, neither is God in the least bound by any promise to hold them up one moment; the devil is waiting for them, hell is gaping for them, the flames gather and flash about them, and would fain lay hold on them, and swallow them up; the fire pent up in their own hearts is struggling to break out: and they have no interest in any Mediator, there are no means within reach that can be any security to them. In short, they have no refuge, nothing to take hold of; all that preserves them every moment is the mere arbitrary will, and uncovenanted, unobliged forbearance of an incensed God.

The application

The use of this awful subject may be for awakening unconverted persons in this congregation. This that you have heard is the case of every one of you that are out of Christ. – That world of misery, that lake of burning brimstone, is extended abroad under you. There is the dreadful pit of the glowing flames of the wrath of God; there is hell's wide gaping mouth open; and you have nothing to stand upon, nor any thing to take hold of; there is nothing between you and hell but the air; it is only the power and mere pleasure of God that holds you up.

You probably are not sensible of this; you find you are kept out of hell, but do not see the hand of God in it; but look at other things, as the good state of your bodily constitution, your care of your own life, and the means you use for your own preservation. But indeed these things are nothing; if God should withdraw his hand, they would avail no more to keep you from falling, than the thin air to hold up a person that is suspended in it.

Your wickedness makes you as it were heavy as lead, and to tend downwards with great weight and pressure towards hell; and if God should let you go, you would immediately sink and swiftly descend and plunge into the bottomless gulf, and your healthy constitution, and your own care and prudence, and best contrivance, and all your righteousness, would have no more influence to uphold you and keep you out of hell, than a spider's web would have to stop a falling rock. Were it not for the sovereign pleasure of God, the earth would not bear you one moment; for you are a burden to it; the creation groans with you; the creature is made subject to the bondage of your corruption, not willingly; the sun does not willingly shine upon you to give you light to serve sin and Satan; the earth does not willingly yield her increase to satisfy your lusts; nor is it willingly a stage for your wickedness to be acted upon; the air does not willingly serve you for breath to maintain the flame of life in your vitals, while you spend your life in the service of God's enemies. God's creatures are good, and were made for men to serve God with, and do not willingly subserve to any other purpose, and groan when they are abused to purposes so directly contrary to their nature and end. And the world would spew you out, were it not for the sovereign hand of him who hath subjected it in hope. There are the black clouds of God's wrath now hanging directly over your heads, full of the dreadful storm, and big with thunder; and were it not for the restraining hand of God, it would immediately burst forth upon you. The sovereign pleasure of God, for the present, stays his rough wind; otherwise it would come with fury, and your destruction would come like a whirlwind, and you would be like the chaff of the summer threshing floor.

The wrath of God is like great waters that are dammed for the present; they increase more and more, and rise higher and higher, till an outlet is given; and the longer the stream is stopped, the more rapid and mighty is its course, when once it is let loose. It is true, that judgment against your evil works has not been executed hitherto; the floods of God's vengeance have been withheld; but your guilt in the mean time is constantly increasing, and you are every day treasuring up more wrath; the waters are constantly rising, and waxing more and more mighty; and there is nothing but the mere pleasure of God, that holds the waters back, that are unwilling to be stopped, and press hard to go forward. If God should only withdraw his hand from the flood-gate, it would immediately fly open, and the fiery floods of the fierceness and wrath of God, would rush forth with inconceivable fury, and would come upon you with omnipotent power; and if your strength were ten thousand times greater than it is, yea, ten thousand times greater than the strength of the stoutest, sturdiest devil in hell, it would be nothing to withstand or endure it.

The bow of God's wrath is bent, and the arrow made ready on the string, and justice bends the arrow at your heart, and strains the bow, and it is nothing but the mere pleasure of God, and that of an angry God, without any promise or obligation at all, that keeps the arrow one moment from being made drunk with your blood. Thus all you that never passed under a great change of heart, by the mighty power of the Spirit of God upon your souls; all you that were never born again, and made new creatures, and raised from being dead in sin, to a state of new, and before altogether unexperienced light and life, are in the hands of an angry God. However you may have reformed your life in many things, and may have had religious affections, and may keep up a form of religion in your families and closets, and in the house of God, it is nothing but his mere pleasure that keeps you from being this moment swallowed up in everlasting destruction. However unconvinced you may now be of the truth of what you hear, by and by you will be fully convinced of it. Those that are gone from being in the like circumstances with you, see that it was so with them; for destruction came suddenly upon most of them; when they expected nothing of it, and while they were saying, Peace and safety: now they see, that those things on which they depended for peace and safety, were nothing but thin air and empty shadows.

The God that holds you over the pit of hell, much as one holds a spider, or some loathsome insect over the fire, abhors you, and is dreadfully provoked: his wrath towards you burns like fire; he looks upon you as worthy of nothing else, but to be cast into the fire; he is of purer eyes than to bear to have you in his sight; you are ten thousand times more abominable in his eyes, than the most hateful venomous serpent is in ours. You have offended him infinitely more than ever a stubborn rebel did his prince; and yet it is nothing but his hand that holds you from falling into the fire every moment. It is to be ascribed to nothing else, that you did not go to hell the last night; that you was suffered to awake again in this world, after you closed your

majesty and strength, and when clothed in their greatest terrors, are but feeble, despicable worms of the dust, in comparison of the great and almighty Creator and King of heaven and earth. It is but little that they can do, when most enraged, and when they have exerted the utmost of their fury. All the kings of the earth, before God, are as grasshoppers; they are nothing, and less than nothing: both their love and their hatred is to be despised. The wrath of the great King of kings, is as much more terrible than theirs, as his majesty is greater. Luke 12:4–5: 'And I say unto you, my friends, Be not afraid of them that kill the body, and after that, have no more that they can do. But I will forewarn you whom you shall fear: fear him, which after he hath killed, hath power to cast into hell: yea, I say unto you, Fear him.'

2. It is the fierceness of his wrath that you are exposed to. We often read of the fury of God; as in Isaiah 59:18: 'According to their deeds, accordingly he will repay fury to his adversaries.' So Isaiah 66:15: 'For behold, the Lord will come with fire, and with his chariots like a whirlwind, to render his anger with fury, and his rebuke with flames of fire.' And in many other places. So, Revelation 19:15, we read of 'the wine press of the fierceness and wrath of Almighty God.' The words are exceeding terrible. If it had only been said, 'the wrath of God,' the words would have implied that which is infinitely dreadful: but it is 'the fierceness and wrath of God.' The fury of God! the fierceness of Jehovah! Oh, how dreadful that must be! Who can utter or conceive what such expressions carry in them! But it is also 'the fierceness and wrath of almighty God.' As though there would be a very great manifestation of his almighty power in what the fierceness of his wrath should inflict, as though omnipotence should be as it were enraged, and exerted, as men are wont to exert their strength in the fierceness of their wrath. Oh! then, what will be the consequence! What will become of the poor

worms that shall suffer it! Whose hands can be strong? And whose heart can endure? To what a dreadful, inexpressible, inconceivable depth of misery must the poor creature be sunk who shall be the subject of this!

Consider this, you that are here present, that yet remain in an unregenerate state. That God will execute the fierceness of his anger, implies, that he will inflict wrath without any pity. When God beholds the ineffable extremity of your case, and sees your torment to be so vastly disproportionate to your strength, and sees how your poor soul is crushed, and sinks down, as it were, into an infinite gloom; he will have no compassion upon you, he will not forbear the executions of his wrath, or in the least lighten his hand; there shall be no moderation or mercy, nor will God then at all stay his rough wind; he will have no regard to your welfare, nor be at all careful lest you should suffer too much in any other sense, than only that you shall not suffer beyond what strict justice requires. Nothing shall be withheld, because it is so hard for you to bear. Ezekiel 8:18: 'Therefore will I also deal in fury: mine eye shall not spare, neither will I have pity; and though they cry in mine ears with a loud voice, yet I will not hear them.' Now God stands ready to pity you; this is a day of mercy; you may cry now with some encouragement of obtaining mercy. But when once the day of mercy is past, your most lamentable and dolorous cries and shrieks will be in vain; you will be wholly lost and thrown away of God, as to any regard to your welfare. God will have no other use to put you to, but to suffer misery; you shall be continued in being to no other end; for you will be a vessel of wrath fitted to destruction; and there will be no other use of this vessel, but to be filled full of wrath. God will be so far from pitying you when you cry to him, that it is said he will only 'laugh and mock' (Prov. 1:25–26).

How awful are those words, Isaiah 63:3, which are the

words of the great God: 'I will tread them in mine anger, and will trample them in my fury, and their blood shall be sprinkled upon my garments, and I will stain all my raiment.' It is perhaps impossible to conceive of words that carry in them greater manifestations of these three things, viz. contempt, and hatred, and fierceness of indignation. If you cry to God to pity you, he will be so far from pitying you in your doleful case, or showing you the least regard or favour, that instead of that, he will only tread you under foot. And though he will know that you cannot bear the weight of omnipotence treading upon you, yet he will not regard that, but he will crush you under his feet without mercy; he will crush out your blood, and make it fly, and it shall be sprinkled on his garments, so as to stain all his raiment. He will not only hate you, but he will have you in the utmost contempt: no place shall be thought fit for you, but under his feet to be trodden down as the mire of the streets.

3. The misery you are exposed to is that which God will inflict to that end, that he might show what that wrath of Jehovah is. God hath had it on his heart to show to angels and men, both how excellent his love is, and also how terrible his wrath is. Sometimes earthly kings have a mind to show how terrible their wrath is, by the extreme punishments they would execute on those that would provoke them. Nebuchadnezzar, that mighty and haughty monarch of the Chaldean empire, was willing to show his wrath when enraged with Shadrach, Meshach, and Abednego; and accordingly gave orders that the burning fiery furnace should be heated seven times hotter than it was before; doubtless, it was raised to the utmost degree of fierceness that human art could raise it. But the great God is also willing to show his wrath, and magnify his awful majesty and mighty power in the extreme sufferings of his enemies. Romans 9:22: 'What if God, willing to show his wrath, and to make his power

known, endured with much long-suffering the vessels of wrath fitted to destruction?' And seeing this is his design, and what he has determined, even to show how terrible the unrestrained wrath, the fury and fierceness of Jehovah is, he will do it to effect. There will be something accomplished and brought to pass that will be dreadful with a witness. When the great and angry God hath risen up and executed his awful vengeance on the poor sinner, and the wretch is actually suffering the infinite weight and power of his indignation, then will God call upon the whole universe to behold that awful majesty and mighty power that is to be seen in it. Isaiah 33:12–14: 'And the people shall be as the burnings of lime, as thorns cut up shall they be burnt in the fire. Hear ye that are far off, what I have done; and ye that are near, acknowledge my might. The sinners in Zion are afraid; fearfulness hath surprised the hypocrites.'

Thus it will be with you that are in an unconverted state, if you continue in it; the infinite might, and majesty, and terribleness of the omnipotent God shall be magnified upon you, in the ineffable strength of your torments. You shall be tormented in the presence of the holy angels, and in the presence of the Lamb; and when you shall be in this state of suffering, the glorious inhabitants of heaven shall go forth and look on the awful spectacle, that they may see what the wrath and fierceness of the Almighty is; and when they have seen it, they will fall down and adore that great power and majesty. Isaiah 66:23–24: 'And it shall come to pass, that from one new moon to another, and from one sabbath to another, shall all flesh come to worship before me, saith the Lord. And they shall go forth and look upon the carcasses of the men that have transgressed against me; for their worm shall not die, neither shall their fire be quenched, and they shall be an abhorring unto all flesh.'

4. It is everlasting wrath. It would be dreadful to suffer this

fierceness and wrath of Almighty God one moment; but you must suffer it to all eternity. There will be no end to this exquisite horrible misery. When you look forward, you shall see a long for ever, a boundless duration before you, which will swallow up your thoughts, and amaze your soul; and you will absolutely despair of ever having any deliverance, any end, any mitigation, any rest at all. You will know certainly that you must wear out long ages, millions of millions of ages, in wrestling and conflicting with this almighty merciless vengeance; and then when you have so done, when so many ages have actually been spent by you in this manner, you will know that all is but a point to what remains. So that your punishment will indeed be infinite. Oh, who can express what the state of a soul in such circumstances is! All that we can possibly say about it, gives but a very feeble, faint representation of it; it is inexpressible and inconceivable: For 'who knows the power of God's anger?'

How dreadful is the state of those that are daily and hourly in the danger of this great wrath and infinite misery! But this is the dismal case of every soul in this congregation that has not been born again, however moral and strict, sober and religious, they may otherwise be. Oh that you would consider it, whether you be young or old! There is reason to think, that there are many in this congregation now hearing this discourse, that will actually be the subjects of this very misery to all eternity. We know not who they are, or in what seats they sit, or what thoughts they now have. It may be they are now at ease, and hear all these things without much disturbance, and are now flattering themselves that they are not the persons, promising themselves that they shall escape. If we knew that there was one person, and but one, in the whole congregation, that was to be the subject of this misery, what an awful thing would it be to think of! If we knew who it was, what an awful sight would it be to see such a person! How might all the rest of the congregation lift up a lamentable and bitter cry over him! But, alas! instead of one, how many is it likely will remember this discourse in hell? And it would be a wonder, if some that are now present should not be in hell in a very short time, even before this year is out. And it would be no wonder if some persons, that now sit here, in some seats of this meeting-house, in health, quiet and secure, should be there before tomorrow morning. Those of you that finally continue in a natural condition, that shall keep out of hell longest will be there in a little time! your damnation does not slumber; it will come swiftly, and, in all probability, very suddenly upon many of you. You have reason to wonder that you are not already in hell. It is doubtless the case of some whom you have seen and known, that never deserved hell more than you, and that heretofore appeared as likely to have been now alive as you. Their case is past all hope; they are crying in extreme misery and perfect despair; but here you are in the land of the living and in the house of God, and have an opportunity to obtain salvation. What would not those poor damned hopeless souls give for one day's opportunity such as you now enjoy!

And now you have an extraordinary opportunity, a day wherein Christ has thrown the door of mercy wide open, and stands in calling and crying with a loud voice to poor sinners; a day wherein many are flocking to him, and pressing into the kingdom of God. Many are daily coming from the east, west, north and south; many that were very lately in the same miserable condition that you are in, are now in a happy state, with their hearts filled with love to him who has loved them, and washed them from their sins in his own blood, and rejoicing in hope of the glory of God. How awful is it to be left behind at such a day! To see so many others feasting, while you are pining and perishing! To see so many rejoicing and singing for joy of the Lord, a day of such great favour to some, will doubtless be a day of as remarkable vengeance to others. Men's hearts harden, and their guilt increases apace at such a day as this, if they neglect their souls; and never was there so great danger of such persons being given up to hardness of heart and blindness of mind. God seems now to be hastily gathering in his elect in all parts of the land; and probably the greater part of adult persons that ever shall be saved, will be brought in now in a little time, and that it will be as it was on the great out-pouring of the Spirit upon the Jews in the apostles' days; the election will obtain, and the rest will be blinded. If this should be the case with you, you will eternally curse this day, and will curse the day that ever you were born, to see such a season of the pouring out of God's Spirit, and will wish that you had died and gone to hell before you had seen it. Now undoubtedly it is, as it was in the days of John the Baptist, the axe is in an extraordinary manner laid at the root of the trees, that every tree which brings not forth good fruit, may be hewn down and cast into the fire.

Therefore, let every one that is out of Christ, now awake and fly from the wrath to come. The wrath of Almighty God is now undoubtedly hanging over a great part of this congregation. Let every one fly out of Sodom: 'Haste and escape for your lives, look not behind you, escape to the mountain, lest you be consumed.'

John Wesley:
1747

'Ye must be born again'

John Wesley (1703–91), an English evangelical preacher and the founder of Methodism, is said to have preached 40,000 sermons in his lifetime, and travelled over 10,000 miles on horseback each year in his evangelistic work.

'Ye must be born again' (John 3:7).

1. If any doctrines within the whole compass of Christianity may be properly termed fundamental, they are doubtless these two – the doctrine of justification, and that of the new birth: The former relating to that great work which God does for us, in forgiving our sins; the latter, to the great work which God does in us, in renewing our fallen nature. In order of time, neither of these is before the other: in the moment we are justified by the grace of God, through the redemption that is in Jesus, we are also 'born of the Spirit'; but in order of thinking, as it is termed, justification precedes the new birth. We first conceive his wrath to be turned away, and then his Spirit to work in our hearts.

2. How great importance then must it be of, to every child of man, thoroughly to understand these fundamental doctrines! From a full conviction of this, many excellent men have wrote very largely concerning justification, explaining every point relating thereto, and opening the Scriptures which treat upon it. Many likewise have wrote on the new birth: And some of them largely enough; but yet not so clearly as might have been desired, nor so deeply and accurately; having either given a dark, abstruse account of it, or a slight and superficial one. Therefore a full, and at the same time a clear, account of the new birth, seems to be wanting still; such as may enable us to give a satisfactory answer to these three questions: First, Why must we

was not made immutable. This would have been inconsistent with the state of trial in which God was pleased to place him. He was therefore created able to stand, and yet liable to fall. And this God himself apprized him of, and gave him a solemn warning against it. Nevertheless, man did not abide in honour: He fell from his high estate. He 'ate of the tree whereof the Lord had commanded him, "Thou shalt not eat thereof."' By this wilful act of disobedience to his Creator, this flat rebellion against his Sovereign, he openly declared that he would no longer have God to rule over him; That he would be governed by his own will, and not the will of Him that created him; and that he would not seek his happiness in God, but in the world, in the works of his hands. Now, God had told him before, 'In the day that thou eatest' of that fruit, 'thou shalt surely die.' And the word of the Lord cannot be broken. Accordingly, in that day he did die: He died to God – the most dreadful of all deaths. He lost the life of God: He was separated from Him, in union with whom his spiritual life consisted. The body dies when it is separated from the soul; the soul, when it is separated from God. But this separation from God, Adam sustained in the day, the hour, he ate of the forbidden fruit. And of this he gave immediate proof; presently showing by his behaviour, that the love of God was extinguished in his soul, which was now 'alienated from the life of God'. Instead of this, he was now under the power of servile fear, so that he fled from the presence of the Lord. Yea, so little did he retain even of the knowledge of Him who filleth heaven and earth, that he endeavoured to 'hide himself from the Lord God among the trees of the garden' (Gen. 3:8). So had he lost both the knowledge and the love of God, without which the image of God could not subsist. Of this, therefore, he was deprived at the same time, and became unholy as well as unhappy. In the room of this, he had sunk into pride and self-will, the very image of the devil; and into sensual appetites and desires, the image of the beasts that perish.

3. If it be said, 'Nay, but that threatening, "In the day that thou eatest thereof, thou shalt surely die," refers to temporal death, and that alone, to the death of the body only'; the answer is plain: To affirm this is flatly and palpably to make God a liar; to aver that the God of truth positively affirmed a thing contrary to truth. For it is evident, Adam did not die in this sense, 'in the day that he ate thereof.' He lived, in the sense opposite to this death, above nine hundred years after. So that this cannot possibly be understood of the death of the body, without impeaching the veracity of God. It must therefore be understood of spiritual death, the loss of the life and image of God.

4. And in Adam all died, all human kind, all the children of men who were then in Adam's loins. The natural consequence of this is, that every one descended from him comes into the world spiritually dead, dead to God, wholly dead in sin; entirely void of the life of God; void of the image of God, of all that righteousness and holiness wherein Adam was created. Instead of this, every man born into the world now bears the image of the devil in pride and self-will; the image of the beast, in sensual appetites and desires. This, then, is the foundation of the new birth – the entire corruption of our nature. Hence it is, that, being born in sin, we must be 'born again'. Hence every one that is born of a woman must be born of the Spirit of God.

II. 1. But how must a man be born again? What is the nature of the new birth? This is the Second question. And a question it is of the highest moment that can be conceived. We ought not, therefore, in so weighty a concern, to be content with a slight inquiry; but to examine it with all possible care, and to ponder it in our hearts, till we fully understand this important point, and clearly see how we are to be born again.

2. Not that we are to expect any minute, philosophical account of the manner how this is done. Our Lord sufficiently guards us against any such expectation, by the words immediately following the text; wherein he reminds Nicodemus of as indisputable a fact as any in the whole compass of nature, which, notwithstanding, the wisest man under the sun is not able fully to explain. 'The wind bloweth where it listeth' – not by thy power or wisdom; 'and thou hearest the sound thereof' – thou art absolutely assured, beyond all doubt, that it doth blow; 'but thou canst not tell whence it cometh, nor whither it goeth' – the precise manner how it begins and ends, rises and falls, no man can tell. 'So is every one that is born of the Spirit' – Thou mayest be as absolutely assured of the fact, as of the blowing of the wind; but the precise manner how it is done, how the Holy Spirit works this in the soul, neither thou nor the wisest of the children of men is able to explain.

3. However, it suffices for every rational and Christian purpose, that, without descending into curious, critical inquiries, we can give a plain scriptural account of the nature of the new birth. This will satisfy every reasonable man, who desires only the salvation of his soul. The expression, 'being born again', was not first used by our Lord in his conversation with Nicodemus: It was well known before that time, and was in common use among the Jews when our Saviour appeared among them. When an adult Heathen was convinced that the Jewish religion was of God, and desired to join therein, it was the custom to baptize him first, before he was admitted to circumcision. And when he was baptized, he was said to be born again; by which they meant, that he who was before a child of the devil was now adopted into the family of God, and accounted one of his children. This expression, therefore, which Nicodemus, being

all these particulars. The 'eyes of his understanding are opened' (such is the language of the great Apostle) and, He who of old 'commanded light to shine out of darkness shining on his heart, he sees the light of the glory of God,' his glorious love, 'in the face of Jesus Christ.' His ears being opened, he is now capable of hearing the inward voice of God, saying, 'Be of good cheer; thy sins are forgiven thee'; 'go and sin no more.' This is the purport of what God speaks to his heart; although perhaps not in these very words. He is now ready to hear whatsoever 'He that teacheth man knowledge' is pleased, from time to time, to reveal to him. He 'feels in his heart', to use the language of our Church, 'the mighty working of the Spirit of God'; not in a gross, carnal sense as the men of the world stupidly and wilfully misunderstand the expression; though they have been told again and again, we mean thereby neither more nor less than this: He feels, is inwardly sensible of, the graces which the Spirit of God works in his heart. He feels, he is conscious of, a 'peace which passeth all understanding.' He many times feels such a joy in God as is 'unspeakable, and full of glory'. He feels 'the love of God shed abroad in his heart by the Holy Ghost which is given unto him'; and all his spiritual senses are then exercised to discern spiritual good and evil. By the use of these, he is daily increasing in the knowledge of God, of Jesus Christ whom he hath sent and to all the things pertaining to his inward kingdom. And now he may be properly said to live: God having quickened him by his Spirit, he is alive to God through Jesus Christ. He lives a life which the world knoweth not of, a 'life which is hid with Christ in God.' God is continually breathing, as it were, upon the soul; and his soul is breathing unto God. Grace is descending into his heart; and prayer and praise ascending to heaven: And by this intercourse between God and man, this fellowship with the Father and the Son, as by a kind of spiritual respiration, the life of God in the soul is sustained; and the child of God grows up, till he comes to the 'full measure of the stature of Christ'.

5. From hence it manifestly appears, what is the nature of the new birth. It is that great change which God works in the soul when he brings it into life; when he raises it from the death of sin to the life of righteousness. It is the change wrought in the whole soul by the almighty Spirit of God when it is 'created anew in Christ Jesus'; when it is 'renewed after the image of God, in righteousness and true holiness'; when the love of the world is changed into the love of God; pride into humility; passion into meekness; hatred, envy, malice, into a sincere, tender, disinterested love for all mankind. In a word, it is that change whereby the earthly, sensual, devilish mind is turned into the 'mind which was in Christ Jesus'. This is the nature of the new birth: 'So is every one that is born of the Spirit.'

III. 1. It is not difficult for any who has considered these things, to see the necessity of the new birth, and to answer the Third question, Wherefore, to what end, is it necessary that we should be born again? It is very easily discerned, that this is necessary, First, in order to holiness. For what is holiness according to the oracles of God? Not a bare external religion, a round of outward duties, how many soever they be, and how exactly soever performed. No: Gospel holiness is no less than the image of God stamped upon the heart; it is no other than the whole mind which was in Christ Jesus; it consists of all heavenly affections and tempers mingled together in one. It implies such a continual, thankful love to Him who hath not withheld from us his Son, his only son, as makes it natural, and in a manner necessary to us, to love every child of man; as fills us 'with bowels of mercies, kindness, gentleness, long-suffering': It is such a love of God as teaches us to be blameless in all manner of conversation; as enables us to present our souls and bodies, all we are and all we have, all our thoughts, words, and actions, a continual sacrifice to God, acceptable through Christ Jesus. Now, this holiness can have no existence till we are renewed in the image of our mind. It cannot commence in the soul till that change be wrought; till, by the power of the Highest overshadowing us, we are 'brought from darkness to light, from the power of Satan unto God'; that is, till we are born again; which, therefore, is absolutely necessary in order to holiness.

2. But 'without holiness no man shall see the Lord', shall see the face of God in glory. Of consequence, the new birth is absolutely necessary in order to eternal salvation. Men may indeed flatter themselves (so desperately wicked and so deceitful is the heart of man!) that they may live in their sins till they come to the last gasp, and yet afterwards live with God; and thousands do really believe, that they have found a broad way which leadeth not to destruction. 'What danger,' say they, 'can a woman be in that is so harmless and so virtuous? What fear is there that so honest a man, one of so strict morality, should miss of heaven; especially if, over and above all this, they constantly attend on church and sacrament?' One of these will ask with all assurance, 'What! Shall not I do as well as my neighbours?' Yes as well as your unholy neighbours; as well as your neighbours that die in their sins! For you will all drop into the pit together, into the nethermost hell! You will all lie together in the lake of fire; 'the lake of fire burning with brimstone'. Then, at length, you will see (but God grant you may see it before!) the necessity of holiness in order to glory; and, consequently, of the new birth, since none can be holy, except he be born again.

3. For the same reason, except he be born again, none can be happy even in this world. For it is not possible, in the nature of things, that a man should be happy who is not holy. Even the poor, ungodly poet could tell us, *Nemo malus felix*: 'no wicked

man is happy.' The reason is plain: All unholy tempers are uneasy tempers: Not only malice, hatred, envy jealousy, revenge, create a present hell in the breast; but even the softer passions, if not kept within due bounds, give a thousand times more pain than pleasure. Even 'hope', when 'deferred' (and how often must this be the case!), 'maketh the heart sick'; and every desire which is not according to the will of God is liable to 'pierce' us 'through with many sorrows': And all those general sources of sin – pride, self-will, and idolatry – are, in the same proportion as they prevail, general sources of misery. Therefore, as long as these reign in any soul, happiness has no place there. But they must reign till the bent of our nature is changed, that is, till we are born again; consequently, the new birth is absolutely necessary in order to obtain happiness in this world, as well as in the world to come.

IV. I proposed in the Last place to subjoin a few inferences, which naturally follow from the preceding observations.

1. And, First, it follows, that baptism is not the new birth: They are not one and the same thing. Many indeed seem to imagine that they are just the same; at least, they speak as if they thought so; but I do not know that this opinion is publicly avowed by any denomination of Christians whatever. Certainly it is not by any within these kingdoms, whether of the established Church, or dissenting from it. The judgment of the latter is clearly declared in the large Catechism: – 'Q. What are the parts of a sacrament? A. The parts of a sacrament are two: The one an outward and sensible sign; the other, and inward and spiritual grace, thereby signified. – Q. What is baptism? A. Baptism is a sacrament, wherein Christ hath ordained the washing with water, to be a sign and seal of regeneration by his Spirit.' Here it is manifest, baptism, the sign, is spoken of as distinct from regeneration, the thing signified.

In the Church Catechism likewise, the judgment of our

Church is declared with the utmost clearness: 'What meanest thou by this word, sacrament? A. I mean an outward and visible sign of an inward and spiritual grace. Q. What is the outward part or form in baptism? A. Water, wherein the person is baptized, in the name of the Father, Son, and Holy Ghost. Q. What is the inward part, or thing signified? A. A death unto sin, and a new birth unto righteousness.' Nothing, therefore, is plainer than that, according to the Church of England, baptism is not the new birth.

But indeed the reason of the thing is so clear and evident, as not to need any other authority. For what can be more plain, than that one is a visible, the other an invisible thing, and therefore wholly different from each other? – the one being an act of man, purifying the body; the other a change wrought by God in the soul: So that the former is just as distinguishable from the latter, as the soul from the body, or water from the Holy Ghost.

2. From the preceding reflections we may, Secondly, observe, that as the new birth is not the same thing with baptism, so it does not always accompany baptism: They do not constantly go together. A man may possibly be 'born of water', and yet not be 'born of the Spirit'. There may sometimes be the outward sign, where there is not the inward grace. I do not now speak with regard to infants: It is certain our Church supposes that all who are baptized in their infancy are at the same time born again; and it is allowed that the whole Office for the Baptism of Infants proceeds upon this supposition. Nor is it an objection of any weight against this, that we cannot comprehend how this work can be wrought in infants. For neither can we comprehend how it is wrought in a person of riper years. But whatever be the case with infants, it is sure all of riper years who are baptized are not at the same time born again. 'The tree is known by its fruits': And hereby it appears too plain to be

denied, that divers of those who were children of the devil before they were baptized continue the same after baptism: 'for the works of their father they do': They continue servants of sin, without any pretence either to inward or outward holiness.

3. A Third inference which we may draw from what has been observed, is, that the new birth is not the same with sanctification. This is indeed taken for granted by many; particularly by an eminent writer, in his late treatise on 'The Nature and Grounds of Christian Regeneration'. To wave several other weighty objections which might be made to that tract, this is a palpable one: It all along speaks of regeneration as a progressive work, carried on in the soul by slow degrees, from the time of our first turning to God. This is undeniably true of sanctification; but of regeneration, the new birth, it is not true. This is a part of sanctification, not the whole; it is the gate to it, the entrance into it. When we are born again, then our sanctification, our inward and outward holiness, begins; and thenceforward we are gradually to 'grow up in Him who is our Head.' This expression of the Apostle admirably illustrates the difference between one and the other, and farther points out the exact analogy there is between natural and spiritual things. A child is born of a woman in a moment, or at least in a very short time: Afterward he gradually and slowly grows, till he attains to the stature of a man. In like manner, a child is born of God in a short time, if not in a moment. But it is by slow degrees that he afterward grows up to the measure of the full stature of Christ. The same relation, therefore, which there is between our natural birth and our growth, there is also between our new birth and our sanctification.

4. One point more we may learn from the preceding observations. But it is a point of so great importance, as may excuse the considering it the more carefully, and prosecuting it at some

length. What must one who loves the souls of men, and is grieved that any of them should perish, say to one whom he sees living in sabbath-breaking, drunkenness, or any other wilful sin? What can he say, if the foregoing observations are true, but, 'You must be born again'? 'No,' says a zealous man, 'that cannot be. How can you talk so uncharitably to the man? Has he not been baptized already? He cannot be born again now.' Can he not be born again? Do you affirm this? Then he cannot be saved. Though he be as old as Nicodemus was, yet 'except he be born again, he cannot see the kingdom of God.' Therefore in saying, 'He cannot be born again', you in effect deliver him over to damnation. And where lies the uncharitableness now? – on my side, or on yours? I say, he may be born again, and so become an heir of salvation. You say, 'He cannot be born again': And if so, he must inevitably perish! So you utterly block up his way to salvation, and send him to hell, out of mere charity!

But perhaps the sinner himself, to whom in real charity we say, 'You must be born again,' has been taught to say, 'I defy your new doctrine; I need not be born again: I was born again when I was baptized. What! Would you have me deny my baptism?' I answer, First, There is nothing under heaven which can excuse a lie; otherwise I should say to an open sinner, If you have been baptized, do not own it. For how highly does this aggravate your guilt! How will it increase your damnation! Was you devoted to God at eight days old, and have you been all these years devoting yourself to the devil? Was you, even before you had the use of reason, consecrated to God the Father, the son, and the Holy Ghost? And have you, ever since you had the use of it, been flying in the face of God, and consecrating yourself to Satan? Does the abomination of desolation – the love of the word, pride, anger, lust, foolish desire, and a whole train of vile affections – stand where it ought not? Have you set up all the accursed things in that soul which was once a temple of the Holy Ghost; set apart for an 'habitation of God, through the Spirit'; yea, solemnly given up to him? And do you glory in this, that you once belonged to God? O be ashamed! blush! hide yourself in the earth! Never boast more of what ought to fill you with confusion, to make you ashamed before God and man!

I answer, Secondly, You have already denied your baptism; and that in the most effectual manner. You have denied it a thousand and a thousand times; and you do so still, day by day. For in your baptism you renounced the devil and all his works. Whenever, therefore, you give place to him again, whenever you do any of the works of the devil, then you deny your baptism. Therefore you deny it by every wilful sin; by every act of uncleanness, drunkenness, or revenge; by every obscene or profane word; by every oath that comes out of your mouth. Every time you profane the day of the Lord, you thereby deny your baptism; yea, every time you do any thing to another which you would not he should do to you.

I answer, Thirdly, Be you baptized or unbaptized, 'you must be born again'; otherwise it is not possible you should be inwardly holy; and without inward as well as outward holiness, you cannot be happy, even in this world, much less in the world to come. Do you say, 'Nay, but I do no harm to any man; I am honest and just in all my dealings; I do not curse, or take the Lord's name in vain; I do not profane the Lord's day; I am no drunkard; I do not slander my neighbour, nor live in any wilful sin?' If this be so, it were much to be wished that all men went as far as you do. But you must go farther yet, or you cannot be saved: Still, 'you must be born again.' Do you add, 'I do go farther yet; for I not only do no harm, but do all the good I can?' I doubt that fact; I fear you have had a thousand opportunities of doing good which you have suffered to pass by unimproved, and for which therefore you are accountable to God. But if you had improved them all, if you really had done all the good you possibly could to all men, yet this does not at all alter the case; still, 'you must be born again.' Without this nothing will do any good to your poor, sinful, polluted soul. 'Nay, but I constantly attend all the ordinances of God: I keep to my church and sacrament.' It is well you do: But all this will not keep you from hell, except you be born again. Go to church twice a day; go to the Lord's table every week; say ever so many prayers in private; hear ever so many good sermons; read ever so many good books; still, 'you must be born again': None of these things will stand in the place of the new birth; no, nor any thing under heaven. Let this therefore, if you have not already experienced this inward work of God, be your continual prayer: 'Lord, add this to all thy blessings – let me be born again! Deny whatever thou pleasest, but deny not this; let me be "born from above"! Take away whatsoever seemeth thee good – reputation, fortune, friends, health – only give me this, to be born of the Spirit, to be received among the children of God! Let me be born, "not of corruptible seed, but incorruptible, by the word of God, which liveth and abideth for ever"; and then let me daily "grow in grace, and in the knowledge of our Lord and Saviour Jesus Christ"!'

William Pitt:

14 January 1766

The Stamp Act

In the following speech William Pitt, first Earl of Chatham, argued against the Bill known as the Stamp Act, which would allow the levying of taxes on British citizens living in America.

Gentlemen, Sir, I have been charged with giving birth to sedition in America. They have spoken their sentiments with freedom against this unhappy act, and that freedom has become their crime. Sorry I am to hear the liberty of speech in this house, imputed as a crime. No gentleman ought to be afraid to exercise it. It is a liberty by which the gentleman who calumniates it might have profited, by which he ought to have profited. He ought to have desisted from this project.

The gentleman tells us, America is obstinate; America is almost in open rebellion. I rejoice that America has resisted. Three million of people so dead to all feelings of liberty, as voluntarily to submit to be slaves, would have been fit instruments to make slaves of the rest. I come not here armed at all points, with law cases and acts of parliament, with the statute book doubled down in dog's-ears, to defend the cause of liberty: if I had, I myself would have cited the two cases of Chester and Durham. I would have cited them, to have shown that even under former arbitrary reigns, parliaments were ashamed of taxing a people without their consent, and allowed them representatives. Why did the gentleman confine himself to Chester and Durham? He might have taken a higher example in Wales; Wales, that never was taxed by parliament till it was incorporated. I would not debate a particular point of law with the gentleman. I know his abilities. I have been obliged to his diligent researches: but, for the defence of liberty, upon a general principle, upon a constitutional principle, it is a ground on which I stand firm; on which I dare meet any man.

The gentleman tells us of many who are taxed, and are not represented. The India Company, merchants, stock-holders, manufacturers. Surely many of these are represented in other capacities, as owners of land, or as freemen of boroughs. It is a misfortune that more are not equally represented: but they are all inhabitants, and as such, are they not virtually represented? ... they have connections with those that elect, and they have influence over them. The gentleman mentioned the stock-holders: I hope he does not reckon the debts of the nation as a part of the national estate. Since the accession of King William, many ministers, some of great, others of more moderate abilities, have taken the lead of government...

None of these thought, or ever dreamed, of robbing the colonies of their constitutional rights. That was to mark the era of the late administration: not that there were wanting some, when I had the honour to serve his majesty, to propose to me to burn my fingers with an American stamp-act. With the enemy at their back, with our bayonets at their breasts, in the day of their distress, perhaps the Americans would have submitted to the imposition: but it would have been taking an ungenerous and unjust advantage.

The gentleman boasts of his bounties to America. Are not those bounties intended finally for the benefit of this kingdom? If they are not, he has misapplied the national treasures. I am no courtier of America; I stand up for this kingdom. I maintain, that the parliament has a right to bind, to restrain America. Our legislative power over the colonies is sovereign and supreme. When it ceases to be sovereign and supreme, I would advise every gentleman to sell his lands, if he can, and embark for that country. When two countries are connected together, like England and her colonies, without being incorporated, the one must necessarily govern; the greater must rule the less; but so rule it, as not to contradict the fundamental principles that are common to both. If the gentleman does not understand the difference between external and internal taxes, I cannot help it; but there is a plain distinction between taxes levied for the purpose of raising a revenue, and duties imposed for the regulation of trade, for the accommodation of the subject; although, in the consequences, some revenue might incidentally arise from the latter.

The gentleman asks, when were the colonies emancipated? But I desire to know, when were they made slaves. But I dwell not upon words. When I had the honour of serving his Majesty, I availed myself of the means of information which I derived from my office: I speak, therefore, from knowledge. My materials were good; I was at pains to collect, to digest, to consider them; and I will be bold to affirm, that the profits to Great Britain from the trade of the colonies, through all its branches, is two millions a year. This is the fund that carried you triumphantly through the last war...

You owe this to America: this is the price America pays you for her protection. And shall a miserable financier come with a boast, that he can bring a pepper-corn into the exchequer, to the loss of millions to the nation? I dare not say, how much higher these profits may be augmented. Omitting the immense increase of people by natural population, and the emigration from every part of Europe, I am convinced the whole commercial system of America may be altered to advantage. You have prohibited where you ought to have encouraged, encouraged where you ought to have prohibited. Improper restraints have been laid on the continent, in favour of the islands. You have but two nations to trade with in America. Would you had twenty! Let acts of parliament in consequence of treaties remain, but let not an English minister become a custom-house officer for Spain, or for any foreign power. Much is wrong; much may be amended for the general good of the whole...

The gentleman must not wonder he was not contradicted, when, as minister, he asserted the right of parliament to tax Ameri-ca. I know not how it is, but there is a modesty in this House, which does not choose to contradict a minister. I wish gentlemen would get the better of this modesty. Even that chair, Sir, sometimes looks towards St James's. If they do not, perhaps the collective body may begin to abate of its respect for the representative...

A great deal has been said without doors of the power, of the strength of America. It is a topic that ought to be cautiously meddled with. In a good cause, on a sound bottom, the force of this country can crush America to atoms. I know the valour of your troops. I know the skill of your officers. There is not a company of foot that has served in America out of which you may not pick a man of sufficient knowledge and experience to make him governor of a colony there. But on this ground, on the Stamp Act, when so many here will think a crying injustice, I am one who will lift up my hands against it.

In such a cause, your success would be hazardous. America, if she fell, would fall like a strong man. She would embrace the pillars of the state, and pull down the constitution along with her. Is this your boasted peace? Not to sheathe the sword in its scabbard, but to sheathe it in the bowels of your countrymen? Will you quarrel with yourselves, now the whole House of Bourbon is united against you...

The Americans have not acted in all things with prudence and temper. They have been wronged. They have been driven to madness by injustice. Will you punish them for the madness you have occasioned? Rather let prudence and temper come first from this side. I will undertake for America, that she will follow the example. There are two lines in a ballad of Prior's, of a man's behaviour to his wife, so applicable to you and your colonies, that I cannot help repeating them:

> Be to her faults a little blind
> Be to her virtues very kind.

Upon the whole, I will beg leave to tell the House what is really my opinion. It is, that the Stamp Act be repealed absolutely, totally, and immediately; that the reason for the repeal should be assigned, because it was founded on an erroneous principle. At the same time, let the sovereign authority of this country over the colonies be asserted in as strong terms as can be devised, and be made to extend every point of legislation whatsoever: that we may bind their trade, confine their manufactures, and exercise every power whatsoever – except that of taking money out of their pockets without their consent.

George Whitefield:

28 January 1770

'For who has despised the day of small things?'

The visits of the Anglican itinerant preacher George Whitefield (1714–70) to the American colonies in the 1730s and 1740s triggered a widespread evangelical revival known as the Great Awakening. This sermon was preached before the Governor, the Council and the House of Assembly in Georgia.

Zechariah 4:10, 31: 'For who has despised the day of small things?'

Men, brethren, and fathers, at sundry times and in diverse manners, God spake to the fathers by the prophets, before he spoke to us in these last days by his Son. And as God is a sovereign agent, and his sacred Spirit bloweth when and where it listeth, surely he may reveal and make known his will to his creatures, when, where, and how he pleaseth; 'and who shall say unto him, what doest thou?' Indeed, this seems to be one reason, to display his sovereignty, why he chose, before the canon of scripture was settled, to make known his mind in such various methods, and to such a variety of his servants and messengers.

Hence it is, that we hear, he talked with Abraham as 'a man talketh with a friend.' To Moses he spoke 'face to face'. To others by 'dreams in the night', or by 'visions' impressed strongly on their imaginations. This seems to be frequently the happy lot of the favorite evangelical prophet Zechariah. I call him evangelical prophet, because his predictions, however they pointed at some approaching or immediate event, ultimately terminated in Him, who is the Alpha and Omega, the beginning and the end of all the lively oracles of God. The chapter from which our text is selected, among many other passages, is a striking proof of this: An angel, that had been more than once sent to him on former occasions, appears again to him, and by way of vision, and 'waked him' (to use his own words) 'as a man that is wakened out of his sleep.' Prophets, and the greatest servants of God, need waking sometimes out of their drowsy frames.

Methinks I see this man of God starting out of his sleep, and being all attention: the angel asked him, 'what seest thou?' He answers, 'I have looked, and behold, a candle-stick all of gold,' an emblem of the church of God, 'with a bowl upon the top of it, and seven lamps thereon, and seven pipes to the seven lamps, which were upon the top thereof'; implying, that the church, however reduced to the lowest ebb, should be preserved, be kept supplied, and shining, through the invisible, but not less real, because invisible aids and operations of the blessed Spirit of God. The occasion of such an extraordinary vision, if we compare this passage with the second chapter of the Prophecy of the prophet Haggai, seems to be this: It was now near eighteen years since the Jewish people had been delivered from their long and grievous Babylonian captivity; and being so long deprived of their temple and its worship, which fabric had been rased even to the ground, one would have imagined, that immediately upon their return, they should have postponed all private works, and with their united strength have first set about rebuilding that once stately and magnificent structure. But they, like too many Christians of a like luke-warm stamp, though all acknowledged that this church-work was a necessary work, yet put themselves and others off, with this godly pretense, 'The time is not come, the time that the Lord's house should be built.' The time is not come! What, not in eighteen years! For so long had they now been returned from their state of bondage: and pray, why was not the time come? The prophet Haggai tells them; their whole time was so taken up building for an habitation for their great and glorious Benefactor, the mighty God of Jacob.

This ingratitude must not be passed by unpunished. Omniscience observes, Omnipotence resents it! And that they might read their sin in their punishment, as they thought it best to get rich, and secure houses and lands and estates for themselves, before they set about unnecessary church-work, the prophet tells them, 'You have sown much, but bring in little: ye eat, but ye have not enough: ye drink, but ye are not filled with drink: ye clothe you, but there is none warm: and he that earneth wages, earneth wages to put it into a bag with holes.' Still he goes on

friends, or all other obstacles whatsoever. If Haggai thunders, Zechariah's message is as lightning. 'This is the word of the Lord unto Zerubbabel, saying, Not by might, not by power [not by barely human power or policy], but by my spirit, saith the Lord of Hosts: Who art thou, O great mountain? [thou Sanballat and thy associates, who have been so long crying out, what mean these feeble Jews? However great, formidable, and seemingly insurmountable] before Zerubbabel thou shalt [not only be lowered and rendered more accessible, but] become a plain'; thy very opposition shall, in the end, promote the work, and help to expedite that very building, which thou intendest to put a stop to, and destroy.

And lest Zerubbabel, through unbelief and outward opposition, or for want of more bodily strength, should think this would be a work of time, and that he should not live to see it completed in his days, 'The word of the Lord came to Zechariah, saying, The hands of Zerubbabel have laid the foundation of this house; his hands also shall finish it, and he shall bring forth the headstone thereof with shoutings, crying, Grace, grace unto it.' Grace! Grace! Unto it: a double acclamation, to show, that out of the abundance of their hearts, their mouth spake; and this with shoutings and crying from all quarters. Even their enemies should see the hand and providence of God in the beginning, continuance, and ending of this seemingly improbable and impracticable work; so that they should be constrained to cry, 'Grace unto it,' and wish both the work and the builders much prosperity: But as for its friends, they should be so transported with heart-felt joy in the reflection upon the signal providences which had attended them through the whole process, that they would shout and cry, 'Grace, grace unto it': or, This is nothing but the Lord's doing; God prosper and bless this work more and more, and make it a place where his free grace and glory may be abundantly displayed.

Then by a beautiful and pungent sarcasm, turning to the insulting enemies, he utters the spirited interrogation in my text, 'Who hath despised the day of small things?' Who are you, that vauntingly said, what can these feeble Jews do, pretending to lay the foundation of a house which they never will have money, or strength, or power to finish? Or, who are you, O timorous, short sighted, doubting, though well-meaning people, who, through unbelief, were discouraged at the small beginnings and feebleness of the attempt to build a second temple? And, because you thought it could not come up to the magnificence of the first, therefore were discouraged from so much as beginning to build a second at all? A close instructive question this; a question, implying, that whenever God intends to bring about any great thing, he generally begins with a day of small things.

As a proof of this, I will not lead you so far back, as to the beginning of time, when the Everlasting 'I AM' spoke all things into existence, by his almighty fiat; and out of a confused chaos, 'without form and void', produced a world worthy of a God to create, and of his favorite creature man, his and representative here below, to inhabit, and enjoy in it both himself and his God. And yet, though the heavens declare his glory, and the firmament showeth his handy work, though there is no speech nor language where their voice is not heard, and their line is gone out through all the earth: and by a dumb, yet persuasive language, proves the hand that made them to be divine; yet there have been, and are now, such fools in the world, as to 'say in their hearts, There is no God'; or so wise, as by their wisdom, not to know God, or own his divine image to be stamped on that book, wherein these grand things are recorded, and that in such legible characters, that he who runs may read.

Neither will I divert your attention, honored fathers, to the histories of Greece and Rome, or any of the great kingdoms and renowned monarchies, which constitute so great a part of ancient history; but whose beginnings were very small (witness Romulus's ditch), their progress as remarkably great, and their declension and downfall, when arrived at their appointed zenith, as sudden, unexpected, and marvelous. These make the chief subjects of the learning of our schools; though they make but a mean figure in sacred history, and would not perhaps have been mentioned at all, had they not been, in some measure, connected with the history of God's people, which is the grand subject of that much despised book, emphatically called, The Scriptures. Whoever hath a mind to inform himself of the one, may read Rollin's *Ancient History*, and whoever would see the connection with the other, may consult the learned Prideaux's admirable and judicious connection. Books which, I hope, will be strenuously recommended, and carefully studied, when this present infant institution gathers more strength, and grows up into a seat of learning. I can hardly forbear mentioning the final beginnings of Great Britain, now so distinguished for liberty, opulence and renown; and the rise and rapid progress of the American colonies, which promises to be one of the most opulent and powerful empires in the world. But my present views, and the honors done this infant institution this day, and the words of my text, as well as the feelings of my own heart, and I trust, of the hearts of all that hear me, lead me to confine your meditations to the history of God's own peculiar people, which for the simplicity and sublimity of its language, the veracity of its author, and the importance and wonders of the facts therein recorded, if weighed in a proper balance, hath not its equal under the sun. And yet, though God himself hath become an author among us, we will not condescend to give his book one thorough reading. Be astonished, O heavens, at this!

Who would have thought that from once, even from Abraham, and from so small a beginning, as the emigration of a single private family, called out of a land wholly given to idolatry, to be sojourners and pilgrims in a strange land; who would have thought, that from a man, who for a long season was written childless, a man whose first possession in this strange land, was by purchasing a burying place for his wife, and in whose grave one might have imagined he would have buried all future expectations; who would have thought, that from this very man and woman, according to the course of nature, both as good as dead, should descend a numerous offspring like unto the stars of heaven for multitude, and as the sand which is upon the sea shore innumerable? Nay, who would have imagined, that against all probability, and in all human appearance impossible, a kingdom should arise? Behold a poor captive slave, even Joseph, who was cruelly separated from his brethren, became second in Pharaoh's kingdom: he was sent before to work out a great deliverance, and to introduce a family which should take root, deep root downwards and bear fruit upwards, and fill the land. How could it enter into the heart of man to conceive, that when oppressed by a king, who knew not Joseph, though they were the best, most loyal, industrious subjects this king had, when an edict was issued forth as impolitic as cruel (since the safety and glory of all kingdoms chiefly consist in the number of its inhabitants), that an outcast, helpless infant should be taken, and bred up in all the learning of the Egyptians, and in that very court from which, and by that very tyrant from whom the edict came, and that the deliverer should be nurtured to be king in Jeshurun?

But time as well as strength would fail me, was I to give you a detail of all the important particulars respecting God's peculiar people; as their miraculous support in the wilderness, the events which took place while they were under a divine theocracy, and during their settlement in Canaan to the time of their return from Babylon, and from thence to the destruction of their second temple, etc. by the Romans. Indeed, considering to whom I am speaking, persons conversant in the sacred and profane history, I have mentioned these things only to stir up your minds by way of remembrance.

But if we descend from the Jewish, to the Christian era, we shall find, that its commencement was, in the eyes of the world, a 'day of small things' indeed. Our blessed Lord compares the beginning of its progress in the world, to a grain of mustard-seed, which though the smallest of all seeds when sown, soon becomes a great tree, and so spread, that the 'birds of the air', or a multitude of every nation, language and tongue, came and lodged in its branches: and its inward progress in the believer's heart, Christ likens to a little leaven which a woman hid in three measures of meal. How both the Jewish and Christian dispensations have been, and even to this day are despised, by the wise disputers of this world, on this very account, is manifest to all who read the lively oracles with a becoming attention. What ridicule, obloquy, and inveterate opposition Christianity meets with, in this our day, not only from the open deist, but from formal professors, is too evident to every truly pious soul.

And what opposition the kingdom of grace meets with in the heart, is well known by all those who are experimentally acquainted with their hearts: they know, to their sorrow, what the great apostle of the Gentiles means, by 'the Spirit striving against the flesh, and the flesh against the Spirit.'

But the sacred Oracles, and the histories of all ages acquaint us, that God brings about the greatest thing, not only by small and unlikely means, but by ways and means directly opposite to the carnal reasonings of unthinking men: he chooses things that be not, to bring to nought those which are. How did

Christianity spread and flourish, by one, who was despised and rejected of men, a man of sorrows, and acquainted with grief, and who expired on a cross? He was despised and rejected, not merely by the vulgar and illiterate, but the Rabbis and Masters of Israel, the Scribes and Pharisees, who by the Jewish churchmen were held too in so high a reputation for their outward sanctity, that it became a common proverb, 'if only two went to heaven, the one would be a Scribe, and the other a Pharisee.' Yet there were they who endeavored to silence the voice of all his miracles and heavenly doctrine with, 'Is not this the Carpenter's son?' Nay, 'He is mad, why hear you him? he hath a devil, and casteth out devils by Beelzebub the prince of the devils.' And their despite not only followed him to, but after death, and when in the grave. 'We remember [said they] that this deceiver said, after three days I will rise again; command therefore that the sepulcher be made sure'; but, maugre all your impotent precautions, in sealing the stone, and setting a watch, he burst the bars of death asunder, and, according to his repeated predictions, proved himself to be the Son of God with power, by rising the third day from the dead. And afterwards, in presence of great multitudes, was he received up into glory; as a proof thereof, he sent down the Holy Ghost (on the mission of whom he pawned all his credit with his disciples), in such an instantaneous, amazing manner, as one would imagine, should have forced and compelled all who saw it to own, that this was indeed the finger of God.

And yet how was this grand transaction treated? With the utmost contempt: when instantaneously the apostles commenced orators and linguists, and with a divine profusion spoke of the wonderful things of God; 'these men [said some] are full of new wine.' And yet by these men, mean fishermen, illiterate men, idiots, in the opinion of the Scribes and Pharisees, and notwithstanding all the opposition of earth and hell, and that too only by the foolishness of preaching, did this grain of mustard-seed grow up, till thousands, ten thousands of thousands, a multitude which no man can number, out of every nation, language and people, came and lodged under the branches of it.

Neither shall it rest here; whatever dark parenthesis may intervene, we are assured, that being still watered by the same divine hand, it shall take deeper and deeper root downward, and bear more and more fruit upward, till the whole earth be filled with the knowledge of the Lord, as the waters cover the sea. Who shall live when God doth this? Hasten O Lord that blessed time! O let this thy kingdom come! Come, not only by the external preaching of the gospel in the world, but by its renovating, heart-renewing, soul-transforming power, to awakened sinners! For want of this, alas! alas! though we understood all mysteries, could speak with the tongues of men and angels, we should be only like sounding brass, or so many tinkling cymbals.

And yet, what a 'day of small things' is the first implantation of the seed of divine life in the soul of man? Well might our Lord, who alone is the author and finisher of our faith, compare it to a little leaven, which a woman took, and hid in three measures of meal, till the whole was leavened. Low similes, mean comparisons these, in the eyes of those, who having eyes, see not; who having ears, hear not; whose heart, being waxed gross, cannot, will not understand! To such, it is despicable, mysterious, and unintelligible in its description; and, if possible, infinitely more so, when made effectual by the power of God, to the salvation of any individual soul. For the wisdom of God will always be foolishness to natural men. As it was formerly, so it is now; they who are born after the flesh, will persecute those that are born after the spirit: the disciple must be as his master: they that will live godly in him; they that live most godly in him, must, shall suffer persecution. This is so interwoven in the very nature and existence of the gospel, that our Lord makes it one part of the beatitudes, in that blessed sermon which he preached, when, to use the words of my old familiar friend the seraphic Hervey, a mount was his pulpit, and the heavens his sounding board. A part, which, like others of the same nature, I believe, will be little relished by such who are always clamoring against those few highly favored souls, who dare stand up and preach the doctrine of JUSTIFICATION BY FAITH ALONE in the imputed righteousness of Jesus Christ, and are reproached with not preaching, like their master, Morality, as they term it, in his glorious sermon on the mount; for did we more preach, and more live it, we should soon find all manner of evil would be spoken against us for Christ's sake.

But shall this hinder the progress, the growth, and consummation? And shall the Christian therefore be dismayed and discouraged? God forbid! On the contrary, the weakest believer may, and ought, to rejoice and be exceeding glad. And why? For a very good reason; because, he that hath begun the good work, hath engaged also to finish it; though Christ found him as black as hell, he shall present him, and every individual purchased with his blood, without spot or wrinkle, or any such-thing, before the Divine Presence. O glorious prospect! How will the saints triumph, and the sons of God then shout for joy? If they shouted when God said, 'Let there by light, and there was light'; and if there is joy in heaven over one sinner only that repenteth, how will the heavenly arches echo and rebound with praise, when all the redeemed of the Lord shall appear together, and the Son of God shall say, 'of all these that thou hast given to me, have I lost nothing.' On the contrary, what weeping, wailing, and gnashing of teeth will there be, not only amongst the devil and his angels, but amongst the fearful and unbelieving, when they see that all the hellish temptations and devices, instead of destroying, were over-ruled to the furtherance of the gospel in general, and to the increase and growth of grace in every individual believer in particular. And how will despisers then behold and wonder and perish, when they shall be obliged to say, 'we fools counted their lives madness, and their end to be without honor; but how are they numbered among the children of God, and how happy is their lot among the saints!'

But whither am I going? Pardon me, my dear hearers, if you think this to be a digression from my main point. It is true, whilst I am musing, the fire begins to kindle: I am flying, but not so high, I trust, as to lose sight of my main subject. And yet, after meditating and talking of the rise and progress of the gospel of the kingdom, I shall find it somewhat difficult to descend so low, as to entertain you with the small beginnings of this infant colony, and of the Orphan-house, in which I am now preaching. But I should judge myself inexcusable on this occasion, if I did not detain you a little longer, in taking a transient view of the traces of divine Providence, in the rise and progress of the colony in general, and the institution of this Orphan-house in particular. Children yet unborn, I trust, will have occasion to bless God for both.

The very design of this settlement, as charity inclines us to hope all things, was, that it might be an Asylum, and a place of business, for as many as were in distress; for foreigners, as well as natives; for Jews and Gentiles. On February 1, a day, the memory of which, I think, should still be perpetuated, the first embarkation was made with forty-five English families; men, who had once lived well in their native country, and who, with many persecuted Saltzburghers, headed by a good old soldier of Jesus lately deceased, the Rev. Mr Boltzius, came to find a refuge here. They came, they saw, they labored, and endeavored to settle; but by an essential, though well-meant defect, in the very beginning of the settlement, too well known by some now present, and too long, and too much felt to bear repeating, prohibiting the importation and use of Negroes, etc. their numbers gradually diminished, and matters were brought to so low an ebb, that the whole colony became a proverb of reproach.

About this time, in the year 1737, being previously stirred up thereto by a strong impulse, which I could by no means resist, I came here, after the example of my worthy and reverend friends, John and Charles Wesley, and Mr Ingham, who, with the most disinterested views, had come hither to serve the colony, by endeavoring to convert the Indians. I came rejoicing to serve the colony also, and to become your willing servant for Christ's sake. My friend and father, good Bishop Bensen, encouraged me, though my brethren and kinsmen after the flesh, as well as religious friends, opposed it. I came, and I saw (you will not be offended with me to speak the truth) the nakedness of the land. Gladly did I distribute about the four hundred pounds sterling, which I had collected in England, among my poor parishioners. The necessity and propriety of erecting an Orphan-house, was mentioned and recommended before my first embarkation. But thinking it a matter of too great importance to be set about unwarily, I deferred the farther prosecution for this laudable design till my return to England in the year 1738, for to have priest's orders.

Miserable was the condition of many grown persons, as well as children, whom I left behind. Their cause I endeavored to plead, immediately upon my arrival; but being denied the churches, in which I had the year before collected many hundreds for the London charity-schools, I endeavored to plead their cause in the fields. The people threw in their mites most willingly; once or twice, I think, twenty-two pounds were collected in copper; the alms were accompanied with many prayers, and which, as I told them, laid, I am persuaded, a blessed foundation to the future charitable superstructure. In a short time, though plucked as it were out of the fire, the collections and charitable contributions amounted to more than a one thousand pounds sterling.

With that I reimbarked, taking Philadelphia in my way, and upon my second arrival, found the spot fixed upon; but, alas! who can describe the low estate to which it was reduced! The whole country almost was left desolate, and the metropolis Savannah, was but like a cottage in a vineyard, or as a lodge in a garden of cucumbers. Many orphans, whose parents had been taken from them by the distresses that naturally attend new settlements, were dispersed here and there in a very forlorn helpless condition; my bowels yearned towards them, and, animated by the example of the great professor Franck, previous to bringing them here, I hired a house, furnished an infirmary, employed all that were capable of employment, and in a few weeks walked to the house of God with a large family of above sixty orphans, and others in as bad a condition.

On March 25, 1740, in full assurance of faith, I laid the foundation of this house; and in the year following, brought in my orphan family, who, with the workmen, now made up the number of one hundred and fifty: by the money which was expended on these, the remaining few were kept in the colony, and were enabled to pay the debts they owed; so that in a representation made to the House of Commons, by some, who for very good reasons wanted the constitution of the colony altered; they declared, that the very existence of the colony was in a great measure, if not totally, owing to the building and supporting of the Orphan House.

Finding the care of such a family, incompatible with the care due to a parish, upon giving previous warning to the then trustees, I gave up the living of Savannah, which without fee or reward I had voluntarily taken upon me: I then ranged through the northern colonies, and afterwards once more returned home. What calumny, what loads of reproach, I for many years was called to undergo, in thus turning beggars for a family, few here present need to be informed; a family, utterly unconnected by any ties of nature; a family, not only to be maintained with food, but clothed and educated also, and that too in the dearest part of his Majesty's dominions, on a pine barren, and in a colony where the use of Negroes was totally denied; this appeared so very improbable, that all beholders looked daily for its decline and annihilation.

But, blessed be God, the building advanced and flourished, and the wished-for period is now come, after having supported the family for thirty-two years, by a change of constitution and the smiles of government, with liberal donations from the northern, and especially the adjacent provinces, the same hands that laid the foundation, are now called to finish it, by making an addition of a seat of learning, the whole products and profits of which, are to go towards the increase of the fund, as at the beginning, for destitute orphans, or such youths as may be called of God to the sacred ministry of his Gospel. I need not call on any here, to cry, 'Grace, grace, unto it.' For on the utmost scrutiny of the intention of those employed, and considering the various exercises they have been called to undergo, and the opposition the building hath every where met with, we may justly say, 'not by might, nor by power, but by thy Spirit, O Lord,' hath this work been carried on thus far; it is his doing, let it be marvelous in our eyes. With humble gratitude, therefore, would we now setup our Ebenezer, and say, 'Hitherto thou,

Lord, hast helped us'; and wherefore should we doubt, but that he, who hath thus far helped, will continue to help, when the weary heads of the first founders and present helpers, are laid in the silent grave.

I am very well aware, what an invidious task it must be to a person in my circumstances, thus to speak on an affair in which he hath been so much concerned. Some may perhaps think, I am become a fool in thus glorying. But as I am now, blessed be God, in the decline of life, and as, in all probability, I shall never be present to celebrate another anniversary, I thought it best to be a little more explicit, that if I have spoken any thing but truth, I may be confronted; and if not, that future ages, and future successors, may see with what a purity of intention, and what various interpositions of Providence, the work was begun, and hath been carried on to its present height.

It was the reading of a like account, written by the late Professor Franck, that encouraged me: who knows but hereafter, the reading something of a similar nature, may encourage others to begin and carry on a like work elsewhere? I have said its present height, for I would humbly hope, that this is, comparatively speaking, only a 'day of small things', only the dawn of brighter scenes. Private geniuses and individuals, as well as collective bodies, have, like the human body, the nonage, puerile, juvenile estate, before they arrive at their zenith, and their lives as gradually they decline. But yet I would hope, that both the province and Bethesda, are but in their puerile or juvenile state. And long, long may they increase, and make large strides, till they arrive at a glorious zenith! I mean not merely in trade, merchandise, and opulence (though I would be far from secluding them from the province, and would be thankful for the advances it hath already made), but a zenith of glorious gospel blessings, without which, all outward emoluments are less than nothing, or as the small dust of the balance: 'For what shall it profit a man, if he shall gain the whole world and lose his own soul.'

Who can imagine, that the prophet Zechariah would be sent to strengthen the hands of Zerubbabel, in building and laying the foundation of the temple, if that temple was not to be frequented with worshippers that worshipped the Father in spirit and truth. The most gaudy fabrics, stately temples, new moon Sabbaths, and solemn assemblies, are only solemn mockeries God cannot away with. This God hath shown by the destruction of both the first and second temples. What is become of the seven churches of Asia? How are all their golden candlesticks overthrown? 'God is a Spirit, and they who worship him must worship him in spirit and truth.' And no longer do I expect that this house will flourish, than when the power of religion is encouraged and promoted, and the persons educated here, prosecute their studies, not only to be great scholars, but good saints.

Blessed be God! I can say with Professor Franck, that it is in a great measure owing to the disinterested spirit of my first fellow-helpers, as well as those who are now employed, that the building hath reached to its present height. This I am bound to speak, not only in honor to those who are now with God, but those at present before me. Nor dare I conclude, without offering to Your Excellency, our pepper corn of acknowledgment for the countenance you have always shown Bethesda's institution, and the honor you did us last year, in laying the first brick of yonder wings: in thus doing, you have honored Bethesda's God. May he long delight to honor you here on earth! And after a life spent to his glory, and your country's good, may he honor you to all eternity, in placing you as Christ's right-hand in the kingdom above!

Next to your Excellency, my dear Mr President, I must beg your acceptance both of thanks and congratulation on the annual return of this festival. For you was not only my dear familiar friend, and first fellow-traveler in this infant province; but you was directed by Providence to this spot, laid the second brick of this house, watched, prayed, and wrought for the family's good: A witness of innumerable trials, partner of my joys and griefs; you will have now the pleasure of seeing the Orphan-house a fruitful bough, its branches running over the wall. For this, no doubt, God hath smiled upon and blessed you, in a manner we could not expect, much less design; and may he continue to bless you with all spiritual blessings in heavenly places in Christ Jesus. Look to the rock from whence you have been hewn, and may your children never be ashamed, that their father left his native country, and married a real Christian, born again under this roof. May Bethesda's Good grant this may be the happy portion of your children, and children's children!

Gentlemen of his Majesty's council, Mr Speaker, and you members of the General Assembly, many thanks are owing to you, for your late address to his Excellency in favor of Bethesda. Your joint recommendation of it, when I was last here, which, though in some measure through the bigotry of some, for the present is rendered abortive, by their wanting to have it confined to a party, yet I trust the event will prove that every thing shall be over-ruled to the furtherance of the work. Here I repeat, what I have often declared, that as far as lies in my power before and after my decease, Bethesda shall be always on a broad bottom. All denominations have freely given; all denominations, all the continent, God being my helper, shall receive benefit from it. May Bethesda's God bless you all! In your private as well as public capacity; and as you are honored to be the representatives of a now flourishing increasing people: may you be directed in all your ways! May truth, justice, religion, and piety be established amongst you through all generations!

LASTLY, My reverend brethren, and you inhabitants of the colony, accept unfeigned thanks for the honor done me, in letting us see you at Bethesda this day. You, Sir, for the sermon preached here last year. Tell it in Germany, tell my great, good friend, Professor Franck, that Bethesda's God, is a God whose mercy endureth for ever. O let us have your earnest prayers! Encourage your people not to 'despise the day of small things.' What hath God wrought? From its infancy, this colony hath been blessed with many faithful gospel ministers: O that this may be a nursery to many more! This hath been the case of the New England College for almost a century, and why not the Orphan-house Academy at Georgia?

Men, brethren, fathers, as many of you, whether inhabitants or strangers, who have honored this day with your presence, give us the additional blessings of your prayers. And O that Bethesda's God may make this day, though but a day of small things, productive of great things to the souls of all amongst whom I have been now preaching the kingdom of God. A great and good day will it be indeed, if Jesus Christ, our great Zerubbabel, should, by the power of the eternal Spirit, bless any thing that hath now been said, to cause every mountain of difficulty, that lies in the way of your conversion, to become a plain. And what art thou, O great mountain, whether the lust of the flesh, the lust of the eye, or the pride of life, sin, or self-righteousness? Before our Bethesda's God, thou shalt become a plain.

Brethren, my heart is enlarged towards you: it is written, blessed be God that it is written, 'In the name of Jesus every knee shall bow, whether things in heaven, or things in earth, or things under the earth.' O that we may be made a willing people in the day of his power! Look, look unto him, all ye that are placed in these ends of the earth. This house hath often been an house of God, a gate of heaven, to some of your fathers. May it be a house of God, a gate of heaven, to the children also! Come unto him, all ye that are weary and heavy laden, he will give you rest; rest from the guilt, rest from the power, rest from the punishment of sin; rest from the fear of divine judgments here, rest with himself eternally hereafter. Fear not, though the beginnings are but small, Christ will not despise the day of small things. A bruised reed will he not break, and the smoking flax will he not quench, until he bring forth judgment unto victory. His hands that laid the foundation, also shall finish it: yet a little while and the top-stone shall be brought forth with shouting, and men and angels join in crying 'Grace! Grace! Unto it.' That all present may be in this happy number, may God of his infinite mercy grant, through Jesus our Lord.

Edmund Burke:

22 March 1775

Conciliation with America

Burke made the following long speech, proposing 13 resolutions for conciliation on behalf of the American colonists, but was heavily defeated when the vote was taken in the House of Commons.

To restore order and repose to an empire so great and so distracted as ours is, merely in the attempt, an undertaking that would ennoble the flights of the highest genius, and obtain pardon for the efforts of the meanest understanding. Struggling a good while with these thoughts, by degrees I felt myself more firm. I derived, at length, some confidence from what in other circumstances usually produces timidity. I grew less anxious, even from the idea of my own insignificance. For, judging of what you are by what you ought to be, I persuaded myself that you would not reject a reasonable proposition because it had nothing but its reason to recommend it.

The proposition is peace. Not peace through the medium of war; not peace to be hunted through the labyrinth of intricate and endless negotiations; not peace to arise out of universal discord, fomented from principle, in all parts of the empire; not peace to depend on the juridical determination of perplexing questions, or the precise marking of the shadowy boundaries of a complex government. It is simple peace, sought in its natural course and in its ordinary haunts.

Let the colonies always keep the idea of their civil rights associated with your government – they will cling and grapple to you, and no force under heaven will be of power to tear them from their allegiance. But let it be once understood that your government may be one thing and their privileges another, that these two things may exist without any mutual relation – the cement is gone, the cohesion is loosened, and everything hastens to decay and dissolution. As long as you have the wisdom to keep the sovereign authority of this country as the sanctuary of liberty, the sacred temple consecrated to our common faith, wherever the chosen race and sons of England worship freedom, they will turn their faces towards you. The more they multiply, the more friends you will have, the more ardently they love liberty, the more perfect will be their obedience. Slavery they can have anywhere. It is a weed that grows in every soil. They may have it from Spain, they may have it from Prussia. But until you become lost to all feeling of your true interest and your natural dignity, freedom they can have from none but you.

This is the commodity of price, of which you have the monopoly. This is the true Act of Navigation, which binds to you the commerce of the colonies, and through them secures to you the wealth of the world. Deny them this participation of freedom, and you break that sole bond which originally made, and must still preserve, the unity of the empire. Do not entertain so weak an imagination as that your registers and your bonds, your affidavits and your sufferances ... are what form the great securities of your commerce. Do not dream that your Letters of office, and your instructions, and your suspending clauses are the things that hold together the great contexture of this mysterious whole. These things do not make your government. Dead instruments, passive tools as they are, it is the spirit of the English communion that gives all their life and efficacy to them. It is the spirit of the English constitution which, infused through the mighty mass, pervades, feeds, unites, invigorates ... every part of the empire, even down to the minutest member.

Is it not the same virtue which does every thing for us here in England? Do you imagine, then, that it is the Land-Tax Act which raises your revenue? that it is the annual vote in the Committee of Supply, which gives you your army? or that it is the Mutiny Bill which inspires it with bravery and discipline? No! surely, no! It is the love of the people; it is their attachment to their government, from the sense of the deep stake they have in such a glorious institution, which gives you your army and your navy, and infuses into both that liberal obedience without which your army would be a base rabble and your navy nothing but rotten timber.

All this, I know well enough, will sound wild and chimerical to the profane herd of those vulgar and mechanical politicians who have no place among us: a sort of people who think that nothing exists but what is gross and material, and who, therefore, far from being qualified to be directors of the great movement of empire, are not fit to turn a wheel in the machine. But to men truly initiated and rightly taught, these ruling and master principles, which in the opinion of such men as I have mentioned have no substantial existence, are in truth everything, and all in all. Magnanimity in politics is not seldom the truest wisdom; and a great empire and little minds go ill together. If we are conscious of our situation, and glow with zeal to fill our places as becomes our station and ourselves, we ought to auspicate all our public proceedings on America with the old warning of the Church, *Sursum corda*! We ought to elevate our minds to the greatness of that trust to which the order of Providence has called us. By adverting to the dignity of this high calling, our ancestors have turned a savage wilderness into a glorious empire, and have made the most extensive and the only honorable conquests, not by destroying, but by promoting the wealth, the number, the happiness of the human race. Let us get an American revenue as we have got an American empire. English privileges have made it all that it is; English privileges alone will make it all it can be.

Patrick Henry:
1775

'Give me liberty or give me death'

At the same time that Edmund Burke was speaking in the British House of Commons on behalf of the American colonies, Patrick Henry (1736–99), a fervent Virginian patriot and lawyer, made the following speech which Thomas Jefferson believed ignited the American Revolution.

No man thinks more highly than I do of the patriotism, as well as abilities, of the very worthy gentlemen who have just addressed the house. But different men often see the same subject in different lights; and, therefore, I hope it will not be thought disrespectful to those gentlemen if, entertaining as I do opinions of a character very opposite to theirs, I shall speak forth my sentiments freely and without reserve. This is no time for ceremony. The question before the house is one of awful moment to this country. For my own part, I consider it as nothing less than a question of freedom or slavery; and in proportion to the magnitude of the subject ought to be the freedom of the debate. It is only in this way that we can hope to arrive at the truth, and fulfill the great responsibility which we hold to God and our country. Should I keep back my opinions at such a time, through fear of giving offense, I should consider myself as guilty of treason towards my country, and of an act of disloyalty toward the Majesty of Heaven, which I revere above all earthly kings.

Mr President, it is natural to man to indulge in the illusions of hope. We are apt to shut our eyes against a painful truth, and listen to the song of that siren till she transforms us into beasts. Is this the part of wise men, engaged in a great and arduous struggle for liberty? Are we disposed to be of the numbers of those who, having eyes, see not, and, having ears, hear not, the things which so nearly concern their temporal salvation? For my part, whatever anguish of spirit it may cost, I am willing to know the whole truth, to know the worst, and to provide for it.

I have but one lamp by which my feet are guided, and that is the lamp of experience. I know of no way of judging of the future but by the past. And judging by the past, I wish to know what there has been in the conduct of the British ministry for the last ten years to justify those hopes with which gentlemen have been pleased to solace themselves and the House. Is it that insidious smile with which our petition has been lately received?

Trust it not, sir; it will prove a snare to your feet. Suffer not yourselves to be betrayed with a kiss. Ask yourselves how this gracious reception of our petition comports with those warlike preparations which cover our waters and darken our land. Are fleets and armies necessary to a work of love and reconciliation? Have we shown ourselves so unwilling to be reconciled that force must be called in to win back our love? Let us not deceive ourselves, sir. These are the implements of war and subjugation; the last arguments to which kings resort. I ask gentlemen, sir, what means this martial array, if its purpose be not to force us to submission? Can gentlemen assign any other possible motive for it? Has Great Britain any enemy, in this quarter of the world, to call for all this accumulation of navies and armies? No, sir, she has none. They are meant for us: they can be meant for no other. They are sent over to bind and rivet upon us those chains which the British ministry have been so long forging. And what have we to oppose to them? Shall we try argument? Sir, we have been trying that for the last ten years. Have we anything new to offer upon the subject? Nothing. We have held the subject up in every light of which it is capable; but it has been all in vain. Shall we resort to entreaty and humble supplication? What terms shall we find which have not been already exhausted? Let us not, I beseech you, sir, deceive ourselves. Sir, we have done everything that could be done to avert the storm which is now coming on. We have petitioned; we have remonstrated; we have supplicated; we have prostrated ourselves before the throne, and have implored its interposition to arrest the tyrannical hands of the ministry and Parliament. Our petitions have been slighted; our remonstrances have produced additional violence and insult; our supplications have been disregarded; and we have been spurned, with contempt, from the foot of the throne! In vain, after these things, may we indulge the fond hope of peace and reconciliation.

There is no longer any room for hope. If we wish to be free – if we mean to preserve inviolate those inestimable privileges for which we have been so long contending – if we mean not basely to abandon the noble struggle in which we have been so long engaged, and which we have pledged ourselves never to abandon until the glorious object of our contest shall be obtained – we must fight! I repeat it, sir, we must fight! An appeal to arms and to the God of hosts is all that is left us! They tell us, sir, that we are weak; unable to cope with so formidable an adversary. But when shall we be stronger? Will it be the next week, or the next year? Will it be when we are totally disarmed, and when a British guard shall be stationed in every house? Shall we gather strength but irresolution and inaction? Shall we acquire the means of effectual resistance by lying supinely on our backs and hugging the delusive phantom of hope, until our enemies shall have bound us hand and foot? Sir, we are not weak if we make a proper use of those means which the God of nature hath placed in our power. The millions of people, armed in the holy cause of liberty, and in such a country as that which we possess, are invincible by any force which our enemy can send against us. Besides, sir, we shall not fight our battles alone. There is a just God who presides over the destinies of nations, and who will raise up friends to fight our battles for us. The battle, sir, is not to the strong alone; it is to the vigilant, the active, the brave. Besides, sir, we have no election. If we were base enough to desire it, it is now too late to retire from the contest. There is no retreat but in submission and slavery! Our chains are forged! Their clanking may be heard on the plains of Boston! The war is inevitable – and let it come! I repeat it, sir, let it come.

It is in vain, sir, to extentuate the matter. Gentlemen may cry, Peace, Peace – but there is no peace. The war is actually begun! The next gale that sweeps from the north will bring to our ears the clash of resounding arms! Our brethren are already in the field! Why stand we here idle? What is it that gentlemen wish? What would they have? Is life so dear, or peace so sweet, as to be purchased at the price of chains and slavery? Forbid it, Almighty God! I know not what course others may take; but as for me, give me liberty or give me death!

Thomas Jefferson:

1782

Commerce between Master and Slave

Thomas Jefferson (1743–1826), the third president of the United States, drafted the Declaration of Independence. In 1779 he became Governor of Virginia, guiding that state through the troubled last years of the American Revolution.

The whole commerce between master and slave is a perpetual exercise of the most boisterous passions, the most unremitting despotism on the one part, and degrading submission on the other. Our children see this and learn to imitate it; for man is an imitative animal. This quality is the germ of all education in him. From his cradle to his grave he is learning to do what he sees others do. If a parent could find no motive either in his philanthropy or his self-love for restraining the intemperance of passion towards his slave, it should always be a sufficient one that his child is present. But generally it is not sufficient. The parent storms, the child looks on, catches the lineaments of his wrath, puts on the same airs in the circle of smaller slaves, gives a loose rein to the worst of passions and thus nursed, educated and daily exercised in tyranny, can not but be stamped by it with odious peculiarities. I tremble for my country when I reflect that God is just: that his justice can not sleep forever...

The man must be a prodigy who can retain his manners and morals undepraved by such circumstances. And with what execrations should the statesman be loaded who, permitting one half the citizens thus to trample on the rights of the other, transforms those into despots and these into enemies, destroys the morals of the one part and the *amor patriae* of the other. For if a slave can have a country in this world, it must be any other in preference to that in which he is born to live and labor for another: in which he must lock up the faculties of his nature, contribute as far as depends on his individual endeavors to the evanishment of the human race or entail his own miserable condition on the endless generations proceeding from him. With the morals of the people, their industry is also destroyed. For in a warm climate, no man will labor for himself who can make another labor for him. This is so true that, of the proprietors of slaves, a very small proportion are ever seen to labor. And can the liberties of a nation be thought secure, when we have removed their only firm basis, a conviction in the minds of the people that these liberties are of the gift of God? That they are not to be violated but with his wrath? Indeed I tremble for my country when I reflect that God is just: that his justice can not sleep forever: that considering numbers, nature and natural means only, a revolution of the wheel of fortune, an exchange of situation is among possible events: that it may become probable by supernatural interference!

The Almighty has no attributes which can take side with us in such a contest. But it is impossible to be temperate and to pursue this subject through the various considerations of policy, of morals, of history natural and civil. We must be contented to hope they will force their way into every one's mind. I think a change already perceptible, since the origin of the present revolution. The spirit of the master is abating, that of the slave rising from the dust, his condition mollifying, the way, I hope, preparing, under the auspices of heaven, for a total emancipation; and that this is disposed, in the order of events, to be with the consent of the masters, rather than by their extirpation.

George Washington Prevents the Revolt of his Officers

15 March 1783

At the end of the Revolutionary War in America, a pivotal moment in the life of the new American democracy occurred as officers of the Continental Army met in Newburgh, New York, to discuss a possible insurrection against the rule of Congress. Washington was not welcome at their meeting, but he spoke to them. This resulted in a unanimous vote to support the Congress.

Gentlemen:

By an anonymous summons, an attempt has been made to convene you together; how inconsistent with the rules of propriety, how unmilitary, and how subversive of all order and discipline, let the good sense of the army decide...

Thus much, gentlemen, I have thought it incumbent on me to observe to you, to show upon what principles I opposed the irregular and hasty meeting which was proposed to have been held on Tuesday last – and not because I wanted a disposition to give you every opportunity consistent with your own honor, and the dignity of the army, to make known your grievances. If my conduct heretofore has not evinced to you that I have been a faithful friend to the army, my declaration of it at this time would be equally unavailing and improper. But as I was among the first who embarked in the cause of our common country. As I have never left your side one moment, but when called from you on public duty. As I have been the constant companion and witness of your distresses, and not among the last to feel and acknowledge your merits. As I have ever considered my own military reputation as inseparably connected with that of the army. As my heart has ever expanded with joy, when I have heard its praises, and my indignation has arisen, when the mouth of detraction has been opened against it, it can scarcely be supposed, at this late stage of the war, that I am indifferent to its interests.

But how are they to be promoted? The way is plain, says the anonymous addresser. If war continues, remove into the unsettled country, there establish yourselves, and leave an ungrateful country to defend itself. But who are they to defend? Our wives, our children, our farms, and other property which we leave behind us. Or, in this state of hostile separation, are we to take the two first (the latter cannot be removed) to perish in a wilderness, with hunger, cold, and nakedness? If peace takes place, never sheathe your swords, says he, until you have obtained full and ample justice; this dreadful alternative, of either deserting our country in the extremest hour of her distress or turning our arms against it (which is the apparent object, unless Congress can be compelled into instant compliance), has something so shocking in it that humanity revolts at the idea. My God! What can this writer have in view, by recommending such measures? Can he be a friend to the army? Can he be a friend to this country? Rather, is he not an insidious foe? Some emissary, perhaps, from New York, plotting the ruin of both, by sowing the seeds of discord and separation between the civil and military powers of the continent? And what a compliment does he pay to our understandings when he recommends measures in either alternative, impracticable in their nature?

I cannot, in justice to my own belief, and what I have great reason to conceive is the intention of Congress, conclude this address, without giving it as my decided opinion, that that honorable body entertain exalted sentiments of the services of the army; and, from a full conviction of its merits and sufferings, will do it complete justice. That their endeavors to discover and establish funds for this purpose have been unwearied, and will not cease till they have succeeded, I have not a doubt. But, like all other large bodies, where there is a variety of different interests to reconcile, their deliberations are slow. Why, then, should we distrust them? And, in consequence of that distrust, adopt measures which may cast a shade over that glory which has been so justly acquired; and tarnish the reputation of an army which is celebrated through all Europe, for its fortitude and patriotism? And for what is this done? To bring the object we seek nearer? No! most certainly, in my opinion, it will cast it at a greater distance.

For myself (and I take no merit in giving the assurance, being induced to it from principles of gratitude, veracity, and justice), a grateful sense of the confidence you have ever placed in me, a recollection of the cheerful assistance and prompt obedience I have experienced from you, under every vicissitude of fortune, and the sincere affection I feel for an army I have so long had the honor to command will oblige me to declare, in this public and solemn manner, that, in the attainment of complete justice for all your toils and dangers, and in the gratification of every wish, so far as may be done consistently with the great duty I owe my country and those powers we are bound to respect, you may freely command my services to the utmost of my abilities.

While I give you these assurances, and pledge myself in the most unequivocal manner to exert whatever ability I am possessed of in your favor, let me entreat you, gentlemen, on your part, not to take any measures which, viewed in the calm light of reason, will lessen the dignity and sully the glory you have hitherto maintained; let me request you to rely on the plighted faith of your country, and place a full confidence in the purity of the intentions of Congress; that, previous to your dissolution as an army, they will cause all your accounts to be fairly liquidated, as directed in their resolutions, which were published to you two days ago, and that they will adopt the most effectual measures in their power to render ample justice to you, for your faithful and meritorious services. And let me conjure you, in the name of our common country, as you value your own sacred honor, as you respect the rights of humanity, and as you regard the military and national character of America, to express your utmost horror and detestation of the man who wishes, under any specious pretenses, to overturn the liberties of our country, and who wickedly attempts to open the floodgates of civil discord and deluge our rising empire in blood.

By thus determining and thus acting, you will pursue the plain and direct road to the attainment of your wishes. You will defeat the insidious designs of our enemies, who are compelled to resort from open force to secret artifice. You will give one more distinguished proof of unexampled patriotism and patient virtue, rising superior to the pressure of the most complicated sufferings. And you will, by the dignity of your conduct, afford occasion for posterity to say, when speaking of the glorious example you have exhibited to mankind, 'Had this day been wanting, the world had never seen the last stage of perfection to which human nature is capable of attaining.'

Jupiter Hammon:

24 September 1786

'God is no respecter of persons'

An address given to the members of the African Society in New York.

> Of a truth I perceive that God is no respecter of persons: But in every Nation, he that feareth him and worketh righteousness, is accepted with him.
>
> Acts 10:34–35

I am Gentlemen, Your Servant, Jupiter Hammon, as I desire to say something to you for your good, and with a view to promote your happiness, I can with truth and sincerity with the apostle Paul, when speaking of his own nation the Jews, and say, 'That I have great heaviness and continual sorrow in my heart for my brethren, my kinsmen according to the flesh.' Yes my dear brethren, when I think of you, which is very often, and of the poor, despised and miserable state you are in, as to the things of this world, and when I think of your ignorance and stupidity, and the great wickedness of the most of you, I am pained to the heart. It is at times, almost too much for human nature to bear, and I am obliged to turn my thoughts from the subject or endeavour to still my mind, by considering that it is permitted thus to be, by that God who governs all things, who setteth up one and pulleth down another. While I have been thinking on this subject, I have frequently had great struggles in my own mind, and have been at a loss to know what to do. I have wanted exceedingly to say something to you, to call upon you with the tenderness of a father and friend, and to give you the last, and I may say, dying advice, of an old man, who wishes our best good in this world, and in the world to come. But while I have had such desires, a sense of my own ignorance, and unfitness to teach others, has frequently discouraged me from attempting to say any thing to you; yet when I thought of your situation, I could not rest easy.

When I was at Hartford in Connecticut, where I lived during the war, I published several pieces which were well received, not only by those of my own colour, but by a number of the white people, who thought they might do good among their servants. This is one consideration, among others, that emboldens me now to publish what I have written to you. Another is, I think you will be more likely to listen to what is said, when you know it comes from a Negro, one your own nation and colour, and therefore can have no interest in deceiving you, or in saying any thing to you, but what he really thinks is your interest and duty to comply with. My age, I think, gives me some right to speak to you, and reason to expect you will hearken to my advice. I am now upwards of seventy years old, and cannot expect, though I am well, and able to do almost any kind of business, to live much longer. I have passed the common bounds set for man, and must soon go the way of all the earth. I have had more experience in the world than the most of you, and I have seen a great deal of the vanity, and wickedness of it. I have great reason to be thankful that my lot has been so much better than most slaves have had. I suppose I have had more advantages and privileges than most of you, who are slaves have ever known, and I believe more than many white people have enjoyed, for which I desire to bless God, and pray that he may bless those who have given them to me. I do not, my dear friends, say these things about myself to make you think that I am wiser or better than others; but that you might hearken, without prejudice, to what I have to say to you on the following particulars.

1. Respecting obedience to masters. Now whether it is

right, and lawful, in the sight of God, for them to make slaves of us or not, I am certain that while we are slaves, it is our duty to obey our masters, in all their lawful commands, and mind them unless we are bid to do that which we know to be sin, or forbidden in God's word. The apostle Paul says, 'Servants be obedient to them that are your masters according to the flesh, with fear and trembling in singleness in your heart as unto Christ: Not with eye service, as men pleasers, but as the servants of Christ doing the will of God from the heart: With good will doing service to the Lord, and not to men: Knowing that whatever thing a man doeth the same shall he receive of the Lord, whether he be bond or free.'

Here is a plain command of God for us to obey our masters. It may seem hard for us, if we think our masters wrong in holding us slaves, to obey in all things, but who of us dare dispute with God! He has commanded us to obey, and we ought to do it chearfully, and freely. This should be done by us, not only because God commands, but because our own peace and comfort depend upon it. As we depend upon our masters, for what we eat and drink and wear, and for all our comfortable things in this world, we cannot be happy, unless we please them. This we cannot do without obeying them freely, without muttering or finding fault. If a servant strives to please his master and studies and takes pains to do it, I believe there are but few masters who would use such a servant cruelly. Good servants frequently make good masters. If your master is really hard, unreasonable and cruel, there is no way so likely for you to convince him of it, as always to obey his commands, and try to serve him, and take care of his interest, and try to promote it all in your power. If you are proud and stubborn and always finding fault, your master will think the fault lies wholly on your side, but if you are humble, and meek, and bear all things patiently, your master may think he is wrong; if he does not, his neighbors will be apt to see it, and will befriend you, and try to alter his conduct. If this does not do, you must cry to him, who has the hearts of all men in his hands, and turneth them as the rivers of waters are turned.

2. The particular I would mention, is honesty and faithfulness. You must suffer me now to deal plainly with you, my dear brethren, for I do not mean to flatter, or omit speaking the truth, whether it is for you, or against you. How many of you are there who allow yourselves in stealing from your masters. It is very wicked for you not to take care of your masters goods, but how much worse is it to pilfer and steal from them, whenever you think you shall not be found out. This you must know is very wicked and provoking to God. There are none of you so ignorant, but that you must know that this is wrong. Though you may try to excuse yourselves, by saying that your masters are unjust to you, and though you may try to quiet your consciences in this way, yet if you are honest in owning the truth you must think it is as wicked, and on some accounts more wicked to steal from your masters, than from others.

We cannot certainly, have any excuse either for taking any thing that belongs to our masters without their leave, or for being unfaithful in their business. It is our duty to be faithful, not with eye service as men pleasers. We have no right to stay when we are sent on errands, any longer than to do the business we were sent upon. All the time spent idly, is spent wickedly, and is unfaithfulness to our masters. In these things I must say, that I think many of you are guilty. I know that many of you endeavour to excuse yourselves, and say that you have nothing that you can call your own, and that you are under great temptations to be unfaithful and take from your masters. But this will not do, God will certainly punish you for stealing and for being unfaithful.

All that we have to mind is our own duty. If God has put us in bad circumstances that is not our fault and he will not punish us for it. If any are wicked in keeping us so, we cannot help it, they must answer to God for it. Nothing will serve as an excuse to us for not doing our duty. The same God will judge both them and us. Pray then my dear friends, fear to offend in this way, but be faithful to God, to your masters, and to your own souls.

The next thing I would mention, and warn you against, is profaneness. This you know is forbidden by God. Christ tells us, 'swear not at all,' and again it is said 'thou shalt not take the name of the Lord thy God in vain, for the Lord will not hold him guiltless, that taketh his name in vain.' Now though the great God has forbidden it, yet how dreadfully profane are many, and I don't know but I may say the most of you? How common is it to hear you take the terrible and awful name of the great God in vain? – To swear by it, and by Jesus Christ, his Son – How common is it to hear you wish damnation to your companions, and to your own souls – and to sport with in the name of Heaven and Hell, as if there were no such places for you to hope for, or to fear. Oh my friends, be warned to forsake this dreadful sin of profaneness. Pray my dear friends, believe and realize, that there is a God – that he is great and terrible beyond what you can think – that he keeps you in life every moment – and that he can send you to that awful Hell, that you laugh at, in an instant, and confine you there for ever, and that he will certainly do it, if you do not repent. You certainly do not believe, that there is a God, or that there is a Heaven or Hell, or you would never trifle with them. It would make you shudder, if you heard others do it, if you believe them as much, as you believe any thing you see with your bodily eyes.

I have heard some learned and good men say, that the heathen, and all that worshiped false Gods, never spoke lightly or irreverently of their Gods, they never took their names in vain, or jested with those things which they held sacred. Now why should the true God, who made all things, be treated worse in this respect, than those false Gods, that were made of wood and stone. I believe it is because Satan tempts men to do it. He tried to make them love their false Gods, and to speak well of them, but he wishes to have men think lightly of the true God, to take his holy name in vain, and to scoff at, and make a jest of all things that are really good. You may think that Satan has not power to do so much, and have so great influence on the minds of men: But the scripture says, 'he goeth about like a roaring Lion, seeking whom he may devour – That he is the prince of the power of the air – and that he rules in the hearts of the children of disobedience – and that wicked men are led captive by him, to do his will.' All those of you who are profane, are serving the Devil. You are doing what he tempts and desires you to do. If you could see him with your bodily eyes, would you like to make an agreement with him, to serve him, and do as he bid you. I believe most of you would be shocked at this, but you may be certain that all of you who allow yourselves in this sin, are as really serving him, and to just as good purpose, as if you met him, and promised to dishonor God, and serve him with all your might. Do you believe this? It is true whether you believe it or not. Some of you to excuse yourselves, may plead the example of others, and say that you hear a great many white people, who know more, than such poor ignorant Negroes, as you are, and some who are rich and great gentlemen, swear, and talk profanely; and some of you may say this of your masters, and say no more than is true. But all this is not a sufficient excuse for you. You know that murder is wicked. If you saw your master kill a man, do you suppose this would be any excuse for you, if you should commit the same crime? You must know it would not;

nor will your hearing him curse and swear, and take the name of God in vain, or any other man, be he ever so great or rich, excuse you.

God is greater than all other beings, and him we are bound to obey. To him we must give an account for every idle word that we speak. He will bring us all, rich and poor, white and black, to his judgment seat. If we are found among those who feared his name, and trembled at his word, we shall be called good and faithful servants. Our slavery will be at an end, and though ever so mean, low, and despited in this world, we shall sit with God in his kingdom as Kings and Priests, and rejoice forever, and ever. Do not then, my dear friends, take God's holy name in vain, or speak profanely in any way. Let not the example of others lead you into the sin, but reverence and fear that great and fearful name, the Lord our God. I might now caution you against other sins to which you are exposed; but as I meant only to mention those you were exposed to, more than others, by your being slaves, I will conclude what I have to say to you, by advising you to become religious, and to make religion the great business of your lives.

Now I acknowledge that liberty is a great thing, and worth seeking for, if we can get it honestly, and by our good conduct, prevail on our masters to set us free: Though for my own part I do not wish to be free, yet I should be glad, if others, especially the young Negroes were to be free, for many of us, who are grown up slaves, and have always had masters to take care of us, should hardly know how to take care of ourselves; and it may be more for our own comfort to remain as we are. That liberty is a great thing we may know from our own feelings, and we may likewise judge so from the conduct of the white-people, in the late war. How much money has been spent, and how many lives has been lost, to defend their liberty. I must say that I have hoped that God would open their eyes, when they were so much engaged for liberty, to think of the state of the poor blacks, and to pity us. He has done it in some measure, and has raised us up many friends, for which we have reason to be thankful, and to hope in his mercy. What may be done further, he only knows, for known unto God are all his ways from the beginning. But this my dear brethren is by no means, the greatest thing we have to be concerned about. Getting our liberty in this world, is nothing to our having the liberty of the children of God. Now the Bible tells us that we are all by nature, sinners, that we are slaves to sin and Satan, and that unless we are converted, or born again, we must be miserable forever. Christ says, except a man be born again, he cannot see the kingdom of God, and all that do not see the kingdom of God, must be in the kingdom of darkness. There are but two places where all go after death, white and black, rich and poor; those places are Heaven and Hell. Heaven is a place made for those, who are born again, and who love God, and it is a place where they will be happy for ever. Hell is a place made for those who hate God, and are his enemies, and where they will be miserable to all eternity. Now you may think you are not enemies to God, and do not hate him: But if your heart has not been changed, and you have not become true Christians, you certainly are enemies to God, and have been opposed to him ever since you were born.

Many of you, I suppose, never think of this, and are almost as ignorant as the beasts that perish. Those of you who can read I must beg you to read the Bible, and whenever you can get time, study the Bible, and if you can get no other time, spare some of your time from sleep, and learn what the mind and will of God is. But what shall I say to them who cannot read. This lay with great weight on my mind, when I thought of writing to my poor brethren, but I hope that those who can read will take pity on them and read what I have to say to them. In hopes of this I will beg of you to spare no pains in trying to learn to read. If you are once engaged you may learn. Let all the time you can get be spent in trying to learn to read. Get those who can read to learn you, but remember, that what you learn for, is to read the Bible. If there was no Bible, it would be no matter whether you could read or not. Reading other books would do you no good. But the Bible is the word of God, and tells you what you must do to please God; it tells you how you may escape misery, and be happy for ever. If you see most people neglect the Bible, and many that can read never look into it, let it not harden you and make you think lightly of it, and that it is a book of no worth. All those who are really good, love the Bible, and meditate on it day and night. In the Bible God has told us every thing it is necessary we should know, in order to be happy here and hereafter. The Bible is a revelation of the mind and will of God to men. Therein we may learn, what God is. That he made all things by the power of his word; and that he made all things for his own glory, and not for our glory. That he is over all, and above all his creatures, and more above them that we can think or conceive – that they can do nothing without him – that he upholds them all, and will over-rule all things for his own glory.

In the Bible likewise we are told what man is. That he was at first made holy, in the image of God, that he fell from that state of holiness, and became an enemy to God, and that since the fall, all the imaginations of the thoughts of his heart, are evil and only evil, and that continually. That the carnal mind is not subject to the law of God, neither indeed can be. And that all mankind, were under the wrath, and curse of God, and must have been for ever miserable, if they had been left to suffer what their sins deserved. It tells us that God, to save some of mankind, sent his Son into this world to die, in the room and stead of sinners, and that now God can save from eternal misery, all that believe in his Son, and take him for their saviour, and that all are called upon to repent, and believe in Jesus Christ. It tells us that those who do repent, and believe, and are friends to Christ, shall have many trials and sufferings in this world, but that they shall be happy forever, after death, and reign with Christ to all eternity. The Bible tells us that this world is a place of trial, and that there is no other time or place for us to alter, but in this life. If we are Christians when we die, we shall awake to the resurrection of life; if not, we shall awake to the resurrection of damnation. It tells us, we must all live in Heaven or Hell, be happy or miserable, and that without end. The Bible does not tell us of but two places, for all to go to. There is no place for innocent folks, that are not Christians. There is no place for ignorant folks, that did not know how to be Christians. What I mean is, that there is no place besides Heaven and Hell. These two places, will receive all mankind, for Christ says, there are but two sorts, he that is not with me is against me, and he that gathereth not with me, scattereth abroad – The Bible likewise tells us that this world, and all things in it shall be burnt up – and that 'God has appointed a day in which he will judge the world, and that he will bring every secret thing whether it be good or bad into judgment – that which is done in secret shall be declared on the house top.' I do not know, nor do I think any can tell, but that the day of judgment may last a thousand years. God could tell the state of all his creatures in a moment, but then every thing that every one has done, through his whole life is to be told, before the whole world of angels, and men. There, Oh how solemn is the thought! You, and I, must stand, and hear every thing we have thought or done, however secret, however wicked and vile, told before all the men and women that ever have been, or ever will be, and before all the angels, good and bad.

Now my dear friends seeing the Bible is the word of God, and every thing in it is true, and it reveals such awful and glorious things, what can be more important than that you should learn to read it; and when you have learned to read, that you should study it day and night. There are some things very encouraging in God's word for such ignorant creatures as we are; for God hath not chosen the rich of this world. Not many rich, not many noble are called, but God hath chosen the weak things of this world, and things which are not, to confound the things that are: And when the great and the rich refused coming to the gospel feast, the servant was told, to go into the highways, and hedges, and compel those poor creatures that he found there to come in. Now my brethren it seems to me, that there are no people that ought to attend to the hope of happiness in another world so much as we do. Most of us are cut off from comfort and happiness here in this world, and can expect nothing from it. Now seeing this is the case, why should we not take care to be happy after death. Why should we spend our whole lives in sinning against God: And be miserable in this world, and in the world to come. If we do thus, we shall certainly be the greatest fools. We shall be slaves here, and slaves forever. We cannot plead so great temptations to neglect religion as others. Riches and honours which drown the greater part of mankind, who have the gospel, in perdition, can be little or no temptations to us.

We live so little time in this world that it is no matter how wretched and miserable we are, if it prepares us for heaven. What is forty, fifty, or sixty years, when compared to eternity. When thousands and millions of years have rolled away, this eternity will be no nigher coming to an end. Oh how glorious is an eternal life of happiness! And how dreadful, an eternity of misery.

Those of us who have had religious masters, and have been taught to read the Bible, and have been brought by their example and teaching to a sense of divine things, how happy shall we be to meet them in heaven, where we shall join them in praising God forever. But if any of us have had such masters, and yet have lived and died wicked, how will it add to our misery to think of our folly. If any of us, who have wicked and profane masters should become religious, how will our estates be changed in another world. Oh my friends, let me intreat of you to think on these things, and to live as if you believed them to be true. If you become Christians you will have reason to bless God forever, that you have been brought into a land where you have heard the gospel, though you have been slaves. If we should ever get to Heaven, we shall find nobody to reproach us for being black, or for being slaves. Let me beg of you my dear African brethren, to think very little of your bondage in this life, for your thinking of it will do you no good. If God designs to set us free, he will do it, in his own time, and way; but think of your bondage to sin and Satan, and do not rest, until you are delivered from it. We cannot be happy if we are ever so free or ever so rich, while we are servants of sin, and slaves to Satan. We must be miserable here, and to all eternity.

I will conclude what I have to say with a few words to those Negroes who have their liberty. The most of what I have said to those who are slaves may be of use to you, but you have more advantages, on some accounts, if you will improve your freedom, as you may do, than they. You have more time to read God's holy word, and to take care of the salvation of your souls. Let me beg of you to spend your time in this way, or it will be better for you, if you had always been slaves. If you think seriously of the matter, you must conclude, that if you do not use your freedom, to promote the salvation of your souls, it will not be of any lasting good to you. Besides all this, if you are idle, and take to bad courses, you will hurt those of your brethren who are slaves, and do all in your power to prevent their being free. One great reason that is given by some for not freeing us, I understand is, that we should not know how to take care of ourselves, and should take to bad courses. That we should be lazy and idle, and get drunk and steal. Now all those of you, who follow any bad courses, and who do not take care to get an honest living by your labour and industry, are doing more to prevent our being free, than any body else. Let me beg of you then for the sake of your own good and happiness, in time, and for eternity, and for the sake of your poor brethren, who are still in bondage 'to lead quiet and peaceable lives in all Godliness and honesty', and may God bless you, and bring you to his kingdom, for Christ's sake, Amen.

George Washington:

30 April 1789

First Inaugural Address

George Washington, the first President of the United States, took his oath of office in April 1789. He had been unanimously elected President by the first electoral college, and John Adams was elected Vice President. Washington gave his inaugural address before a joint session of the two Houses of Congress at the Senate Chamber in Federal Hall on Wall Street, New York City.

Fellow-Citizens of the Senate and of the House of Representatives: among the vicissitudes incident to life no event could have filled me with greater anxieties than that of which the notification was transmitted by your order, and received on the 14th day of the present month. On the one hand, I was summoned by my country, whose voice I can never hear but with veneration and love, from a retreat which I had chosen with the fondest predilection, and, in my flattering hopes, with an immutable decision, as the asylum of my declining years – a retreat which was rendered every day more necessary as well as more dear to me by the addition of habit to inclination, and of frequent interruptions in my health to the gradual waste committed on it by time. On the other hand, the magnitude and difficulty of the trust to which the voice of my country called me, being sufficient to awaken in the wisest and most experienced of her citizens a distrustful scrutiny into his qualifications, could not but overwhelm with despondence one who (inheriting inferior endowments from nature and unpracticed in the duties of civil administration) ought to be peculiarly conscious of his own deficiencies. In this conflict of emotions all I dare aver is that it has been my faithful study to collect my duty from a just appreciation of every circumstance by which it might be affected. All I dare hope is that if, in executing this task, I have been too much swayed by a grateful remembrance of former instances, or by an affectionate sensibility to this transcendent proof of the confidence of my fellow-citizens, and have thence too little consulted my incapacity as well as disinclination for the weighty and untried cares before me, my error will be palliated by the motives which mislead me, and its consequences be judged by my country with some share of the partiality in which they originated.

Such being the impressions under which I have, in obedience to the public summons, repaired to the present station, it would be peculiarly improper to omit in this first official act my fervent supplications to that Almighty Being who rules over the universe, who presides in the councils of nations, and whose providential aids can supply every human defect, that His benediction may consecrate to the liberties and happiness of the people of the United States a Government instituted by themselves for these essential purposes, and may enable every instrument employed in its administration to execute with success the functions allotted to his charge. In tendering this homage to the Great Author of every public and private good, I assure myself that it expresses your sentiments not less than my own, nor those of my fellow-citizens at large less than either. No people can be bound to acknowledge and adore the Invisible Hand which conducts the affairs of men more than those of the United States. Every step by which they have advanced to the character of an independent nation seems to have been distinguished by some token of providential agency; and in the important revolution just accomplished in the system of their united government the tranquil deliberations and voluntary consent of so many distinct communities from which the event has resulted can not be compared with the means by which most governments have been established without some return of pious gratitude, along with an humble anticipation of the future blessings which the past seem to presage. These reflections, arising out of the present crisis, have forced themselves too strongly on my mind to be suppressed. You will join with me, I trust, in thinking that there are none under the influence of which the proceedings of a new and free government can more auspiciously commence.

By the article establishing the executive department it is made the duty of the President 'to recommend to your consideration such measures as he shall judge necessary and expedient.' The circumstances under which I now meet you will acquit me from entering into that subject further than to refer to the great constitutional charter under which you are assembled, and which, in defining your powers, designates the objects to which your attention is to be given. It will be more consistent with those circumstances, and far more congenial with the feelings which actuate me, to substitute, in place of a recommendation of particular measures, the tribute that is due to the talents, the rectitude, and the patriotism which adorn the characters selected to devise and adopt them. In these honorable qualifications I behold the surest pledges that as on one side no local prejudices or attachments, no separate views nor party animosities, will misdirect the comprehensive and equal eye which ought to watch over this great assemblage of communities and interests, so, on another, that the foundation of our national policy will be laid in the pure and immutable principles of private morality, and the pre-eminence of free government be exemplified by all the attributes which can win the affections of its citizens and command the respect of the world. I dwell on this prospect with every satisfaction which an ardent love for my country can inspire, since there is no truth more thoroughly established than that there exists in the economy and course of nature an indissoluble union between virtue and happiness; between duty and advantage; between the genuine maxims of an honest and magnanimous policy and the solid rewards of public prosperity and felicity; since we ought to be no less persuaded that the propitious smiles of Heaven can never be expected on a nation that disregards the eternal rules of order and right which Heaven itself has ordained; and since the preservation of the sacred fire of liberty and the destiny of the republican model of government are justly considered, perhaps, as deeply, as finally, staked on the experiment entrusted to the hands of the American people.

Besides the ordinary objects submitted to your care, it will remain with your judgment to decide how far an exercise of the occasional power delegated by the fifth article of the Constitution is rendered expedient at the present juncture by the nature of objections which have been urged against the system, or by the degree of inquietude which has given birth to them. Instead of undertaking particular recommendations on this subject, in which I could be guided by no lights derived from official opportunities, I shall again give way to my entire confidence in your discernment and pursuit of the public good; for I assure myself that whilst you carefully avoid every alteration which might endanger the benefits of an united and effective government, or which ought to await the future lessons of experience, a reverence for the characteristic rights of freemen and a regard for the public harmony will sufficiently influence your deliberations on the question how far the former can be impregnably fortified or the latter be safely and advantageously promoted.

To the foregoing observations I have one to add, which will be most properly addressed to the House of Representatives. It concerns myself, and will therefore be as brief as possible. When I was first honored with a call into the service of my country, then on the eve of an arduous struggle for its liberties, the light in which I contemplated my duty required that I should renounce every pecuniary compensation. From this resolution I have in no instance departed; and being still under the impressions which produced it, I must decline as inapplicable to myself any share in the personal emoluments which may be indispensably included in a permanent provision for the executive department, and must accordingly pray that the pecuniary estimates for the station in which I am placed may during my continuance in it be limited to such actual expenditures as the public good may be thought to require.

Having thus imparted to you my sentiments as they have been awakened by the occasion which brings us together, I shall take my present leave; but not without resorting once more to the benign Parent of the Human Race in humble supplication that, since He has been pleased to favor the American people with opportunities for deliberating in perfect tranquillity, and dispositions for deciding with unparalleled unanimity on a form of government for the security of their union and the advancement of their happiness, so His divine blessing may be equally conspicuous in the enlarged views, the temperate consultations, and the wise measures on which the success of this Government must depend.

Edmund Burke:

1793

On the Death of Marie Antoinette

Edmund Burke (1729–97) was born in Dublin, Ireland, and became a member of the British House of Commons. He made many speeches which have become classics. After the French Revolution of 1789 had destroyed the French monarchy, and especially after the beheading of Queen Marie Antoinette, Burke became an outspoken critic of the excesses of the Revolution.

It is now sixteen or seventeen years since I saw the queen of France, then the dauphiness, at Versailles; and surely never lighted on this orb, which she hardly seemed to touch, a more delightful vision. I saw her just above the horizon, decorating and cheering the elevated sphere she had just begun to move in, glittering like the morning star full of life and splendor and joy. O, what a revolution! and what a heart must I have, to contemplate without emotion that elevation and that fall! Little did I dream, when she added titles of veneration to those of enthusiastic, distant, respectful love, that she should ever be obliged to carry the sharp antidote against disgrace concealed in that bosom; little did I dream that I should have lived to see such disasters fallen upon her, in a nation of gallant men, in a nation of men of honour, and of cavaliers! I thought ten thousand swords must have leaped from their scabbards, to avenge even a look that threatened her with insult.

But the age of chivalry is gone; that of sophisters, economists, and calculators has succeeded, and the glory of Europe is extinguished forever. Never, never more, shall we behold that generous loyalty to rank and sex, that proud submission, that dignified obedience, that subordination of the heart, which kept alive, even in servitude itself, the spirit of an exalted freedom! The unbought grace of life, the cheap defence of nations, the nurse of manly sentiment and heroic enterprise is gone. It is gone, that sensibility of principle, that chastity of honour, which felt a stain like a wound, which inspired courage whilst it mitigated ferocity, which ennobled whatever it touched, and under which vice itself lost half its evil, by losing all its grossness.

Maximilien Robespierre:

1794

Republican Frenchmen

Maximilien Robespierre (1758–94), one of the leaders and orators of the French Revolution of 1789, is best known for his involvement in the Reign of Terror that followed. He developed great love for power and a reputation for intolerance and cruelty. Shortly after delivering this speech, Robespierre was arrested and sent to the guillotine on 28 July 1794.

The day forever fortunate has arrived, which the French people have consecrated to the Supreme Being. Never has the world which He created offered to Him a spectacle so worthy of His notice. He has seen reigning on the earth tyranny, crime, and imposture. He sees at this moment a whole nation, grappling with all the oppressions of the human race, suspend the course of its heroic labours to elevate its thoughts and vows toward the great Being who has given it the mission it has undertaken and the strength to accomplish it.

Is it not He whose immortal hand, engraving on the heart of man the code of justice and equality, has written there the death sentence of tyrants? Is it not He who, from the beginning of time, decreed for all the ages and for all peoples liberty, good faith, and justice?

He did not create kings to devour the human race. He did not create priests to harness us, like vile animals, to the chariots of kings and to give to the world examples of baseness, pride, perfidy, avarice, debauchery, and falsehood. He created the universe to proclaim His power. He created men to help each other, to love each other mutually, and to attain to happiness by the way of virtue.

It is He who implanted in the breast of the triumphant oppressor remorse and terror, and in the heart of the oppressed and innocent calmness and fortitude. It is He who impels the just man to hate the evil one, and the evil man to respect the just one. It is He who adorns with modesty the brow of beauty, to make it yet more beautiful. It is He who makes the mother's heart beat with tenderness and joy. It is He who bathes with delicious tears the eyes of the son pressed to the bosom of his mother. It is He who silences the most imperious and tender passions before the sublime love of the fatherland. It is He who has covered nature with charms, riches, and majesty. All that is good is His work, or is Himself. Evil belongs to the depraved man who oppresses his fellow man or suffers him to be oppressed.

The Author of Nature has bound all mortals by a boundless chain of love and happiness. Perish the tyrants who have dared to break it!

Republican Frenchmen, it is yours to purify the earth which they have soiled, and to recall to it the justice that they have banished! Liberty and virtue together came from the breast of Divinity. Neither can abide with mankind without the other.

O generous People, would you triumph over all your enemies? Practise justice, and render the Divinity the only worship worthy of Him. O People, let us deliver ourselves today, under His auspices, to the just transports of a pure festivity. Tomorrow we shall return to the combat with vice and tyrants. We shall give to the world the example of republican virtues. And that will be to honour Him still.

The monster which the genius of kings had vomited over France has gone back into nothingness. May all the crimes and all the misfortunes of the world disappear with it! Armed in turn with the daggers of fanaticism and the poisons of atheism, kings have always conspired to assassinate humanity. If they are able no longer to disfigure Divinity by superstition, to associate it with their crimes, they try to banish it from the earth, so that they may reign there alone with crime.

O People, fear no more their sacrilegious plots! They can no more snatch the world from the breast of its Author than remorse from their own hearts. Unfortunate ones, uplift your eyes toward heaven! Heroes of the fatherland, your generous devotion is not a brilliant madness. If the satellites of tyranny can assassinate you, it is not in their power entirely to destroy you. Man, whoever thou mayest be, thou canst still conceive high thoughts for thyself. Thou canst bind thy fleeting life to God, and to immortality. Let nature seize again all her splendour, and wisdom all her empire! The Supreme Being has not been annihilated.

It is wisdom above all that our guilty enemies would drive from the republic. To wisdom alone it is given to strengthen the prosperity of empires. It is for her to guarantee to us the rewards of our courage. Let us associate wisdom, then, with all our enterprises. Let us be grave and discreet in all our deliberations, as men who are providing for the interests of the world. Let us be ardent and obstinate in our anger against conspiring tyrants, imperturbable in dangers, patient in labours, terrible in striking back, modest and vigilant in successes. Let us be generous toward the good, compassionate with the unfortunate, inexorable with the evil, just toward every one. Let us not count on an unmixed prosperity, and on triumphs without attacks, nor on all that depends on fortune or the perversity of others. Sole, but infallible guarantors of our independence, let us crush the impious league of kings by the grandeur of our character, even more than by the strength of our arms.

Frenchmen, you war against kings; you are therefore worthy to honour Divinity. Being of Beings, Author of Nature, the brutalized slave, the vile instrument of despotism, the perfidious and cruel aristocrat, outrages Thee by his very invocation of Thy name. But the defenders of liberty can give themselves up to Thee, and rest with confidence upon Thy paternal bosom. Being of Beings, we need not offer to Thee unjust prayers. Thou knowest Thy creatures, proceeding from Thy hands. Their needs do not escape Thy notice, more than their secret thoughts. Hatred of bad faith and tyranny burns in our hearts, with love of justice and the fatherland. Our blood flows for the cause of humanity. Behold our prayer. Behold our sacrifices. Behold the worship we offer Thee.

George Washington:

17 September 1796

'Cultivate peace and harmony with all'

In his farewell address Washington bequeathed to America a summary of his political ideas. Each year on 22 February this speech is read in the Senate and the House of Representatives at noon, to remind the nation of Washington's beliefs.

Friends and fellow-citizens: the period for a new election of a citizen to administer the executive government of the United States being not far distant, and the time actually arrived when your thoughts must be employed in designating the person who is to be clothed with that important trust, it appears to me proper, especially as it may conduce to a more distinct expression of the public voice, that I should now apprise you of the resolution I have formed, to decline being considered among the number of those out of whom a choice is to be made.

I beg you, at the same time, to do me the justice to be assured that this resolution has not been taken without a strict regard to all the considerations appertaining to the relation which binds a dutiful citizen to his country; and that in withdrawing the tender of service which silence, in my situation, might imply, I am influenced by no diminution of zeal for your future interest, no deficiency of grateful respect for your past kindness, but am supported by a full conviction that the step is compatible with both.

The acceptance of, and continuance hitherto, in the office to which your suffrages have twice called me, have been a uniform sacrifice of inclination to the opinion of duty, and to a deference for what appeared to be your desire. I constantly hoped that it would have been much earlier in my power, consistently with motives which I was not at liberty to disregard, to return to that retirement from which I had been reluctantly drawn. The strength of my inclination to do this, previous to the last election, had even led to the preparation of an address, to declare it to you; but mature reflection on the then perplexed and critical posture of our affairs with foreign nations, and the unanimous advice of persons entitled to my confidence, impelled me to abandon the idea...

Here, perhaps, I ought to stop. But a solicitude for your welfare, which cannot end but with my life, and the apprehension of danger, natural to that solicitude, urge me, on an occasion like the present, to offer to your solemn contemplation, and to recommend to your frequent review, some sentiments, which are the result of much reflection, of no inconsiderable observation, and which appear to me all-important to the permanency of your felicity as a people. These will be offered to you with the more freedom, as you can only see in them the disinterested warnings of a parting friend, who can possibly have no personal motive to bias his counsel. Now can I forget, as an encouragement to it, your indulgent reception of my sentiments on a former and not dissimilar occasion.

Interwoven as is the love of liberty with every ligament of your hearts, no recommendation of mine is necessary to fortify or confirm the attachment.

The unity of government which constitutes you one people is also now dear to you. It is justly so, for it is a main pillar in the edifice of your real independence, the support of your tranquility at home, your peace abroad, of your safety, of your prosperity, of that very liberty which you so highly prize. But as it is easy to foresee, that from different causes and from different quarters, much pains will be taken, many artifices employed, to weaken in your minds the convictions of this truth; as this is the point in your political fortress against which the batteries of internal and external enemies will be most constantly and actively (though often covertly and insidiously) directed, it is of infinite moment that you should properly estimate the immense value of your national union, to your collective and individual happiness; that you should cherish a cordial, habitual, and immovable attachment to it; accustoming yourselves to think and speak of it as of the palladium of your political safety and prosperity, watching for its preservation with jealous anxiety; discountenancing whatever may suggest even a suspicion that it can in any event be abandoned; and indignantly frowning upon the first dawning of every attempt to alienate any portion of our country from the rest, or to enfeeble the sacred ties which now link together the various parts.

For this you have every inducement of sympathy and interest. Citizens, by birth or choice, of a common country, that country has a right to concentrate your affections. The name of America, which belongs to you in your national capacity, must always exalt the just pride of patriotism more than any appellation derived from local discriminations. With slight shades of difference, you have the same religion, manners, habits and political principles. You have, in a common cause, fought and triumphed together; the independence and liberty you possess are the work of joint councils and joint efforts, of common dangers, sufferings, and successes...

Let me now warn you, in the most solemn manner, against the baneful effects of the spirit of party, generally.

This spirit, unfortunately, is inseparable from our nature, having its root in the strongest passions of the human mind. It exists under different shapes, in all governments, more or less stifled, controlled, or repressed. But in those of the popular form, it is seen in its greatest rankness, and is truly their worst enemy.

The alternate domination of one faction over another, sharpened by the spirit of revenge, natural to party dissensions, which, in different ages and countries, has perpetuated the most horrid enormities, is itself a frightful despotism...

Observe good faith and justice towards all nations; cultivate peace and harmony with all; religion and morality enjoin this conduct; and can it be that good policy does not equally enjoin it? It will be worthy of a free, enlightened, and at no distant period, a great nation, to give to mankind the magnanimous and too novel example of a people always guided by an exalted justice and benevolence. Who can doubt that, in the course of time and things, the fruits of such a plan would richly repay any temporary advantages that might be lost by a steady adherence to it? Can it be, that Providence has not connected the permanent felicity of a nation with its virtue. The experiment, at least, is recommended by every sentiment which ennobles human nature. Alas! is it rendered impossible by its vices?

In the execution of such a plan, nothing is more essential than that permanent, inveterate antipathies against particular nations, and passionate attachments for others, should be excluded; and that in place of them, just and amicable feelings towards all should be cultivated. The nation, which indulges towards another an habitual hatred, or an habitual fondness, is in some degree a slave. It is a slave to its animosity or to its affection, either of which is sufficient to lead it astray from its duty and its interest. Antipathy in one nation against another, disposes each more readily to offer insult and injury, to lay hold of slight causes of umbrage, and to be haughty and intractable, when accidental or trifling occasions of dispute occur.

Hence frequent collisions, obstinate, envenomed, and bloody contests. The nation, prompted by ill-will and resentment, sometimes impels to war the government, contrary to the best calculations of policy. The government sometimes participates in the national propensity, and adopts through passion what reason would reject; at other times, it makes the animosity of the nation subservient to projects of hostility instigated by pride, ambition and other sinister and pernicious motives. The peace often, and sometimes, perhaps, the liberty of nations, has been the victim.

So, likewise, a passionate attachment of one nation for another produces a variety of evils. Sympathy for the favorite nation facilitating the illusion of an imaginary common interest in cases where no real common interest exists, and infusing into one the enmities of the other, betrays the former into a participation in the quarrels and wars of the latter, without adequate inducement or justification...

Against the insidious wiles of foreign influence (I conjure you to believe me, fellow-citizens), the jealousy of a free people ought to be constantly awake; since history and experience prove, that foreign influence is one of the most baneful foes of republican government...

The great rule of conduct for us, in regard to foreign nations is, in extending our commercial relations, to have with them as little political connection as possible. So far as we have already formed engagements, let them be fulfilled with perfect good faith. Here let us stop...

Though, in reviewing the incidents of my administration, I an unconscious of intentional error, I am, nevertheless, too sensible of my defects, not to think it probable that I may have committed many errors. Whatever they may be, I fervently beseech the Almighty to avert or mitigate the evils to which they may tend. I shall also carry with me the hope that my country will never cease to view them with indulgence, and that after forty-five years of my life dedicated to its service, with an upright zeal, the faults of incompetent abilities will be consigned to oblivion, as myself must soon be to the mansions of rest.

Relying on its kindness in this, as in other things, and actuated by that fervent love towards it, which is so natural to a man who views in it the native soil of himself and his progenitors for several generations, I anticipate, with pleasing expectations, that retreat in which I promise myself to realize, without alloy, the sweet enjoyment of partaking, in the midst of my fellow-citizens, the benign influence of good laws under a free government – the ever favorite object of my heart, and the happy reward, as I trust, of our mutual cares, labors, and dangers.

PART IV

The Nineteenth Century

Thomas Jefferson:
1800

'Let us pursue our own Federal and Republican principles'

The outcome of the American election of 1800 had been in doubt until late February because the two leading candidates, Thomas Jefferson and Aaron Burr, both received 73 electoral votes. After 30 hours of debate and after a ballot in the House of Representatives, Jefferson emerged as the President and Burr as the Vice President.

Friends and Fellow-Citizens:

Called upon to undertake the duties of the first executive office of our country, I avail myself of the presence of that portion of my fellow-citizens which is here assembled to express my grateful thanks for the favor with which they have been pleased to look toward me, to declare a sincere consciousness that the task is above my talents, and that I approach it with those anxious and awful presentiments which the greatness of the charge and the weakness of my powers so justly inspire. A rising nation, spread over a wide and fruitful land, traversing all the seas with the rich productions of their industry, engaged in commerce with nations who feel power and forget right, advancing rapidly to destinies beyond the reach of mortal eye – when I contemplate these transcendent objects, and see the honor, the happiness, and the hopes of this beloved country committed to the issue, and the auspices of this day, I shrink from the contemplation, and humble myself before the magnitude of the undertaking. Utterly, indeed, should I despair did not the presence of many whom I here see remind me that in the other high authorities provided by our Constitution I shall find resources of wisdom, of virtue, and of zeal on which to rely under all difficulties. To you, then, gentlemen, who are charged with the sovereign functions of legislation, and to those associated with you, I look with encouragement for that guidance and support which may enable us to steer with safety the vessel in which we are all embarked amidst the conflicting elements of a troubled world. During the contest of opinion through which we have passed the animation of discussions and of exertions has sometimes worn an aspect which might impose on strangers unused to think freely and to speak and to write what they think; but this being now decided by the voice of the nation, announced according to the rules of the Constitution, all will, of course, arrange themselves under the will of the law, and unite in common efforts for the common good. All, too, will bear in mind this sacred principle, that though the will of the majority is in all cases to prevail, that will to be rightful must be reasonable; that the minority possess their equal rights, which equal law must protect, and to violate would be oppression.

Let us, then, fellow-citizens, unite with one heart and one mind. Let us restore to social intercourse that harmony and affection without which liberty and even life itself are but dreary things. And let us reflect that, having banished from our land that religious intolerance under which mankind so long bled and suffered, we have yet gained little if we countenance a political intolerance as despotic, as wicked, and capable of as bitter and bloody persecutions. During the throes and convulsions of the ancient world, during the agonizing spasms of infuriated man, seeking through blood and slaughter his long-lost liberty, it was not wonderful that the agitation of the billows should reach even this distant and peaceful shore; that this should be more felt and feared by some and less by others, and should divide opinions as to measures of safety. But every difference of opinion is not a difference of principle. We have called by different names brethren of the same principle. We are all

Republicans, we are all Federalists. If there be any among us who would wish to dissolve this Union or to change its republican form, let them stand undisturbed as monuments of the safety with which error of opinion may be tolerated where reason is left free to combat it. I know, indeed, that some honest men fear that a republican government can not be strong, that this Government is not strong enough; but would the honest patriot, in the full tide of successful experiment, abandon a government which has so far kept us free and firm on the theoretic and visionary fear that this Government, the world's best hope, may by possibility want energy to preserve itself? I trust not. I believe this, on the contrary, the strongest Government on earth. I believe it the only one where every man, at the call of the law, would fly to the standard of the law, and would meet invasions of the public order as his own personal concern. Sometimes it is said that man can not be trusted with the government of himself. Can he, then, be trusted with the government of others? Or have we found angels in the forms of kings to govern him? Let history answer this question.

Let us, then, with courage and confidence pursue our own Federal and Republican principles, our attachment to union and representative government. Kindly separated by nature and a wide ocean from the exterminating havoc of one quarter of the globe; too high-minded to endure the degradations of the others; possessing a chosen country, with room enough for our descendants to the thousandth and thousandth generation; entertaining a due sense of our equal right to the use of our own faculties, to the acquisitions of our own industry, to honor and confidence from our fellow-citizens, resulting not from birth, but from our actions and their sense of them; enlightened by a benign religion, professed, indeed, and practiced in various forms, yet all of them inculcating honesty, truth, temperance, gratitude, and the love of man; acknowledging and adoring an overruling Providence, which by all its dispensations proves that it delights in the happiness of man here and his greater happiness hereafter – with all these blessings, what more is necessary to make us a happy and a prosperous people? Still one thing more, fellow-citizens – a wise and frugal Government, which shall restrain men from injuring one another, shall leave them otherwise free to regulate their own pursuits of industry and improvement, and shall not take from the mouth of labor the bread it has earned. This is the sum of good government, and this is necessary to close the circle of our felicities.

About to enter, fellow-citizens, on the exercise of duties which comprehend everything dear and valuable to you, it is proper you should understand what I deem the essential principles of our Government, and consequently those which ought to shape its Administration. I will compress them within the narrowest compass they will bear, stating the general principle, but not all its limitations. Equal and exact justice to all men, of whatever state or persuasion, religious or political; peace, commerce, and honest friendship with all nations, entangling alliances with none; the support of the State governments in all their rights, as the most competent administrations for our domestic concerns and the surest bulwarks against antirepublican tendencies; the preservation of the General Government in its whole constitutional vigor, as the sheet anchor of our peace at home and safety abroad; a jealous care of the right of election by the people – a mild and safe corrective of abuses which are lopped by the sword of revolution where peaceable remedies are unprovided; absolute acquiescence in the decisions of the majority, the vital principle of republics, from which is no appeal but to force, the vital principle and immediate parent of despotism; a well disciplined militia, our best reliance in peace and for the first moments of war, till regulars may relieve them; the supremacy of the civil over the military authority; economy in the public expense, that labor may be lightly burthened; the honest payment of our debts and sacred preservation of the public faith; encouragement of agriculture, and of commerce as its handmaid; the diffusion of information and arraignment of all abuses at the bar of the public reason; freedom of religion; freedom of the press, and freedom of person under the protection of the habeas corpus, and trial by juries impartially selected.

These principles form the bright constellation which has gone before us and guided our steps through an age of revolution and reformation. The wisdom of our sages and blood of our heroes have been devoted to their attainment. They should be the creed of our political faith, the text of civic instruction, the touchstone by which to try the services of those we trust; and should we wander from them in moments of error or of alarm, let us hasten to retrace our steps and to regain the road which alone leads to peace, liberty, and safety. I repair, then, fellow-citizens, to the post you have assigned me. With experience enough in subordinate offices to have seen the difficulties of this the greatest of all, I have learnt to expect that it will rarely fall to the lot of imperfect man to retire from this station with the reputation and the favor which bring him into it. Without pretensions to that high confidence you reposed in our first and greatest revolutionary character, whose pre-eminent services had entitled him to the first place in his country's love and destined for him the fairest page in the volume of faithful history, I ask so much confidence only as may give firmness and effect to the legal administration of your affairs. I shall often go wrong through defect of judgment. When right, I shall often be thought wrong by those whose positions will not command a view of the whole ground. I ask your indulgence for my own errors, which will never be intentional, and your support against the errors of others, who may condemn what they would not if seen in all its parts. The approbation implied by your suffrage is a great consolation to me for the past, and my future solicitude will be to retain the good opinion of those who have bestowed it in advance, to conciliate that of others by doing them all the good in my power, and to be instrumental to the happiness and freedom of all. Relying, then, on the patronage of your good will, I advance with obedience to the work, ready to retire from it whenever you become sensible how much better choice it is in your power to make. And may that Infinite Power which rules the destinies of the universe lead our councils to what is best, and give them a favorable issue for your peace and prosperity.

Thomas Jefferson:

4 March 1805

'I shall need the favor of that Being ...'

President Thomas Jefferson's second Inaugural Address.

Proceeding, fellow-citizens, to that qualification which the Constitution requires before my entrance on the charge again conferred on me, it is my duty to express the deep sense I entertain of this new proof of confidence from my fellow-citizens at large, and the zeal with which it inspires me so to conduct myself as may best satisfy their just expectations. On taking this station on a former occasion I declared the principles on which I believed it my duty to administer the affairs of our Commonwealth. My conscience tells me I have on every occasion acted up to that declaration according to its obvious import and to the understanding of every candid mind.

In the transaction of your foreign affairs we have endeavored to cultivate the friendship of all nations, and especially of those with which we have the most important relations. We have done them justice on all occasions, favored where favor was lawful, and cherished mutual interests and intercourse on fair and equal terms. We are firmly convinced, and we act on that conviction, that with nations as with individuals our interests soundly calculated will ever be found inseparable from our moral duties, and history bears witness to the fact that a just nation is trusted on its word when recourse is had to armaments and wars to bridle others.

At home, fellow-citizens, you best know whether we have done well or ill. The suppression of unnecessary offices, of useless establishments and expenses, enabled us to discontinue our internal taxes. These, covering our land with officers and opening our doors to their intrusions, had already begun that process of domiciliary vexation which once entered is scarcely to be restrained from reaching successively every article of property and produce. If among these taxes some minor ones fell which had not been inconvenient, it was because their amount would not have paid the officers who collected them, and because, if they had any merit, the State authorities might adopt them instead of others less approved.

The remaining revenue on the consumption of foreign articles is paid chiefly by those who can afford to add foreign luxuries to domestic comforts, being collected on our seaboard and frontiers only, and incorporated with the transactions of our mercantile citizens, it may be the pleasure and the pride of an American to ask, What farmer, what mechanic, what laborer ever sees a taxgatherer of the United States? These contributions enable us to support the current expenses of the Government, to fulfill contracts with foreign nations, to extinguish the native right of soil within our limits, to extend those limits, and to apply such a surplus to our public debts as places at a short day their final redemption, and that redemption once effected the revenue thereby liberated may, by a just repartition of it among the States and a corresponding amendment of the Constitution, be applied in time of peace to rivers, canals, roads, arts, manufactures, education, and other great objects within each State. In time of war, if injustice by ourselves or others must sometimes produce war, increased as the same revenue will be by increased population and consumption, and aided by other resources reserved for that crisis, it may meet within the year all the expenses of the year without encroaching on the rights of future generations by burthening them with the debts of the past. War will then be but a suspension of useful works, and a return to a state of peace, a return to the progress of improvement.

I have said, fellow-citizens, that the income reserved had enabled us to extend our limits, but that extension may possibly pay for itself before we are called on, and in the meantime may keep down the accruing interest; in all events, it will replace the advances we shall have made. I know that the acquisition of Louisiana had been disapproved by some from a candid apprehension that the enlargement of our territory would endanger its union. But who can limit the extent to which the federative principle may operate effectively? The larger our association the less will it be shaken by local passions; and in any view is it not better that the opposite bank of the Mississippi should be settled by our own brethren and children than by strangers of another family? With which should we be most likely to live in harmony and friendly intercourse?

In matters of religion I have considered that its free exercise is placed by the Constitution independent of the powers of the General Government. I have therefore undertaken on no occasion to prescribe the religious exercises suited to it, but have left them, as the Constitution found them, under the direction and discipline of the church or state authorities acknowledged by the several religious societies.

The aboriginal inhabitants of these countries I have regarded with the commiseration their history inspires. Endowed with the faculties and the rights of men, breathing an ardent love of liberty and independence, and occupying a country which left them no desire but to be undisturbed, the stream of overflowing population from other regions directed itself on these shores; without power to divert or habits to contend against it, they have been overwhelmed by the current or driven before it; now reduced within limits too narrow for the hunter's state, humanity enjoins us to teach them agriculture and the domestic arts; to encourage them to that industry which alone can enable them to maintain their place in existence and to prepare them in time for that state of society which to bodily comforts adds the improvement of the mind and morals. We have therefore liberally furnished them with the implements of husbandry and household use; we have placed among them instructors in the arts of first necessity, and they are covered with the aegis of the law against aggressors from among ourselves.

But the endeavors to enlighten them on the fate which awaits their present course of life, to induce them to exercise their reason, follow its dictates, and change their pursuits with the change of circumstances have powerful obstacles to encounter; they are combated by the habits of their bodies, prejudices of their minds, ignorance, pride, and the influence of interested and crafty individuals among them who feel themselves something in the present order of things and fear to become nothing in any other. These persons inculcate a sanctimonious reverence for the customs of their ancestors; that whatsoever they did must be done through all time; that reason is a false guide, and to advance under its counsel in their physical, moral, or political condition is perilous innovation; that their duty is to remain as their Creator made them, ignorance being safety and knowledge full of danger; in short, my friends, among them also is seen the action and counteraction of good sense and of bigotry; they too have their antiphilosophists who find an interest in keeping things in their present state, who dread reformation, and exert all their faculties to maintain the ascendancy of habit over the duty of improving our reason and obeying its mandates.

In giving these outlines I do not mean, fellow-citizens, to arrogate to myself the merit of the measures. That is due, in the first place, to the reflecting character of our citizens at large, who, by the weight of public opinion, influence and strengthen the public measures. It is due to the sound discretion with which they select from among themselves those to whom they confide the legislative duties. It is due to the zeal and wisdom of the characters thus selected, who lay the foundations of public happiness in wholesome laws, the execution of which alone remains for others, and it is due to the able and faithful auxiliaries, whose patriotism has associated them with me in the executive functions.

During this course of administration, and in order to disturb it, the artillery of the press has been leveled against us, charged with whatsoever its licentiousness could devise or dare. These abuses of an institution so important to freedom and science are deeply to be regretted, inasmuch as they tend to lessen its usefulness and to sap its safety. They might, indeed, have been corrected by the wholesome punishments reserved to and provided by the laws of the several States against falsehood and defamation, but public duties more urgent press on the time of public servants, and the offenders have therefore been left to find their punishment in the public indignation.

Nor was it uninteresting to the world that an experiment should be fairly and fully made, whether freedom of discussion, unaided by power, is not sufficient for the propagation and protection of truth – whether a government conducting itself in the true spirit of its constitution, with zeal and purity, and doing no act which it would be unwilling the whole world should witness, can be written down by falsehood and defamation. The experiment has been tried; you have witnessed the scene; our fellow-citizens looked on, cool and collected; they saw the latent source from which these outrages proceeded; they gathered around their public functionaries, and when the Constitution called them to the decision by suffrage, they pronounced their verdict, honorable to those who had served them and consolatory to the friend of man who believes that he may be trusted with the control of his own affairs.

No inference is here intended that the laws provided by the States against false and defamatory publications should not be enforced; he who has time renders a service to public morals and public tranquillity in reforming these abuses by the salutary coercions of the law; but the experiment is noted to prove that, since truth and reason have maintained their ground against false opinions in league with false facts, the press, confined to truth, needs no other legal restraint; the public judgment will correct false reasoning and opinions on a full hearing of all parties; and no other definite line can be drawn between the inestimable liberty of the press and its demoralizing licentiousness. If there be still improprieties which this rule would not restrain, its supplement must be sought in the censorship of public opinion.

Contemplating the union of sentiment now manifested so generally as auguring harmony and happiness to our future course, I offer to our country sincere congratulations. With those, too, not yet rallied to the same point the disposition to do so is gaining strength; facts are piercing through the veil drawn over them, and our doubting brethren will at length see that the mass of their fellow-citizens with whom they can not yet resolve to act as to principles and measures, think as they think and desire what they desire; that our wish as well as theirs is that the public efforts may be directed honestly to the public good, that peace be cultivated, civil and religious liberty unassailed, law and order preserved, equality of rights maintained, and that state of property, equal or unequal, which results to every man from his own industry or that of his father's. When satisfied of these views it is not in human nature that they should not approve and support them. In the meantime let us cherish them with patient affection, let us do them justice, and more than justice, in all competitions of interest; and we need not doubt that truth, reason, and their own interests will at length prevail, will gather them into the fold of their country, and will complete that en-tire union of opinion which gives to a nation the blessing of harmony and the benefit of all its strength.

I shall now enter on the duties to which my fellow-citizens have again called me, and shall proceed in the spirit of those principles which they have approved. I fear not that any motives of interest may lead me astray; I am sensible of no passion which could seduce me knowingly from the path of justice, but the weaknesses of human nature and the limits of my own understanding will produce errors of judgment sometimes injurious to your interests. I shall need, therefore, all the indulgence which I have heretofore experienced from my constituents; the want of it will certainly not lessen with increasing years. I shall need, too, the favor of that Being in whose hands we are, who led our fathers, as

Israel of old, from their native land and planted them in a country flowing with all the necessaries and comforts of life; who has covered our infancy with His providence and our riper years with His wisdom and power, and to whose goodness I ask you to join in supplications with me that He will so enlighten the minds of your servants, guide their councils, and prosper their measures that whatsoever they do shall result in your good, and shall secure to you the peace, friendship, and approbation of all nations.

Napoleon Bonaparte:

20 April 1814

Farewell to the Old Guard

Having been defeated by the Allies, the Emperor Napoleon Bonaparte of France says goodbye to his Old Guard at Fontainebleau.

Soldiers of my Old Guard: I bid you farewell. For twenty years I have constantly accompanied you on the road to honour and glory. In these latter times, as in the days of our prosperity, you have invariably been models of courage and fidelity. With men such as you our cause could not be lost; but the war would have been interminable; it would have been civil war, and that would have entailed deeper misfortunes on France.

I have sacrificed all of my interests to those of the country.

I go, but you, my friends, will continue to serve France. Her happiness was my only thought. It will still be the object of my wishes. Do not regret my fate; if I have consented to survive, it is to serve your glory. I intend to write the history of the great achievements we have performed together. Adieu, my friends. Would I could press you all to my heart.

Daniel O'Connell:

4 February 1836

'Here am I calling for justice to Ireland'

Daniel O'Connell (1775–1847), a great Irish statesman who became known as the Liberator of Ireland, led a movement that forced the British to pass the Catholic Emancipation Act of 1829. This allowed Roman Catholics to become members of the British House of Commons. This is the speech he gave in the House of Commons calling for equal justice to Ireland.

It appears to me impossible to suppose that the House will consider me presumptuous in wishing to be heard for a short time on this question, especially after the distinct manner in which I have been alluded to in the course of the debate. If I had no other excuse, that would be sufficient; but I do not want it; I have another and a better – the question is one in the highest degree interesting to the people of Ireland. It is, whether we mean to do justice to that country – whether we mean to continue the injustice which has been already done to it, or to hold out the hope that it will be treated in the same manner as England and Scotland. That is the question. We know what 'lip service' is; we do not want that. There are some men who will even declare that they are willing to refuse justice to Ireland; while there are others who, though they are ashamed to say so, are ready to consummate the iniquity, and they do so.

England never did do justice to Ireland – she never did. What we have got of it we have extorted from men opposed to us on principle – against which principle they have made us such concessions as we have obtained from them. The right honourable baronet opposite [Sir Robert Peel] says he does not distinctly understand what is meant by a principle. I believe him.

which, adopted in practice, will be most salutary not only to the British Empire, but to the world. When speaking of our foreign policy, it rejoices in the cooperation between France and this country; but it abstains from conveying any ministerial approbation of alterations in the domestic laws of that country which aim at the suppression of public liberty, and the checking of public discussion, such as call for individual reprobation, and which I reprobate as much as any one. I should like to know whether there is a statesman in the country who will get up in this House and avow his approval of such proceedings on the part of the French government. I know it may be done out of the House amid the cheers of an assembly of friends; but the government have, in my opinion, wisely abstained from reprobating such measures in the speech, while they have properly exulted in such a union of the two countries as will contribute to the national independence and the public liberty of Europe.

Years are coming over me, but my heart is as young and as ready as ever in the service of my country, of which I glory in being the pensionary and the hired advocate. I stand in a situation in which no man ever stood yet – the faithful friend of my country – its servant – its stave, if you will – I speak its sentiments by turns to you and to itself. I require no £20,000,000 on behalf of Ireland – I ask you only for justice: will you – can you – I will not say dare you refuse, because that would make you turn the other way. I implore you, as English gentlemen, to take this matter into consideration now, because you never had such an opportunity of conciliating. Experience makes fools wise; you are not fools, but you have yet to be convinced. I cannot forget the year 1825. We begged then as we would for a beggar's boon; we asked for emancipation by all that is sacred amongst us, and I remember how my speech and person were treated on the Treasury Bench, when I had no opportunity of reply. The other place turned us out and sent us back again, but we showed that justice was with us. The noble lord says the other place has declared the same sentiments with himself; but he could not use a worse argument. It is the very reason why we should acquiesce in the measure of reform, for we have no hope from that House – all our hopes are centred in this; and I am the living representative of those hopes.

I have no other reason for adhering to the ministry than because they, the chosen representatives of the people of England, are anxiously determined to give the same measure of reform to Ireland as that which England has received. I have not fatigued myself, but the House, in coming forward upon this occasion. I may be laughed and sneered at by those who talk of my power; but what has created it but the injustice that has been done in Ireland? That is the end and the means of the magic, if you please – the groundwork of my influence in Ireland. If you refuse justice to that country, it is a melancholy consideration to me to think that you are adding substantially to that power and influence, while you are wounding my country to its very heart's core; weakening that throne, the monarch who sits upon which, you say you respect; severing that union which, you say, is bound together by the tightest links, and withholding that justice from Ireland which she will not cease to seek till it is obtained; every man must admit that the course I am taking is the legitimate and proper course – I defy any man to say it is not. Condemn me elsewhere as much as you please, but this you must admit. You may taunt the ministry with having coalesced me, you may raise the vulgar cry of 'Irishman and Papist' against me, you may send out men called ministers of God to slander and calumniate me; they may assume whatever garb they please, but the question comes into this narrow compass. I demand, I respectfully insist: on equal justice for Ireland, on the same principle by which it has been administered to Scotland and England. I will not take less. Refuse me that if you can.

Charles Dickens:

February 1842

'Virtue in rags and patches'

A speech given by Charles Dickens to the young men of Boston.

Gentlemen – If you had given this splendid entertainment to anyone else in the whole wide world – if I were to-night to exult in the triumph of my dearest friend – if I stood here upon my defence, to repel any unjust attack – to appeal as a stranger to your generosity and kindness as the freest people on the earth – I could, putting some restraint upon myself, stand among you as self-possessed and unmoved as I should be alone in my own room in England. But when I have the echoes of your cordial greeting ringing in my ears; when I see your kind faces beaming a welcome so warm and earnest as never man had – I feel, it is my nature, so vanquished and subdued, that I have hardly fortitude enough to thank you. If your President, instead of pouring forth that delightful mixture of humour and pathos which you have just heard, had been but a caustic, ill-natured man – if he had only been a dull one – if I could only have doubted or distrusted him or you, I should have had my wits at my fingers' ends, and, using them, could have held you at arm's-length. But you have given me no such opportunity; you take advantage of me in the tenderest point; you give me no chance of playing at company, or holding you at a distance, but flock about me like a host of brothers, and make this place like home. Indeed, gentlemen,

that few persons have been more interested in mine than I, and if it be a general principle in nature that a lover's love is blind, and that a mother's love is blind, I believe it may be said of an author's attachment to the creatures of his own imagination, that it is a perfect model of constancy and devotion, and is the blindest of all. But the objects and purposes I have had in view are very plain and simple, and may be easily told. I have always had, and always shall have, an earnest and true desire to contribute, as far as in me lies, to the common stock of healthful cheerfulness and enjoyment. I have always had, and always shall have, an invincible repugnance to that mole-eyed philosophy which loves the darkness, and winks and scowls in the light. I believe that Virtue shows quite as well in rags and patches, as she does in purple and fine linen. I believe that she and every beautiful object in external nature, claims some sympathy in the breast of the poorest man who breaks his scanty loaf of daily bread. I believe that she goes barefoot as well as shod. I believe that she dwells rather oftener in alleys and by-ways than she does in courts and palaces, and that it is good, and pleasant, and profitable to track her out, and follow her. I believe that to lay one's hand upon some of those rejected ones whom the world has too long forgotten, and too often misused, and to say to the proudest and most thoughtless – 'These creatures have the same elements and capacities of goodness as yourselves, they are moulded in the same form, and made of the same clay; and though ten times worse than you, may, in having retained anything of their original nature amidst the trials and distresses of their condition, be really ten times better'; I believe that to do this is to pursue a worthy and not useless vocation. Gentlemen, that you think so too, your fervent greeting sufficiently assures me. That this feeling is alive in the Old World as well as in the New, no man should know better than I – I, who have found such wide and ready sympathy in my own dear land.

no chance of spoiling me. I feel as though we were agreeing – as indeed we are, if we substitute for fictitious characters the classes from which they are drawn – about third parties, in whom we had a common interest. At every new act of kindness on your part, I say to myself 'That's for Oliver; I should not wonder if that was meant for Smike; I have no doubt that is intended for Nell'; and so I become a much happier, certainly, but a more sober and retiring man than ever I was before.

Gentlemen, talking of my friends in America, brings me back, naturally and of course, to you. Coming back to you, and being thereby reminded of the pleasure we have in store in hearing the gentlemen who sit about me, I arrive by the easiest, though not by the shortest course in the world, at the end of what I have to say. But before I sit down, there is one topic on which I am desirous to lay particular stress. It has, or should have, a strong interest for us all, since to its literature every country must look for one great means of refining and improving its people, and one great source of national pride and honour. You have in America great writers – great writers – who will live in all time, and are as familiar to our lips as household words. Deriving (as they all do in a greater or less degree, in their several walks) their inspiration from the stupendous country that gave them birth, they diffuse a better knowledge of it, and a higher love for it, all over the civilized world. I take leave to say, in the presence of some of those gentlemen, that I hope the time is not far distant when they, in America, will receive of right some substantial profit and return in England from their labours; and when we, in England, shall receive some substantial profit and return in America for ours. Pray do not misunderstand me. Securing to myself from day to day the means of an honourable subsistence, I would rather have the affectionate regard of my fellow men, than I would have heaps and mines of gold. But the two things do not seem to me incompatible. They cannot be, for nothing good is incompatible with justice; there must be an international arrangement in this respect: England has done her part, and I am confident that the time is not far distant when America will do hers. It becomes the character of a great country; FIRSTLY, because it is justice; SECONDLY, because without it you never can have, and keep, a literature of your own.

Gentlemen, I thank you with feelings of gratitude, such as are not often awakened, and can never be expressed. As I understand it to be the pleasant custom here to finish with a toast, I would beg to give you: AMERICA AND ENGLAND, and may they never have any division but the Atlantic between them.

Elizabeth Cady Stanton:

20 July 1848

The Declaration of Sentiments

The following Declaration of Sentiments was made at the Woman's Rights Convention held in the Wesleyan Chapel at Senecca Falls, New York. This was the first formal action by women in the United States to gain civil rights and suffrage. Women gained the federal guarantee of the vote in 1920 after 72 years of campaigning – the largest civil rights movement in the history of the world.

I should feel exceedingly diffident to appear before you at this time, having never before spoken in public, were I not nerved by a sense of right and duty, did I not feel the time had fully come for the question of woman's wrongs to be laid before the public, did I not believe that woman herself must do this work; for woman alone can understand the height, the depth, the length, and the breadth of her own degradation. Man cannot speak for her, because he has been educated to believe that she differs from him so materially, that he cannot judge of her thoughts, feelings, and opinions by his own. Moral beings can only judge of others by themselves. The moment they assume a different nature for any of their own kind, they utterly fail. The drunkard was hopelessly lost until it was discovered that he was governed by the same laws of mind as the sober man. Then with what magic power, by kindness and love, was he raised from the slough of despond and placed rejoicing on high land.

Let a man once settle the question that a woman does not think and feel like himself, and he may as well undertake to judge of the amount of intellect and sensation of any of the animal creation as of woman's nature. He can know but little with certainty, and that but by observation.

Among the many important questions which have been brought before the public, there is none that more vitally affects the whole human family than that which is technically called Woman's Rights. Every allusion to the degraded and inferior position occupied by women all over the world has been met by scorn and abuse. From the man of highest mental cultivation to the most degraded wretch who staggers in the streets do we meet ridicule, and coarse jests, freely bestowed upon those who dare assert that woman stands by the side of man, his equal, placed here by her God, to enjoy with him the beautiful earth, which is her home as it is his, having the same sense of right and wrong, and looking to the same Being for guidance and support. So long has man exercised tyranny over her, injurious to himself and benumbing to her faculties, that few can nerve themselves to meet the storm; and so long has the chain been about her that she knows not there is a remedy.

The whole social, civil and religious condition of woman is a subject too vast to be brought within the limits of one short lecture. Suffice it to say, for the present, wherever we turn, the history of woman is sad and dark, without any alleviating circumstances, nothing from which we can draw consolation.

The world has never yet seen a truly great and virtuous nation, because in the degradation of woman the very fountains of life are poisoned at their source. It is vain to look for silver and gold from mines of copper and lead. It is the wise mother that has the wise son. So long as your women are slaves you may throw your colleges and churches to the winds. You can't have scholars and saints so long as your mothers are ground to powder between the upper and nether millstone of tyranny and lust. How seldom, now, is a father's pride gratified, his fond hopes realized, in the budding genius of his son. The wife is degraded, made the mere creature of caprice, and the foolish son is heaviness to his heart. Truly are the sins of the fathers visited upon the children to the third and fourth generation. God, in his wisdom, has so linked the whole human family together, that any violence done at one end of the chain is felt throughout its length, and here, too, is the law of restoration, as in woman all have fallen, so in her elevation shall the race be recreated. 'Voices' were the visitors and advisers of Joan of Arc. Do not 'voices' come to us daily from the haunts of poverty, sorrow, degradation and despair, already too long unheeded. Now is the time for the women of this country, if they would save our free institutions, to defend the right, to buckle on the armour that can best resist the keenest weapons of the enemy – contempt and ridicule. The same religious enthusiasm that nerved Joan of Arc to her work nerves us to ours. In every generation God calls some men and women for the utterance of truth, a heroic action, and our work to-day is the fulfilling of what has long since been foretold by the prophet –

Joel 2:28: 'And it shall come to pass afterward that I will pour out my spirit upon all flesh, and your sons and your daughters shall prophesy.' We do not expect our path will be strewn with the flowers of popular applause, but over the thorns of bigotry and prejudice will be our way, and on our banners will beat the dark stormclouds of opposition from those who have entrenched themselves behind the stormy bulwarks of custom and authority, and who have fortified their position by every means, holy and unholy. But we will steadfastly abide the result. Unmoved we will bear it aloft. Undauntedly we will unfurl it to the gale, for we know that the storm cannot rend from it a shred, that the electric flash will but more clearly show to us the glorious words inscribed upon it, 'Equality of Rights'...

When in the course of human events, it becomes necessary for one portion of the family of man to assume among the people of the earth a position different from that which they have hither to occupied, but one to which the laws of nature and of nature's God entitle them, a decent respect to the opinions of mankind requires that they should declare the causes that impel them to such a course.

We hold these truths to be self-evident: that all men and women are created equal; that they are endowed by their creator with certain inalienable rights; among these are life, liberty, and the pursuit of happiness; that to secure these rights governments are instituted, deriving their just powers from the consent of the governed.

Whenever any form of government becomes destructive of these ends, it is the right of those who suffer from it to refuse allegiance to it, and to insist upon the institution of a new government, laying its foundation on such principles, and organizing its powers in such form, as to them shall seem most likely to effect their safety and happiness.

Prudence indeed, will dictate that governments long established should not be changed for light and transient causes; and accordingly all experience hath shown that mankind are more disposed to suffer, while evils are sufferable, than to right themselves by abolishing the forms to which they were accustomed. But when a long train of abuses and usurpations, pursuing invariably the same object evinces a design to reduce them under absolute despotism, it is their duty to throw off such government, and to provide new guards for their future security. Such has been the patient sufferance of the women under this government and such is now the necessity which constrains them to demand the equal station to which they are entitled.

The history of mankind is a history of repeated injuries and usurpations on the part of man toward woman, having in direct object the establishment of an absolute tyranny over her. To prove this, let facts be submitted to a candid world.

He has never permitted her to exercise her inalienable right to the elective franchise.

He has compelled her to submit to laws, in the formation of which she had no voice.

He has withheld from her rights which are given to the most ignorant and degraded men – both natives and foreigners. Having deprived her of this first right of a citizen, the elective franchise, thereby leaving her without representation in the halls of legislation, he has oppressed her on all sides.

He has made her, if married, in the eye of the law, civilly dead.

He has taken from her all right in property, even to the wages she earns.

He has made her, morally, an irresponsible being, as she can commit many crimes with impunity, provided they be done in the presence of her husband. In the covenant of marriage, she is compelled to promise obedience to her husband, he becoming, to all intents and purposes, her master – the law giving him power to deprive her of her liberty and to administer chastisement.

He has so framed the laws of divorce, as to what shall be the proper causes, and in case of separation, to whom the guardianship of the children shall be given, as to be wholly regardless of the happiness of women – the law, in all cases, going upon a false supposition of the supremacy of man and giving all power into his hands.

After depriving her of all rights as a married woman, if single, and the owner of property, he has taxed her to support a government which recognizes her only when her property can be made profitable to it.

He has monopolized nearly all the profitable employments, and from those she is permitted to follow, she receives but a scanty remuneration.

He closes against her all the avenues to wealth and distinction which he considers most honorable to himself. As a teacher of theology, medicine, or law, she is not known.

He has denied her the facilities for obtaining a thorough education, all colleges being closed against her.

He allows her in Church, as well as State, but a subordinate position, claiming Apostolic authority for her exclusion from the ministry, and, with some exceptions, from any public participation in the affairs of the Church.

He has created a false public sentiment by giving to the world a different code of morals for men and women, by which moral delinquencies by which exclude women from society, are not only tolerated, but deemed of little account in man.

He has usurped the prerogative of Jehovah himself, claiming it as his right to assign for her a sphere of action, when that belongs to her conscience and to her God.

He has endeavored, in every way that he could, to destroy her confidence in her own powers, to lessen her self-respect, and to make her willing to lead a dependent and abject life.

Now in view of this entire disfranchisement of one-half the people of this country, their social and religious degradation – in view of the unjust laws above mentioned, and because women do feel themselves aggrieved, oppressed, and fraudulently deprived of their most sacred rights, we insist that they have immediate admission to all the rights and privileges which belong to them as citizens of the United States.

In entering upon the great work before us, we anticipate no small amount of misconception, misrepresentation, and ridicule; but we shall use every instrumentality without our power to effect our object.

We shall employ agents, circulate tracts, petition the State and National legislatures, and endeavor to enlist the pulpit and the press on our behalf. We hope this Convention will be followed by a series of Conventions embracing every part of the country.

Sojourner Truth:

28 May 1851

'Ain't I A Woman?'

Sojourner Truth (c. 1797–1883), evangelist, abolitionist and feminist, is remembered for her unschooled but remarkable voice raised in support of abolitionism, the freedmen and women's rights. This address was delivered at the Women's Convention in Akron, Ohio.

Well, children, where there is so much racket there must be something out of kilter. I think that 'twixt the Negroes of the South and the women at the North, all talking about rights, the white men will be in a fix pretty soon. But what's all this here talking about?

That man over there says that women need to be helped into carriages, and lifted over ditches, and to have the best place everywhere. Nobody ever helps me into carriages, or over mud-puddles, or gives me any best place! And ain't I a woman? Look at me! Look at my arm! I have ploughed and planted, and gathered into barns, and no man could head me! And ain't I a woman? I could work as much and eat as much as a man – when I could get it – and bear the lash as well! And ain't I a woman? I have borne thirteen children, and seen most all sold off to slavery, and when I cried out with my mother's grief, none but Jesus heard me! And ain't I a woman? Then they talk about this thing in the head; what's this they call it? [A member of the audience whispers, 'Intellect.'] That's it, honey. What's that got to do with women's rights or Negroes' rights? If my cup won't hold but a pint, and yours holds a quart, wouldn't you be mean not to let me have my little half measure full? Then that little man in black there, he says women can't have as much rights as men, 'cause Christ wasn't a woman! Where did your Christ come

the most beneficial results that have ever taken place in the annals of human history. And to him that can trace the various epochs in human life, it is as cheering as it is interesting to mark the onward movement of the race towards higher states of human progression – that while nations strive against nations, people against people to attain the same amount of freedom already possessed in this country, Woman is rising in the full dignity of her being to claim the recognition of her rights. And though the first public demonstration has been here, already has the voice of woman in behalf of her sex been carried as it were on the wings of lightning to all parts of Europe, whose echo has brought back the warmest and most heartfelt responses from our sisters there.

Among the many encouraging letters received at the recent Woman's Convention at Worcester, there was one exceeding all the rest in the soul-stirring interest it created. It spoke, through the dungeon walls, the cheering and encouraging words of sympathy from two incarcerated women of Paris, to the hearts of their sisters in America. The cause of their imprisonment was their practically claiming the fulfillment of that glorious motto, 'Liberty, Equality, and Fraternity', destined to shake the thrones, break the sceptres and bow down the mitres of Europe. One of them presented herself as candidate for Mayor of an Arrondissement, the other (to the honor of the genuine Republicans of Paris, be it said) was nominated by the Industrial Union, consisting of two hundred and twenty Societies, as a member of the Assembly. For these offences they were cast into prison. Oh! France, where is the glory of thy revolutions? Is the blood thy children poured out on the altar of freedom so effaced, that thy daughters dare not lift their voices in behalf of their rights? But a long as might constitutes right, every good cause must have its martyrs. Why then, should woman not be a martyr to her cause? But how can we wonder that France, governed as it is by Russian and Austrian despotism, does not recognize the higher laws of humanity in the recognition of the rights of woman, when even here, in this far-famed land of freedom and of knowledge, under a republic that has inscribed on its banner the great truth that all men are created free and equal and are endowed with inalienable rights to life, liberty, and the pursuit of happiness – a Declaration wafted like the voice of Hope on the breezes of heaven to the remotest parts of earth, to whisper freedom and equality to the oppressed and downtrodden children of men – a Declaration that lies at the very foundation of human freedom and happiness, yet in the very face of that eternal truth, woman, the mockingly so-called 'better half of man', has yet to plead for her rights, nay, for her life; for what is life without liberty? and what is liberty without equality of rights; and as for the pursuit of happiness, she is not allowed to pursue any line of life that might promote it; she has only thankfully to accept what man, in the plentitude of his wisdom and generosity, decides as proper for her to do, and that is, what he does not choose to do himself. Is woman then not included in that Declaration? Answer, ye wise men of the nation, and answer truly; add not hypocrisy to your other sins. Say she is not created free and equal, and therefore (for the sequence follows on the premises) she is not entitled to life, liberty, and the pursuit of happiness. But you dare not answer this simple question. With all the audacity arising from an assumed superiority, you cannot so libel and insult humanity as to say she is not; and if she is, then what right has man, except that of might, to deprive her of the same rights and privileges he claims for himself? And why, in the name of reason and justice, I ask, why should she not have the same rights as man? Because she is woman? Humanity recognizes no sex – mind recognizes no sex

– virtue recognizes no sex – life and death, pleasure and pain, happiness and misery recognize no sex. Like him she comes involuntarily into existence; like him she possesses physical, mental, and moral powers, on the proper cultivation of which depends her happiness; like him she is subject to all the vicissitudes of life; like him she has to pay the penalty for disobeying nature's laws, and far greater penalties has she to suffer from ignorance of her far more complicated nature than he; like him she enjoys or suffers with her country.

Yet she is not recognized as his equal. In the laws of the land she has no rights; in government she has no voice, and in spite of another principle recognized in this republic, namely, that taxation without representation is tyranny, woman is taxed without being represented; her property may be consumed by heavy taxes, to defray the expenses of that unholy and unrighteous thing called war, yet she cannot give her veto against it. From the cradle to the grave, she is subject to the power and control of man, father, guardian and husband. One conveys her like some piece of merchandise over to the other. At marriage she loses her entire identity. Her being is said to be merged in her husband. Has nature there merged it? Has she ceased to exist or feel pleasure and pain? When she violates the laws of her being, does he pay the penalty? When she breaks the laws of the land, does he suffer the punishment? When his wants are supplied, is it sufficient to satisfy the wants of her nature? Or when, at his nightly orgies, in the grog-shop, the oyster cellar, or the gaming table, he spends the means she helped by her co-operation and economy to accumulate and she awakens to penury and destitution, will it supply the wants of her children to tell them, that owing to the superiority of man she has no redress by law? – and that as her being was merged in him, so also ought theirs to be? But it will be said that the husband provides for the wife, or in other words, he is bound to feed, clothe, and shelter her. Oh! the degradation of that idea! Yes, he keeps her, so he does his horse. By law both are considered his property; both can, when the cruelty of the owner compels them to run away, be brought back by the strong arm of the law; and according to a still extant law of England, both may be led by the halter to the market place and sold.

This is humiliating indeed, but nevertheless true, and the sooner these things are known and understood the better for humanity. It is no fancy sketch. I know that some endeavor to throw the mantle of romance over the subject, and treat woman like some ideal existence not subject to the ills of life. Let those deal in fancy that have nothing better to deal in. We have to do with sober, sad realities, with stubborn facts. But again it will be said, the law presumes the husband would be kind, affectionate, that he would provide for and protect the wife; but I ask, what right has the law to presume at all on the subject? What right has the law to intrust the interest and happiness of one being to the power of another? And if this merging of interests is so indispensable, then why should woman always be on the losing side? Turn the tables; let the identity and interest of the husband be merged in the wife, think you she would act less generous towards him than he towards her? – that she would be incapable of as much justice, disinterested devotion, and abiding affection as him? Oh! how grossly you misunderstand and wrong her nature. But we desire no such undue power over man. It would be as wrong in her, as it now is in him; all we claim is our own rights. – We have nothing to do with individual man, be he good or bad, but with the laws that oppress woman. Bad and unjust laws must in the nature of things make man so too. If he acts better, if he is kind, affectionate, and consistent, it is because the kindlier feelings instilled by a mother, kept warm by a sister, and cherished by a wife, will not allow him to carry out the barbarous laws against woman; but the estimation she is generally held in is as degrading as it is unjust. Not long ago, I saw an account of two offenders brought before a Justice in New York; one, for stealing a pair of boots, for which offence he was sentenced to six months imprisonment; the other, for an assault and battery on his wife, for which offence he was let off with a reprimand from the Judge! With my principles entirely opposed to punishment, I hold to reforming the erring, and removing the causes, as being much more efficient as well as just than punishing; but the Judge showed the comparative value he set on these two kinds of property. But you must remember that the boots were taken by a stranger, while the wife was insulted by her legal owner. Yet it will be said that such degrading cases are few. For the sake of humanity, I hope they are; but as long as woman is wronged by unequal laws, so long will she be degraded by man. We can hardly have an adequate idea how all-powerful law is in forming public opinion, in giving tone and character to the mass of society.

To illustrate this point, look at that inhuman, detestable law, written in human blood, signed and sealed with life and liberty, that eternal stain on the statute books of this country, the Fugitive Slave Law. Think you, that before its passage you could have found any in the free States, except a few politicians in the market, base enough to desire such a law? No, no! Even those that took no interest in the subject, would have shrunk from so barbarous a thing; but no sooner is it passed, than the ignorant mass, the rabble of the self-styled Union Safety Committee, found out we were a law-loving and law-abiding people. Such is the magic power of law; hence the necessity to guard against bad ones, hence also the reason why we call on the nation to remove the legal shackles from woman. Set her politically and civilly free, and it will have a more beneficial effect on that still greater tyrant she has to contend with, public opinion. Carry out the Republican principle of universal suffrage, or strike it from your banner, and substitute freedom and power to one half of society, and submission and slavery to the other. Give women then the elective franchise. Let married women have the same right to property that man has; for whatever the difference in their respective occupations, the duties of the wife are as indispensable and far more arduous than the husband's. Why, then, should the wife at the death of her husband, not be his heir to the same extent that he is to her? In this legal inequality there is involved another wrong. When the wife dies, the husband is left in the undisturbed possession of all, and the children are left with him. No change is made, no stranger intrudes on his home and his affliction; but when the husband dies, not only is she, as is too often the case, deprived of all, or at best receives but a mere pittance, but strangers assume authority denied to the wife and mother. The sanctuary of affliction must be desecrated by executors, every thing must be ransacked and assessed, lest she should steal something out of her own house, and to cap the climax, the children are taken from her and placed under guardians. When he dies poor, no guardian is required, the children are left with the mother to care and toil for them as best she may; but when any thing is left for the maintenance and education of the children, then it must be placed in the hands of strangers for safe keeping, lest the mother might defraud them.

The whole care and bringing up of the children are left with the mother, and safe they are in her hands; but a few hundred or thousand dollars cannot be intrusted with her. But it will be said, that in case of a second marriage, the children must be protected in their possession. Does that reason not hold as good in his case? Oh! no! – When he marries again, he still retains his identity and power to act, but she becomes merged once more into a mere nonentity, and therefore the first husband must rob her to prevent the second from doing it. But we say, make the laws regulating marriage, if any are required at all, equal for both, and all these difficulties would be obviated. According to a late act, the wife has a right to the property she brings at marriage, or received in any way after marriage. Here is some provision for the favored few, but for the laboring many there is none. The mass of the people commence life with no other capital than the head, heart, and hand. To the result of this best of all capital, the wife has no right. If they are unsuccessful in married life, who suffers more the bitter consequences of poverty than the wife? But if successful, she cannot call a dollar her own. He may will away every dollar (of his personal property) and leave her destitute and pennyless, and she has no redress by law; and even when real estate is left, she receives but a life interest in a third part of it, and at her death she cannot leave it to any of her relations; it falls back even to the remotest of his relations. This is law, but where is the justice of it? Well might we say, that laws were made to prevent, but not promote the ends of justice. Or, in case of separation, why should the children be taken from the protecting care of the mother? Who has a better right to them than she?

How much do fathers generally do towards the bringing them up? When he comes home from business, and the child is in good humor and handsome trim, he takes the little darling on his knee and plays with it; but when the wife, with the care of the whole household on her shoulders, with little or no help, was not able to put them in the best order and trim, how much does the father do towards it? Oh! no! Fathers like to have children good-natured, well-behaved, and comfortable; but how to put them in that desirable condition is out of their philosophy.

Children always depend more on the tender, watchful care of the mother, than the father. Whether from nature or habit, or both, the mother is more capable of administering to their health and comfort than the father, and therefore she has the best right to them; and where there is property, it ought to be divided equally between them with an additional provision from the father towards the maintenance and education of the children. Much is said about the burdens and responsibilities of married men. Responsibilities there are, if they only felt them; but as to burdens, what are they? The sole province of man seems to be centered in that one thing, attending to some business. I grant that owing to the present unequal and unjust reward for labor, some have to work too hard for a subsistence; but whatever his vocation, he has to attend to it as much before as after marriage. Look at your bachelors, and see if they do not strive as much for wealth, and attend as steadily to business as married men. No; the husband has little or no increase of burden, and every increase of comfort after marriage, while all the burdens, cares, pains, and penalties of married life fall entirely on the wife. How unjust and cruel, then, to have all the laws in his favor! – If any difference ought to be made by law between husband and wife, reason, justice, and humanity, if their voices were heard, would dictate it in her favor. It is high time, then, to denounce such gross injustice, to compel man by the might of right to give woman her political, legal, and social rights. Open to her all the avenues of emolument, distinction, and greatness; give her an object for which to cultivate her powers, and a fair chance to do so, and there will be no need to speculate as to her proper sphere. She will find her own sphere in accordance with her capacities, powers, and tastes; and yet she will be woman still. Her rights will not change, but strengthen, develop, and elevate her nature. Away with that folly that her rights would be detrimental to her character – that if she is recognized as the equal to man, she would cease to be woman! – Have his rights as a citizen of a republic, the elective franchise with all its advantages, so changed his nature that he has ceased to be man? Oh! no! But woman could not bare such a degree of power; what has benefitted him would injure her; what has strengthened him would weaken her; what prompted him to the performance of his duties would make her neglect hers!

Such is the superficial mode of reasoning, if it deserves that name, that is brought against the subject. It reminds me of two reasons given by a minister of Milton, on the North River. Having heard I had spoken on the rights of woman, he took the subject up the following Sunday, to prove that woman ought not to have equal rights with man, first, because Adam was created before Eve, and secondly, man was compared to the fore wheel, and woman to the hind wheel of a wagon! These reasons are about as philosophical as any that can be brought on the subject. Man forgets, or he never knew, that our duties spring from our rights; and in proportion to the rights we enjoy, are the duties we owe, and he that enjoys the most rights owes in return the most duties; though until now, while man enjoys the rights, he preaches all the duties to woman. But, say some, in point of principle we grant it is right enough, but would you expose woman to the contact of rough, rude, drinking, swearing, fighting men at the ballot-box? What a humiliating confession lies in this plea for keeping women in the back-ground! Is the brutality of some men, then, a reason why woman should be kept from her rights? If man, in his superior wisdom, cannot devise means to enable woman to deposit her vote without having her finer sensibilities shocked by such disgraceful conduct, then there is an additional reason as well as necessity why she should be there to civilize, refine, and purify him, even at the ballot-box. Yes, in addition to the principle of right, this is one of the reasons why women should participate in all the important duties of life; for, with all due respect to the other sex, she is the true civilizer of man. Without her, he is at best a semi-barbarian. From my very heart do I pity the man who has grown up and lives without the benign influence of woman! Even now, in spite of being considered the inferior, she has a most beneficial effect on man.

Look at your annual festivities where woman is excluded, and you will find more or less drunkenness, disorder, vulgarity, and excess to be the order of the day. Compare them with such, where woman is the equal participant with man, and you will find rational social enjoyment and decorum prevail; and if this is the case now – and who can deny it? – how much more beneficial would be her influence, if, as the equal to man, she would take her stand by his side, to cheer, counsel, and aid him in the drama of life, in the Legislative Halls, in the Senate Chamber, in the Judge's chair, in the Jury box, on the Forum, in the Laboratory of the Arts and Sciences, and wherever duty would call her for the benefit of herself, her county, her race. In every step she would carry a humanizing influence. And why, I would ask, should she not occupy all these stations? Why would one half of the race legislate for the other? In this country it is considered wrong for one nation to enact laws and enforce them against another. Does the same wrong not hold good of the sexes? – Is she a being like him? Then she is entitled to the same rights – is she not? Then how can he legislate rightfully against a being whose nature he cannot understand, whose motives he cannot appreciate, and whose feelings he cannot realize? How can he sit in judgment and pronounce a verdict against a being so entirely different? No, there are no reasons for it, but there are deep-rooted, hoary-headed prejudices against her. The main cause of them is, that pernicious falsehood propagated against her being, viz.: – that she is inferior by her nature. Inferior in what? What has man ever done, that woman, under the same advantages, could not be made to do? In morals, bad as she is, she is generally considered his superior.

In intellect, give her a fair chance before you pronounce a verdict against her. Cultivate that portion of the brain as much as that of man's, and she will stand his equal, at least. Even now, where her mind has been called out at all, her intellect is as bright, as capacious, and as powerful as his. Will you tell me, we have no Newtons, Shakespeares, and Byrons? Greater natural powers than even these possessed, have been destroyed in woman for want of proper culture – a just appreciation and reward for merit, as an incentive to exertion and freedom of action, without which, mind becomes cramped and stifled. It cannot expand under bolts and bats; and yet, under all these blighting, crushing circumstances, confined within the narrowest possible limits, trampled upon by prejudice and injustice, from her education and position forced to occupy herself almost exclusively with the most trivial affairs – in spite of all these difficulties, her intellect is as good as man's. The few bright meteors in man's intellectual horizon could well be matched by woman, were she allowed to occupy the same elevated poison. There is no need of naming the De Staels, the Rolands, the Somervilles, the Wollstonecrafts, the Wrights, the Fullers, the Martineaus, the Hemanses, the Sigourneys, the Jagiellos, and the many more of modern as well as ancient times, to prove her mental powers, her patriotism, her heroism, her self-sacrificing devotion to the cause of humanity – the eloquence that gushes from her pen or from her tongue.

These things are too well known to require repetition. And do you ask for fortitude of mind, energy, and perseverance? Then look at woman under suffering, reverse of fortune, and affliction, when the strength and power of man has sunk to the lowest ebb, when his mind is overwhelmed by the dark waters of despair. – She, like the tender plant, bent but not broken by the storms of life, now only upholds her own hopeful courage, but, like the tender shoots of the ivy, clings around the tempest-fallen oak, to bind up the wounds, peak hope to his faltering spirit, and shelter him from the returning blast of the storm.

Wherein, then, is man so much her superior that he must forever remain her master? In physical strength? Then allow me to say that the ox and the elephant is his superior! But, even on this point, why is she the feeble, sickly, suffering being we behold her? Look at the most defective and irrational education, and you will find the solution of the problem. Is the girl allowed to expand her limbs and chest in healthful exercise in the fresh breezes of heaven? Is she allowed to inflate her lungs and make the welkin ring with her cheerful expanded voice, like the boy? Whoever heard a girl committing such improprieties? Strongly developed limbs in a girl is unfashionable – a healthy, sound voice is vulgar – a ruddy glow on the cheek is coarse; and when life within her is so strong as to show itself in spite of bolts and bars, then she has to undergo a bleaching process, eat lemons and slate pencils – drink vinegar, and keep in the shade! And do you know why these irrationalities are practised? Because man wishes them so, and whatever he mostly admires in woman will she possess. That is the influence man has over woman, for she has been made to believe that she was created for his benefit only. – 'It was not well for man to be alone,' therefore she was made as a play-thing to pass away an idle hour, or a drudge to do his bidding; and until this falsehood is eradicated from her mind, until she feels that the necessities, services, and obligations of the sexes are mutual – that she is as independent of him as he is of her – that she is formed for the same aims and ends in life that he is – until, in fact, she has all her rights equal with man, there will be no other object in her education except to get married, and what will best promote that a desirable end will be cultivated in her. When a boy arrives at the age of twelve or so, the parents consult as to the kind of education that shall best fit him for all the purposes of life, to enable him to become a useful, respectable, independent member of society; and in accordance with the knowledge and means of the parents, and the capacities of the boy, so do they direct his education to make him a farmer, mechanic, merchant, lawyer, doctor, or, if the boy is not bright enough for any of these callings or professions, then he is destined for the ministry.

But for what purpose is the girl educated? Do parents ever direct the education of a daughter for any such purposes? Oh! no! The rich man's daughter is taught to dance, to play on the piano, to draw and paint (which she sometimes practises on her own face), to speak a little bad French, etc., etc., not for the intrinsic value and beauty of these accomplishments, but to attract, and ultimately catch a beau and get married; for no sooner is she married than these things are all laid aside as some idle things to be thought of no more. How many ladies past the age of fifty use these accomplishments from a pure love of them, and the gratification of the family around them? Among the musical nations of Europe you may find some, but here these accomplishments are acquired as a means to an end – that end once obtained, there is no further use for them. The working classes educate their daughters in accordance with what would now be required of them – namely, to cook a dinner good enough for a poor man, darn his stockings, sew on buttons, etc. Now these things are a very good in themselves; every girl ought to know them, and know them well, yet it is not enough for a healthy, happy, rational, intellectual life, but then it is all man now requires of woman. When he will look for higher and nobler mental accomplishments and powers, she will possess them. Do you not yet understand what has made woman what she is? Then see what the sickly taste and perverted judgment of man now admires in woman. Not health and strength of body and mind, but a pale delicate face; hands too small to grasp a broom, for that were treason in a lady; a voice so sickly, sentimental, and depressed, as to hear what she says only by the moving of her half-parted lips; and, above all, that nervous sensibility that sees a ghost in every passing shadow – that beautiful diffidence that dare not take a step without the arm of a man to support her tender frame, and that shrinking (mock) modesty that faints at the mention of the leg of a table.

I know there are many noble exceptions that see and deplore these irrationalities, but as a general thing it is so, or else why set up the hue-and-cry of 'manish', 'unfeminine', 'out of her sphere' etc., whenever she evinces any strength of body or mind and takes part in any thing deserving of a rational being? Oh! the crying injustice towards woman! She is crushed in every step she takes, and then insulted for being what a most pernicious education and corrupt public sentimental has made her. But there is no confidence in her powers nor principles. After last year's Convention of women, I saw an article in a Unitarian paper edited by the Rev. Mr Bellows of New York, where, in reply to a correspondent on the subject of woman's rights, in which he strenuously opposed her taking part in any thing in public, he said, 'Public woman unbonneted and unshawled before the public gaze, and what becomes of her modesty and her virtue?' In his benighted mind, the modesty and virtue of woman is but shawl deep, and, when in contact with the atmosphere, evaporates like chloroform. But I refrain to comment on the subject; it carries its own condemnation with it. When I read the article, I earnestly wished I had the ladies of his congregation before me to see whether they could realize the estimation their pastor held them in; yet I hardly know which sentiment was strongest in me, contempt for such foolish opinions, or pity for the writer; for a man that has such a degrading opinion of woman, of the being that gave him life and sustenance – that sustained his helpless infancy with her ever watchful care; and laid the very foundation for the little mind he may possess – of the being he took to his bosom as the partner of his joys and sorrows – the one whom, when he strove to win her affections, he courted as all such men court woman, like some divinity – such a man deserves our pity, for I cannot realize that man purposely and willingly degrades his mother, sister, wife, and daughter. No! my better nature, my best knowledge and convictions forbid me to believe it. It is from ignorance, not malice, man acts as he does. In ignorance of her nature, and the interest and happiness of both, he conceived ideas, laid down rules, and enacted laws concerning her destiny and rights. The same ignorance, strengthened by age, sanctified by superstition, ingrafted into his being by habit, makes him still carry them out to the detriment of his own as well as her happiness; for is he not the loser by it? Oh! how severely he suffers. Who can fathom the depth of suffering and misery to society from the subjugation and injury inflicted on woman?

The race is elevated in excellence and power, or kept back in progression, in accordance with the scale of woman's position in society. The attainment of woman's co-equality with man, is, in itself, not the end, but the means towards a still higher elevation of the race, without which, it never can attain. But so firmly has prejudice closed the eyes of man to the light of truth, that though he feels the evils, he knows not the cause. Those that have their eyes already open to these facts, earnestly desire the restoration of her rights, to enable her to take her proper position in the scale of humanity. If all could see it, all would desire it as they desire their own happiness, for the interest and happiness of the sexes cannot be divided. Nature has too closely united them to permit one to oppress the other with impunity, and therefore I can cast no more blame or reproach on man than on woman; for she, from habit based on the same errors, is as much opposed to her interest and happiness as he is. Yes; I will do man the justice to say, that I never mentioned the subject to any man capable of reflection, but he acknowledged the justice of it; and how long is it since any of us have advocated this righteous cause? – how long since any of us have come out of the darkness into the light of day? The longest period is but as it were since yesterday, and why? From the same reason that so many of both sexes are opposed to it yet – ignorance. Both have to be aroused from that deathly lethargy in which they slumber. That worse than Egyptian darkness must be dispelled from their minds before the pure rays of the sun can penetrate them. And therefore while I feel it my duty – aye, a painful duty, to point out the wrong done to woman and its evil consequences, and would do all in my power to aid in her deliverance, I can have no more ill feelings towards him than for the same errors towards her. Both are the victims of error and ignorance, and both suffer; and hence the necessity for active, earnest endeavors to enlighten their minds; hence the necessity to protest against the wrong and claim our rights, and in doing our duty we must not heed the taunts, ridicule, and stigma cast upon us.

We must remember we have a crusade before us far holier and more righteous than led warrior to Palestine – a crusade not to deprive any one of his rights, but to claim our own; and as our cause is a better one, so also must be the means to achieve it. We therefore must put on the armor of charity, carry before us the banner of truth, and defend ourselves with the shield of right against the invaders of our liberty. And yet, like the knights of old, we must enlist in this holy cause with a disinterested devotion, energy, and determination never to turn back until we have conquered, not indeed to drive the Turk from his possession, but to claim our rightful inheritance for his benefit as well as our own. To achieve this great victory of right over might, woman has much to do. She must not sit idle and wait till man inspired by justice and humanity will work out her redemption. It has well been said, 'He that would be free, himself must strike the blow.' It is with nations as with individuals, if they do not strive to help themselves no one will help them. Man may, and in the nature of things will, remove the legal, political, and civil disabilities from woman, and recognize her as his equal with himself, and it will do much towards her elevation; but the laws cannot compel her to cultivate her physical and mental powers, and take a stand as a free and independent being. All that, she has to do. She must investigate and take an interest in every thing on which the welfare of society depends, for the interest and happiness of every member of society is connected with that of society. She must at once claim and exercise those rights and privileges with which the laws do not interfere, and it will aid her to obtain all the rest. She must, therefore, throw off that heavy yoke that like a nightmare weighs down her best energies, viz., the fear of public opinion.

It has been said, that 'The voice of the People is the voice of God.' If that voice is on the side of justice and humanity, then it is true, if the term God means the principle of Truth and of Right. But if the public voice is oppressive and unjust, then it ought to be spurned like the voice of falsehood and corruption; and woman, instead of implicitly and blindly following the dictates of public opinion, must investigate for herself what is right or wrong – act in accordance with her best convictions and let the rest take care of itself, for obedience to wrong is wrong itself, and opposition to it is virtue alike in woman as in man, even though she should incur the ill will of bigotry, superstition, and priestcraft, for the approval of our fellow-being is valuable only when it does not clash with our own sense of right, and no further. The priests well know the influence and value of women when warmly engaged in any cause, and therefore as long as they can keep them steeped in superstitious darkness, so long are they safe; and hence the horror and anathema against every woman that has intelligence, spirit, and moral courage to cast off the dark and oppressive yoke of superstition. But she must do it, or she will ever remain a slave, for of all tyranny that of superstition is the greatest, and he is the most abject slave who tamely submits to its yoke. Woman, then, must ease it off as her greatest enemy; and the time I trust will come when she will aid man to remove the political, civil, and religious evils that have swept over the earth like some malignant scourge to lay waste and destroy so much of the beauty, harmony, and happiness of man; and the old fable of the fall of man through a woman will be superseded by the glorious fact that she was instrumental in the elevation of the race towards a higher, nobler, and happier destiny.

Frederick Douglass:

4 July 1852

'What to the American slave is your Fourth of July?'

Frederick Douglass (1817–95) was the most influential African American leader of the 1800s and was the leading figure in the New England anti-slavery movement. In 1852 he was asked to give a speech as part of

Rochester's Fourth of July celebrations. In his speech he delivered a scathing attack on the hypocrisy of a nation which celebrated freedom and independence with speeches, parades and platitudes while nearly four million of its people were slaves.

Fellow citizens, pardon me, and allow me to ask, why am I called upon to speak here today? What have I or those I represent to do with your national independence? Are the great principles of political freedom and of natural justice, embodied in that Declaration of Independence, extended to us? And am I, therefore, called upon to bring our humble offering to the national altar, and to confess the benefits, and express devout gratitude for the blessings resulting from your independence to us?

Would to God, both for your sakes and ours, that an affirmative answer could be truthfully returned to these questions. Then would my task be light, and my burden easy and delightful. For who is there so cold that a nation's sympathy could not warm him? Who so obdurate and dead to the claims of gratitude, that would not thankfully acknowledge such priceless benefits? Who so stolid and selfish that would not give his voice to swell the hallelujahs of a nation's jubilee, when the chains of servitude had been torn from his limbs? I am not that man. In a case like that, the dumb might eloquently speak, and the 'lame man leap as an hart.'

But such is not the state of the case. I say it with a sad sense of disparity between us. I am not included within the pale of this glorious anniversary! Your high independence only reveals the immeasurable distance between us. The blessings in which you this day rejoice are not enjoyed in common. The rich inheritance of justice, liberty, prosperity, and independence bequeathed by your fathers is shared by you, not by me. The sunlight that brought life and healing to you has brought stripes and death to me. This Fourth of July is yours, not mine. You may rejoice, I must mourn. To drag a man in fetters into the grand illuminated temple of liberty, and call upon him to join you in joyous anthems, were inhuman mockery and sacrilegious irony. Do you mean, citizens, to mock me, by asking me to speak today? If so, there is a parallel to your conduct. And let me warn you, that it is dangerous to copy the example of a nation (Babylon) whose crimes, towering up to heaven, were thrown down by the breath of the Almighty, burying that nation in irrecoverable ruin.

Fellow citizens, above your national, tumultuous joy, I hear the mournful wail of millions, whose chains, heavy and grievous yesterday, are today rendered more intolerable by the jubilant shouts that reach them. If I do forget, if I do not remember those bleeding children of sorrow this day, 'may my right hand forget her cunning, and may my tongue cleave to the roof of my mouth!'

To forget them, to pass lightly over their wrongs and to chime in with the popular theme would be treason most scandalous and shocking, and would make me a reproach before God and the world.

My subject, then, fellow citizens, is 'American Slavery'. I shall see this day and its popular characteristics from the slave's point of view. Standing here, identified with the American bondman, making his wrongs mine, I do not hesitate to declare, with all my soul, that the character and conduct of this nation never looked blacker to me than on this Fourth of July.

Whether we turn to the declarations of the past, or to the professions of the present, the conduct of the nation seems equally hideous and revolting. America is false to the past, false to the present, and solemnly binds herself to be false to the future. Standing with God and the crushed and bleeding slave on this occasion, I will, in the name of humanity, which is outraged, in the name of liberty, which is fettered, in the name of the Constitution and the Bible, which are disregarded and trampled upon, dare to call in question and to denounce, with all the emphasis I can command, everything that serves to perpetuate slavery – the great sin and shame of America! 'I will not equivocate – I will not excuse.' I will use the severest language I can command, and yet not one word shall escape me that any man, whose judgment is not blinded by prejudice, or who is not at heart a slave-holder, shall not confess to be right and just.

But I fancy I hear some of my audience say it is just in this circumstance that you and your brother Abolitionists fail to make a favorable impression on the public mind. Would you argue more and denounce less, would you persuade more and rebuke less, your cause would be much more likely to succeed. But, I submit, where all is plain there is nothing to be argued. What point in the anti-slavery creed would you have me argue? On what branch of the subject do the people of this country need light? Must I undertake to prove that the slave is a man? That point is conceded already. Nobody doubts it. The slaveholders themselves acknowledge it in the enactment of laws for their government. They acknowledge it when they punish disobedience on the part of the slave. There are seventy-two crimes in the State of Virginia, which, if committed by a black man (no matter how ignorant he be), subject him to the punishment of death; while only two of these same crimes will subject a white man to like punishment.

What is this but the acknowledgment that the slave is a moral, intellectual, and responsible being? The manhood of the slave is conceded. It is admitted in the fact that Southern statute books are covered with enactments, forbidding, under severe fines and penalties, the teaching of the slave to read and write.

When you can point to any such laws in reference to the beasts of the field, then I may consent to argue the manhood of the slave. When the dogs in your streets, when the fowls of the air, when the cattle on your hills, when the fish of the sea, and the reptiles that crawl, shall be unable to distinguish the slave from a brute, then I will argue with you that the slave is a man!

For the present it is enough to affirm the equal manhood of the Negro race. Is it not astonishing that, while we are plowing, planting, and reaping, using all kinds of mechanical tools, erecting houses, constructing bridges, building ships, working in metals of brass, iron, copper, silver, and gold; that while we are reading, writing, and ciphering, acting as clerks, merchants, and secretaries, having among us lawyers, doctors, ministers, poets, authors, editors, orators, and teachers; that we are engaged in all the enterprises common to other men – digging gold in California, capturing the whale in the Pacific, feeding sheep and cattle on the hillside, living, moving, acting, thinking, planning, living in families as husbands, wives, and children, and above all, confessing and worshipping the Christian God, and looking hopefully for life and immortality beyond the grave – we are called upon to prove that we are men?

Would you have me argue that man is entitled to liberty? That he is the rightful owner of his own body? You have already declared it. Must I argue the wrongfulness of slavery? Is that a question for republicans? Is it to be settled by the rules of logic and argumentation, as a matter beset with great difficulty, involving a doubtful application of the principle of justice, hard to understand? How should I look today in the presence of Americans, dividing and subdividing a discourse, to show that men have a natural right to freedom, speaking of it relatively and positively, negatively and affirmatively? To do so would be to make myself ridiculous, and to offer an insult to your understanding.

There is not a man beneath the canopy of heaven who does not know that slavery is wrong for him.

What! Am I to argue that it is wrong to make men brutes, to rob them of their liberty, to work them without wages, to keep them ignorant of their relations to their fellow men, to beat them with sticks, to flay their flesh with the lash, to load their limbs with irons, to hunt them with dogs, to sell them at auction, to sunder their families, to knock out their teeth, to burn their flesh, to starve them into obedience and submission to their masters? Must I argue that a system thus marked with blood and stained with pollution is wrong? No – I will not. I have better employment for my time and strength than such arguments would imply.

What, then, remains to be argued? Is it that slavery is not divine; that God did not establish it; that our doctors of divinity are mistaken? There is blasphemy in the thought. That which is inhuman cannot be divine. Who can reason on such a proposition? They that can, may – I cannot. The time for such argument is past.

At a time like this, scorching irony, not convincing argument, is needed. Oh! had I the ability, and could I reach the nation's ear, I would today pour out a fiery stream of biting ridicule, blasting reproach, withering sarcasm, and stern rebuke. For it is not light that is needed, but fire; it is not the gentle shower, but thunder. We need the storm, the whirlwind, and the earthquake. The feeling of the nation must be quickened; the conscience of the nation must be roused; the propriety of the nation must be startled; the hypocrisy of the nation must be exposed; and its crimes against God and man must be denounced.

What to the American slave is your Fourth of July? I answer, a day that reveals to him more than all other days of the year, the

myself. The circumstances under which I have been called for a limited period to preside over the destinies of the Republic fill me with a profound sense of responsibility, but with nothing like shrinking apprehension. I repair to the post assigned me not as to one sought, but in obedience to the unsolicited expression of your will, answerable only for a fearless, faithful, and diligent exercise of my best powers. I ought to be, and am, truly grateful for the rare manifestation of the nation's confidence; but this, so far from lightening my obligations, only adds to their weight. You have summoned me in my weakness; you must sustain me by your strength. When looking for the fulfillment of reasonable requirements, you will not be unmindful of the great changes which have occurred, even within the last quarter of a century, and the consequent augmentation and complexity of duties imposed in the administration both of your home and foreign affairs. Whether the elements of inherent force in the Republic have kept pace with its unparalleled progression in territory, population, and wealth has been the subject of earnest thought and discussion on both sides of the ocean.

Less than sixty-four years ago the Father of this Country made the then 'recent accession of the important State of North Carolina to the Constitution of the United States' one of the subjects of his special congratulation. At that moment, however, when the agitation consequent upon the Revolutionary struggle had hardly subsided, when we were just emerging from the weakness and embarrassments of the Confederation, there was an evident consciousness of vigor equal to the great mission so wisely and bravely fulfilled by our fathers. It was not a presumptuous assurance, but a calm faith, springing from a clear view of the sources of power in a government constituted like ours. It is no paradox to say that although comparatively weak the new-born nation was intrinsically strong. Inconsiderable in population and apparent resources, it was upheld by a broad and intelligent comprehension of rights and an all-pervading purpose to maintain them, stronger than armaments. It came from the furnace of the Revolution, tempered to the necessities of the times. The thoughts of the men of that day were as practical as their sentiments were patriotic. They wasted no portion of their energies upon idle and delusive speculations, but with a firm and fearless step advanced beyond the governmental landmarks which had hitherto circumscribed the limits of human freedom and planted their standard, where it has stood against dangers which have threatened from abroad, and internal agitation, which has at times fearfully menaced at home. They proved themselves equal to the solution of the great problem, to understand which their minds had been illuminated by the dawning lights of the Revolution. The object sought was not a thing dreamed of; it was a thing realized. They had exhibited only the power to achieve, but, what all history affirms to be so much more unusual, the capacity to maintain.

The oppressed throughout the world from that day to the present have turned their eyes hitherward, not to find those lights extinguished or to fear lest they should wane, but to be constantly cheered by their steady and increasing radiance. In this our country has, in my judgment, thus far fulfilled its highest duty to suffering humanity. It has spoken and will continue to speak, not only by its words, but by its acts, the language of sympathy, encouragement, and hope to those who earnestly listen to tones which pronounce for the largest rational liberty. But after all, the most animating encouragement and potent appeal for freedom will be its own history – its trials and its triumphs. Pre-eminently, the power of our advocacy reposes in our example; but no example, be it remembered, can be powerful for lasting good, whatever apparent advantages may be gained, which is not based upon eternal principles of right and justice. Our fathers decided for themselves, both upon the hour to declare and the hour to strike. They were their own judges of the circumstances under which it became them to pledge to each other 'their lives, their fortunes, and their sacred honor' for the acquisition of the priceless inheritance transmitted to us. The energy with which that great conflict was opened and, under the guidance of a manifest and beneficent Providence the uncomplaining endurance with which it was prosecuted to its consummation were only surpassed by the wisdom and patriotic spirit of concession which characterized all the counsels of the early fathers.

One of the most impressive evidences of that wisdom is to be found in the fact that the actual working of our system has dispelled a degree of solicitude which at the outset disturbed bold hearts and far-reaching intellects. The apprehension of dangers from extended territory, multiplied States, accumulated wealth, and augmented population has proved to be unfounded. The stars upon your banner have become nearly threefold their original number; your densely populated possessions skirt the shores of the two great oceans; and yet this vast increase of people and territory has not only shown itself compatible with the harmonious action of the States and Federal Government in their respective constitutional spheres, but has afforded an additional guaranty of the strength and integrity of both. With an experience thus suggestive and cheering, the policy of my Administration will not be controlled by any timid forebodings of evil from expansion. Indeed, it is not to be disguised that our attitude as a nation and our position on the globe render the acquisition of certain possessions not within our jurisdiction eminently important for our protection, if not in the future essential for the preservation of the rights of commerce and the peace of the world. Should they be obtained, it will be through no grasping spirit, but with a view to obvious national interest and security, and in a manner entirely consistent with the strictest observance of national faith. We have nothing in our history or position to invite aggression; we have everything to beckon us to the cultivation of relations of peace and amity with all nations. Purposes, therefore, at once just and pacific will be significantly marked in the conduct of our foreign affairs.

I intend that my Administration shall leave no blot upon our fair record, and trust I may safely give the assurance that no act within the legitimate scope of my constitutional control will be tolerated on the part of any portion of our citizens which can not challenge a ready justification before the tribunal of the civilized world. An Administration would be unworthy of confidence at home or respect abroad should it cease to be influenced by the conviction that no apparent advantage can be purchased at a price so dear as that of national wrong or dishonor. It is not your privilege as a nation to speak of a distant past. The striking incidents of your history, replete with instruction and furnishing abundant grounds for hopeful confidence, are comprised in a period comparatively brief. But if your past is limited, your future is boundless. Its obligations throng the unexplored pathway of advancement, and will be limitless as duration. Hence a sound and comprehensive policy should embrace not less the distant future than the urgent present. The great objects of our pursuit as a people are best to be attained by peace, and are entirely consistent with the tranquillity and interests of the rest of mankind. With the neighboring nations upon our continent we should cultivate kindly and fraternal relations. We can desire nothing in regard to them so much as to see them consolidate their strength and pursue the paths of prosperity and happiness. If in the course of their growth we should open new channels of trade and create additional facilities for friendly intercourse, the benefits realized will be equal and mutual.

Of the complicated European systems of national polity we have heretofore been independent. From their wars, their tumults, and anxieties we have been, happily, almost entirely exempt. Whilst these are confined to the nations which gave them existence, and within their legitimate jurisdiction, they can not affect us except as they appeal to our sympathies in the cause of human freedom and universal advancement. But the vast interests of commerce are common to all mankind, and the advantages of trade and international intercourse must always present a noble field for the moral influence of a great people. With these views firmly and honestly carried out, we have a right to expect, and shall under all circumstances require, prompt reciprocity. The rights which belong to us as a nation are not alone to be regarded, but those which pertain to every citizen in his individual capacity, at home and abroad, must be sacredly maintained. So long as he can discern every star in its place upon that ensign, without wealth to purchase for him preferment or title to secure for him place, it will be his privilege, and must be his acknowledged right, to stand unabashed even in the presence of princes, with a proud consciousness that he is himself one of a nation of sovereigns and that he can not in legitimate pursuit wander so far from home that the agent whom he shall leave behind in the place which I now occupy will not see that no rude hand of power or tyrannical passion is laid upon him with impunity. He must realize that upon every sea and on every soil where our enterprise may rightfully seek the protection of our flag American citizenship is an inviolable panoply for the security of American rights.

And in this connection it can hardly be necessary to reaffirm a principle which should now be regarded as fundamental. The rights, security, and repose of this Confederacy reject the idea of interference or colonization on this side of the ocean by any foreign power beyond present jurisdiction as utterly inadmissible. The opportunities of observation furnished by my brief experience as a soldier confirmed in my own mind the opinion, entertained and acted upon by others from the formation of the Government, that the maintenance of large standing armies in our country would be not only dangerous, but unnecessary. They also illustrated the importance – I might well say the absolute necessity – of the military science and practical skill furnished in such an eminent degree by the institution which has made your Army what it is, under the discipline and instruction of officers not more distinguished for their solid attainments, gallantry, and devotion to the public service than for unobtrusive bearing and high moral tone. The Army as organized must be the nucleus around which in every time of need the strength of your military power, the sure bulwark of your defense – a national militia – may be readily formed into a well-disciplined and efficient organization. And the skill and self-devotion of the Navy assure you that you may take the performance of the past as a pledge for the future, and may confidently expect that the flag which has waved its untarnished folds over every sea will still float in undiminished honor. But these, like many other subjects, will be appropriately brought at a future time to the attention of the coordinate branches of the Government, to which I shall always look with profound respect and with trustful confidence that they will accord to me the aid and support which I shall so much need and which their experience and wisdom will readily suggest.

In the administration of domestic affairs you expect a devoted integrity in the public service and an observance of rigid economy in all departments, so marked as never justly to be questioned. If this reasonable expectation be not realized, I frankly confess that one of your leading hopes is doomed to disappointment, and that my efforts in a very important particular must result in a humiliating failure. Offices can be properly regarded only in the light of aids for the accomplishment of these objects, and as occupancy can confer no prerogative nor importunate desire for preferment any claim, the public interest imperatively demands that they be considered with sole reference to the duties to be performed. Good citizens may well claim the protection of good laws and the benign influence of good government, but a claim for office is what the people of a republic should never recognize. No reasonable man of any party will expect the Administration to be so regardless of its responsibility and of the obvious elements of success as to retain persons known to be under the influence of political hostility and partisan prejudice in positions which will require not only severe labor, but cordial cooperation. Having no implied engagements to ratify, no rewards to bestow, no resentments to remember, and no personal wishes to consult in selections for official station, I shall fulfill this difficult and delicate trust, admitting no motive as worthy either of my character or position which does not contemplate an efficient discharge of duty and the best interests of my country. I acknowledge my obligations to the masses of my countrymen, and to them alone. Higher objects than personal aggrandizement gave direction and energy to their exertions in the late canvass, and they shall not be disappointed. They require at my hands diligence, integrity, and capacity wherever there are duties to be performed. Without these qualities in their public servants, more stringent laws for the prevention or punishment of fraud, negligence, and peculation will be vain. With them they will be unnecessary.

But these are not the only points to which you look for vigi-

it what are we individually or collectively? What becomes of the noblest field ever opened for the advancement of our race in religion, in government, in the arts, and in all that dignifies and adorns mankind? From that radiant constellation which both illumines our own way and points out to struggling nations their course, let but a single star be lost, and, if these be not utter darkness, the luster of the whole is dimmed. Do my countrymen need any assurance that such a catastrophe is not to overtake them while I possess the power to stay it? It is with me an earnest and vital belief that as the Union has been the source, under Providence, of our prosperity to this time, so it is the surest pledge of a continuance of the blessings we have enjoyed, and which we are sacredly bound to transmit undiminished to our children. The field of calm and free discussion in our country is open, and will always be so, but never has been and never can be traversed for good in a spirit of sectionalism and uncharitableness.

The founders of the Republic dealt with things as they were presented to them, in a spirit of self-sacrificing patriotism, and, as time has proved, with a comprehensive wisdom which it will always be safe for us to consult. Every measure tending to strengthen the fraternal feelings of all the members of our Union has had my heartfelt approbation. To every theory of society or government, whether the offspring of feverish ambition or of morbid enthusiasm, calculated to dissolve the bonds of law and affection which unite us, I shall interpose a ready and stern resistance. I believe that involuntary servitude, as it exists in different States of this Confederacy, is recognized by the Constitution. I believe that it stands like any other admitted right, and that the States where it exists are entitled to efficient remedies to enforce the constitutional provisions. I hold that the laws of 1850, commonly called the 'compromise measures', are strictly constitutional and to be unhesitatingly carried into effect. I believe that the constituted authorities of this Republic are bound to regard the rights of the South in this respect as they would view any other legal and constitutional right, and that the laws to enforce them should be respected and obeyed, not with a reluctance encouraged by abstract opinions as to their propriety in a different state of society, but cheerfully and according to the decisions of the tribunal to which their exposition belongs. Such have been, and are, my convictions, and upon them I shall act. I fervently hope that the question is at rest, and that no sectional or ambitious or fanatical excitement may again threaten the durability of our institutions or obscure the light of our prosperity.

But let not the foundation of our hope rest upon man's wisdom. It will not be sufficient that sectional prejudices find no place in the public deliberations. It will not be sufficient that the rash counsels of human passion are rejected. It must be felt that there is no national security but in the nation's humble, acknowledged dependence upon God and His overruling providence. We have been carried in safety through a perilous crisis. Wise counsels, like those which gave us the Constitution, prevailed to uphold it. Let the period be remembered as an ad-monition, and not as an encouragement, in any section of the Union, to make experiments where experiments are fraught with such fearful hazard. Let it be impressed upon all hearts that, beautiful as our fabric is, no earthly power or wisdom could ever reunite its broken fragments. Standing, as I do, almost within view of the green slopes of Monticello, and, as it were, within reach of the tomb of Washington, with all the cherished memories of the past gathering around me like so many eloquent voices of exhortation from heaven, I can express no better hope for my country than that the kind Providence which smiled upon our fathers may enable their children to preserve the blessings they have inherited.

which now have a few tucks in them, will be let out, and then this hall, which now sits so easily upon us, will be too tight and small for us.

'Nevertheless, it is likely that even we are not without our experience now and then of spoilt children. I do not mean of our own spoilt children, because nobody's own children ever were spoilt, but I mean the disagreeable children of our particular friends. We know by experience what it is to have them down after dinner, and, across the rich perspective of a miscellaneous dessert to see, darkly, the family doctor looming in the distance. We know, I have no doubt we all know, what it is to assist at those little maternal anecdotes and table entertainments illustrated with imitations and descriptive dialogue which might not be inaptly called, after the manner of my friend Mr Albert Smith, the toilsome ascent of Miss Mary and the eruption (cutaneous) of Master Alexander. We know what it is when those children won't go to bed; we know how they prop their eyelids open with their forefingers when they will sit up; how, when they become fractious, they say aloud that they don't like us, and our nose is too long, and why don't we go? And we are perfectly acquainted with those kicking bundles which are carried off at last protesting. An eminent eye-witness told me that he was one of a company of learned pundits who assembled at the house of a very distinguished philosopher of the last generation to hear him expound his stringent views concerning infant education and early mental development, and he told me that while the philosopher did this in very beautiful and lucid language, the philosopher's little boy, for his part, edified the assembled sages by dabbling up to the elbows in an apple pie which had been provided for their entertainment, having previously anointed his hair with the syrup, combed it with his fork, and brushed it with his spoon. It is probable that we also have our similar experiences sometimes, of principles that are not quite practice, and that we know people claiming to be very wise and profound about nations of men who show themselves to be rather weak and shallow about units of babies.

But, ladies and gentlemen, the spoilt children whom I have to present to you after this dinner of to-day are not of this class. I have glanced at these for the easier and lighter introduction of another, a very different, a far more numerous, and a far more serious class. The spoilt children whom I must show you are the spoilt children of the poor in this great city, the children who are, every year, for ever and ever irrevocably spoilt out of this breathing life of ours by tens of thousands, but who may in vast numbers be preserved if you, assisting and not contravening the ways of Providence, will help to save them. The two grim nurses, Poverty and Sickness, who bring these children before you, preside over their births, rock their wretched cradles, nail down their little coffins, pile up the earth above their graves. Of the annual deaths in this great town, their unnatural deaths form more than one-third. I shall not ask you, according to the custom as to the other class – I shall not ask you on behalf of these children to observe how good they are, how pretty they are, how clever they are, how promising they are, whose beauty they most resemble – I shall only ask you to observe how weak they are, and how like death they are! And I shall ask you, by the remembrance of everything that lies between your own infancy and that so miscalled second childhood when the child's graces are gone and nothing but its helplessness remains; I shall ask you to turn your thoughts to THESE spoilt children in the sacred names of Pity and Compassion.

Some years ago, being in Scotland, I went with one of the most humane members of the humane medical profession, on a morning tour among some of the worst lodged inhabitants of the old town of Edinburgh. In the closes and wynds of that picturesque place – I am sorry to remind you what fast friends picturesqueness and typhus often are – we saw more poverty and sickness in an hour than many people would believe in a life. Our way lay from one to another of the most wretched dwellings, reeking with horrible odours; shut out from the sky, shut out from the air, mere pits and dens. In a room in one of these places, where there was an empty porridge-pot on the cold hearth, with a ragged woman and some ragged children crouching on the bare ground near it – where, I remember as I speak, that the very light, refracted from a high damp-stained and lime-stained house-wall, came trembling in, as if the fever which had shaken everything else there had shaken even it – there lay, in an old egg-box which the mother had begged from a shop, a little feeble, wasted, wan, sick child. With his little wasted face, and his little hot, worn hands folded over his breast, and his little bright, attentive eyes, I can see him now, as I have seen him for several years, look in steadily at us. There he lay in his little frail box, which was not at all a bad emblem of the little body from which he was slowly parting – there he lay, quite quiet, quite patient, saying never a word. He seldom cried, the mother said; he seldom complained; 'he lay there, seemin' to woonder what it was a'boot.'

God knows, I thought, as I stood looking at him, he had his reasons for wondering – reasons for wondering how it could possibly come to be that he lay there, left alone, feeble and full of pain, when he ought to have been as bright and as brisk as the birds that never got near him – reasons for wondering how he came to be left there, a little decrepid old man pining to death, quite a thing of course, as if there were no crowds of healthy and happy children playing on the grass under the summer's sun within a stone's throw of him, as if there were no bright, moving sea on the other side of the great hill overhanging the city;

as if there were no great clouds rushing over it; as if there were no life, and movement, and vigour anywhere in the world – nothing but stoppage and decay. There he lay looking at us, saying, in his silence, more pathetically than I have ever heard anything said by any orator in my life, 'Will you please to tell me what this means, strange man? and if you can give me any good reason why I should be so soon, so far advanced on my way to Him who said that children were to come into His presence and were not to be forbidden, but who scarcely meant, I think, that they should come by this hard road by which I am travelling; pray give that reason to me, for I seek it very earnestly and wonder about it very much'; and to my mind he has been wondering about it ever since. Many a poor child, sick and neglected, I have seen since that time in this London; many a poor sick child I have seen most affectionately and kindly tended by poor people, in an unwholesome house and under untoward circumstances, wherein its recovery was quite impossible; but at all such times I have seen my poor little drooping friend in his egg-box, and he has always addressed his dumb speech to me, and I have always found him wondering what it meant, and why, in the name of a gracious God, such things should be!

Now, ladies and gentlemen, such things need not be, and will not be, if this company, which is a drop of the life-blood of the great compassionate public heart, will only accept the means of rescue and prevention which it is mine to offer. Within a quarter of a mile of this place where I speak, stands a courtly old house, where once, no doubt, blooming children were born, and grew up to be men and women, and married, and brought their own blooming children back to patter up the old oak staircase which stood but the other day, and to wonder at the old oak carvings on the chimney-pieces. In the airy wards into which the old state drawing-rooms and family bedchambers of that house are now converted are such little patients that the attendant nurses look like reclaimed giantesses, and the kind medical practitioner like an amiable Christian ogre. Grouped about the little low tables in the centre of the rooms are such tiny convalescents that they seem to be playing at having been ill. On the doll's beds are such diminutive creatures that each poor sufferer is supplied with its tray of toys; and, looking round, you may see how the little tired, flushed cheek has toppled over half the brute creation on its way into the ark; or how one little dimpled arm has mowed down (as I saw myself) the whole tin soldiery of Europe. On the walls of these rooms are graceful, pleasant, bright, childish pictures. At the bed's heads, are pictures of the figure which is the universal embodiment of all mercy and compassion, the figure of Him who was once a child himself, and a poor one.

Besides these little creatures on the beds, you may learn in that place that the number of small Out-patients brought to that house for relief is no fewer than ten thousand in the compass of one single year. In the room in which these are received, you may see against the wall a box, on which it is written, that it has been calculated, that if every grateful mother who brings a child there will drop a penny into it, the Hospital funds may possibly be increased in a year by so large a sum as forty pounds. And you may read in the Hospital Report, with a glow of pleasure, that these poor women are so respondent as to have made, even in a toiling year of difficulty and high prices, this estimated forty, fifty pounds. In the printed papers of this same Hospital, you may read with what a generous earnestness the highest and wisest members of the medical profession testify to the great need of it; to the immense difficulty of treating children in the same hospitals with grown-up people, by reason of their different ailments and requirements, to the vast amount of pain that will be assuaged, and of life that will be saved, through this Hospital;

not only among the poor, observe, but among the prosperous too, by reason of the increased knowledge of children's illnesses, which cannot fail to arise from a more systematic mode of studying them.

Lastly, gentlemen, and I am sorry to say, worst of all – (for I must present no rose-coloured picture of this place to you – I must not deceive you;) lastly, the visitor to this Children's Hospital, reckoning up the number of its beds, will find himself perforce obliged to stop at very little over thirty; and will learn, with sorrow and surprise, that even that small number, so forlornly, so miserably diminutive, compared with this vast London, cannot possibly be maintained, unless the Hospital be made better known; I limit myself to saying better known, because I will not believe that in a Christian community of fathers and mothers, and brothers and sisters, it can fail, being better known, to be well and richly endowed.

Now, ladies and gentlemen, this, without a word of adornment – which I resolved when I got up not to allow myself – this is the simple case. This is the pathetic case which I have to put to you; not only on behalf of the thousands of children who annually die in this great city, but also on behalf of the thousands of children who live half developed, racked with preventible pain, shorn of their natural capacity for health and enjoyment. If these innocent creatures cannot move you for themselves, how can I possibly hope to move you in their name? The most delightful paper, the most charming essay, which the tender imagination of Charles Lamb conceived, represents him as sitting by his fireside on a winter night telling stories to his own dear children, and delighting in their society, until he suddenly comes to his old, solitary, bachelor self, and finds that they were but dream-children who might have been, but never were. 'We are nothing,' they say to him; 'less than nothing, and dreams. We are only what might have been, and we must wait upon the tedious shore of Lethe, millions of ages, before we have existence and a name.' 'And immediately awaking,' he says, 'I found myself in my arm chair.' The dream-children whom I would now raise, if I could, before every one of you, according to your various circumstances, should be the dear child you love, the dearer child you have lost, the child you might have had, the child you certainly have been. Each of these dream-children should hold in its powerful hand one of the little children now lying in the Child's Hospital, or now shut out of it to perish. Each of these dream-children should say to you, 'O, help this little suppliant in my name; O, help it for my sake!' Well! – And immediately awaking, you should find yourselves in the Freemasons' Hall, happily arrived at the end of a rather long speech, drinking 'Prosperity to the Hospital for Sick Children', and thoroughly resolved that it shall flourish.

Frederick Douglass:

4 December 1860

A Plea for Free Speech in Boston

Douglass gave this speech at Boston's Music Hall the week after an anti-slavery meeting had been broken up by a mob of 'gentlemen'.

Boston is a great city – and Music Hall has a fame almost as extensive as that of Boston. Nowhere more than here have the principles of human freedom been expounded. But for the circumstances already mentioned, it would seem almost presumption for me to say anything here about those principles. And yet, even here, in Boston, the moral atmosphere is dark and heavy. The principles of human liberty, even if correctly apprehended, find but limited support in this hour of trial. The world moves slowly, and Boston is much like the world. We thought the principle of free speech was an accomplished fact. Here, if nowhere else, we thought the right of the people to assemble and to express their opinion was secure. Dr Channing had defended the right, Mr Garrison had practically asserted the right, and Theodore Parker had maintained it with steadiness and fidelity to the last.

But here we are to-day contending for what we thought we gained years ago. The mortifying and disgraceful fact stares us in the face, that though Faneuil Hall and Bunker Hill Monument stand, freedom of speech is struck down. No lengthy detail of facts is needed. They are already notorious; far more so than will be wished ten years hence.

The world knows that last Monday a meeting assembled to discuss the question: 'How Shall Slavery Be Abolished?' The world also knows that that meeting was invaded, insulted, captured by a mob of gentlemen, and thereafter broken up and dispersed by the order of the mayor, who refused to protect it, though called upon to do so. If this had been a mere outbreak of passion and prejudice among the baser sort, maddened by rum and hounded on by some wily politician to serve some immediate purpose – a mere exceptional affair – it might be allowed to rest with what has already been said. But the leaders of the mob were gentlemen. They were men who pride themselves upon their respect for law and order.

These gentlemen brought their respect for the law with them and proclaimed it loudly while in the very act of breaking the law. Theirs was the law of slavery. The law of free speech and the law for the protection of public meetings they trampled under foot, while they greatly magnified the law of slavery.

The scene was an instructive one. Men seldom see such a

blending of the gentleman with the rowdy, as was shown on that occasion. It proved that human nature is very much the same, whether in tarpaulin or broadcloth. Nevertheless, when gentlemen approach us in the character of lawless and abandoned loafers – assuming for the moment their manners and tempers – they have themselves to blame if they are estimated below their quality. 'Liberty is meaningless where the right to utter one's thoughts and opinions has ceased to exist.'

No right was deemed by the fathers of the Government more sacred than the right of speech. It was in their eyes, as in the eyes of all thoughtful men, the great moral renovator of society and government. Daniel Webster called it a homebred right, a fireside privilege. Liberty is meaningless where the right to utter one's thoughts and opinions has ceased to exist. That, of all rights, is the dread of tyrants. It is the right which they first of all strike down. They know its power. Thrones, dominions, principalities, and powers, founded in injustice and wrong, are sure to tremble, if men are allowed to reason of righteousness, temperance, and of a judgment to come in their presence. Slavery cannot tolerate free speech. Five years of its exercise would banish the auction block and break every chain in the South. They will have none of it there, for they have the power. But shall it be so here?

Even here in Boston, and among the friends of freedom, we hear two voices: one denouncing the mob that broke up our meeting on Monday as a base and cowardly outrage; and another, deprecating and regretting the holding of such a meeting, by such men, at such a time. We are told that the meeting was ill-timed, and the parties to it unwise.

Why, what is the matter with us? Are we going to palliate and excuse a palpable and flagrant outrage on the right of speech, by implying that only a particular description of persons should exercise that right? Are we, at such a time, when a great principle has been struck down, to quench the moral indignation which the deed excites, by casting reflections upon those on whose persons the outrage has been committed? After all the arguments for liberty to which Boston has listened for more than a quarter of a century, has she yet to learn that the time to assert a right is the time when the right itself is called in question, and that the men of all others to assert it are the men to whom the right has been denied?

It would be no vindication of the right of speech to prove that certain gentlemen of great distinction, eminent for their learning and ability, are allowed to freely express their opinions on all subjects – including the subject of slavery. Such a vindication would need, itself, to be vindicated. It would add insult to injury. Not even an old-fashioned abolition meeting could vindicate that right in Boston just now. There can be no right of speech where any man, however lifted up, or however humble, however young, or however old, is overawed by force, and compelled to suppress his honest sentiments.

'It is just as criminal to rob a man of his right to speak and hear as it would be to rob him of his money.' Equally clear is the right to hear. To suppress free speech is a double wrong. It violates the rights of the hearer as well as those of the speaker. It is just as criminal to rob a man of his right to speak and hear as it would be to rob him of his money. I have no doubt that Boston will vindicate this right. But in order to do so, there must be no concessions to the enemy. When a man is allowed to speak because he is rich and powerful, it aggravates the crime of denying the right to the poor and humble.

The principle must rest upon its own proper basis. And until the right is accorded to the humblest as freely as to the most exalted citizen, the government of Boston is but an empty name, and its freedom a mockery. A man's right to speak does not depend upon where he was born or upon his color. The simple quality of manhood is the solid basis of the right – and there let it rest forever.

Abraham Lincoln:

4 March 1861

First Inaugural Address

Lincoln made this address against the backdrop of national upheaval caused by the grim reality of secession. Two weeks earlier Jefferson Davis had been inaugurated as the President of the Confederacy.

Fellow-Citizens of the United States:

In compliance with a custom as old as the Government itself, I appear before you to address you briefly and to take in your presence the oath prescribed by the Constitution of the United States to be taken by the President 'before he enters on the execution of this office.' I do not consider it necessary at present for me to discuss those matters of administration about which there is no special anxiety or excitement. Apprehension seems to exist among the people of the Southern States that by the accession of a Republican Administration their property and their peace and personal security are to be endangered. There has never been any reasonable cause for such apprehension. Indeed, the most ample evidence to the contrary has all the while existed and been open to their inspection. It is found in nearly all the published speeches of him who now addresses you. I do but quote from one of those speeches when I declare that:

I have no purpose, directly or indirectly, to interfere with the institution of slavery in the States where it exists. I believe

I have no lawful right to do so, and I have no inclination to do so. Those who nominated and elected me did so with full knowledge that I had made this and many similar declarations and had never recanted them; and more than this, they placed in the platform for my acceptance, and as a law to themselves and to me, the clear and emphatic resolution which I now read:

Resolved, That the maintenance inviolate of the rights of the States, and especially the right of each State to order and control its own domestic institutions according to its own judgment exclusively, is essential to that balance of power on which the perfection and endurance of our political fabric depend; and we denounce the lawless invasion by armed force of the soil of any State or Territory, no matter what pretext, as among the gravest of crimes. I now reiterate these sentiments, and in doing so I only press upon the public attention the most conclusive evidence of which the case is susceptible that the property, peace, and security of no section are to be in any wise endangered by the now incoming Administration. I add, too, that all the protection which, consistently with the Constitution and the laws, can be given will be cheerfully given to all the States when lawfully demanded, for whatever cause – as cheerfully to one section as to another. There is much controversy about the delivering up of fugitives from service or labor. The clause I now read is as plainly written in the Constitution as any other of its provisions:

No person held to service or labor in one State, under the laws thereof, escaping into another, shall in consequence of any law or regulation therein be discharged from such service or labor, but shall be delivered up on claim of the party to whom such service or labor may be due. It is scarcely questioned that this provision was intended by those who made it for the reclaiming of what we call fugitive slaves; and the intention of the lawgiver is the law. All members of Congress swear their support to the whole Constitution – to this provision as much as to any other. To the proposition, then, that slaves whose cases come within the terms of this clause 'shall be delivered up' their oaths are unanimous. Now, if they would make the effort in good temper, could they not with nearly equal unanimity frame and pass a law by means of which to keep good that unanimous oath? There is some difference of opinion whether this clause should be enforced by national or by State authority, but surely that difference is not a very material one. If the slave is to be surrendered, it can be of but little consequence to him or to others by which authority it is done. And should anyone in any case be content that his oath shall go unkept on a merely unsubstantial controversy as to how it shall be kept?

Again: In any law upon this subject ought not all the safeguards of liberty known in civilized and humane jurisprudence to be introduced, so that a free man be not in any case surrendered as a slave? And might it not be well at the same time to provide by law for the enforcement of that clause in the Constitution which guarantees that 'the citizens of each State shall be entitled to all privileges and immunities of citizens in the several States'? I take the official oath to-day with no mental reservations and with no purpose to construe the Constitution or laws by any hypercritical rules; and while I do not choose now to specify particular acts of Congress as proper to be enforced, I do suggest that it will be much safer for all, both in official and private stations, to conform to and abide by all those acts which stand unrepealed than to violate any of them trusting to find impunity in having them held to be unconstitutional. It is seventy-two years since the first inauguration of a President under our National Constitution. During that period fifteen different and greatly distinguished citizens have in succession administered the executive branch of the Government. They have conducted it through many perils, and generally with great success. Yet, with all this scope of precedent, I now enter upon the same task for the brief constitutional term of four years under great and peculiar difficulty. A disruption of the Federal Union, heretofore only menaced, is now formidably attempted. I hold that in contemplation of universal law and of the Constitution the Union of these States is perpetual. Perpetuity is implied, if not expressed, in the fundamental law of all national governments. It is safe to assert that no government proper ever had a provision in its organic law for its own termination. Continue to execute all the express provisions of our National Constitution, and the Union will endure forever, it being impossible to destroy it except by some action not provided for in the instrument itself.

Again: If the United States be not a government proper, but an association of States in the nature of contract merely, can it, as a contract, be peaceably unmade by less than all the parties who made it? One party to a contract may violate it – break it, so to speak – but does it not require all to lawfully rescind it? Descending from these general principles, we find the proposition that in legal contemplation the Union is perpetual confirmed by the history of the Union itself. The Union is much older than the Constitution. It was formed, in fact, by the Articles of Association in 1774. It was matured and continued by the Declaration of Independence in 1776. It was further matured, and the faith of all the then thirteen States expressly plighted and engaged that it should be perpetual, by the Articles of Confederation in 1778. And finally, in 1787, one of the declared objects for ordaining and establishing the Constitution was 'to form a more perfect Union.' But if destruction of the Union by one or by a part only of the States be lawfully possible, the Union is less perfect than before the Constitution, having lost the vital element of perpetuity. It follows from these views that no State upon its own mere motion can lawfully get out of the Union; that resolves and ordinances to that effect are legally void, and that acts of violence within any State or States against the authority of the United States are insurrectionary or revolutionary, according to circumstances. I therefore consider that in view of the Constitution and the laws the Union is unbroken, and to the extent of my ability, I shall take care, as the Constitution itself expressly enjoins upon me, that the laws of the Union be faithfully executed in all the States. Doing this I deem to be only a simple duty on my part, and I shall perform it so far as practicable unless my rightful masters, the American people, shall withhold the requisite means or in some authoritative manner direct the contrary. I trust this will not be regarded as a menace, but only as the declared purpose of the Union that it will constitutionally defend and maintain itself. In doing this there needs to be no bloodshed or violence, and there shall be none unless it be forced upon the national authority. The power confided to me will be used to hold, occupy, and possess the property and places belonging to the Government and to collect the duties and imposts; but beyond what may be necessary for these objects, there will be no invasion, no using of force against or among the people anywhere. Where hostility to the United States in any interior locality shall be so great and universal as to prevent competent resident citizens from holding the Federal offices, there will be no attempt to force obnoxious strangers among the people for that object. While the strict legal right may exist in the Government to enforce the exercise of these offices, the attempt to do so would be so irritating and so nearly impracticable withal that I deem it better to forego for the time the uses of such offices. The mails, unless repelled, will continue to be furnished in all parts of the Union. So far as possible the people everywhere shall have that sense of perfect security which is most favorable to calm thought and reflection. The course here indicated will be followed unless current events and experience shall show a modification or change to be proper, and in every case and exigency my best discretion will be exercised, according to circumstances actually existing and with a view and a hope of a peaceful solution of the national troubles and the restoration of fraternal sympathies and affections.

That there are persons in one section or another who seek to destroy the Union at all events and are glad of any pretext to do it I will neither affirm nor deny; but if there be such, I need address no word to them. To those, however, who really love the Union may I not speak? Before entering upon so grave a matter as the destruction of our national fabric, with all its benefits, its memories, and its hopes, would it not be wise to ascertain precisely why we do it? Will you hazard so desperate a step while there is any possibility that any portion of the ills you fly from have no real existence? Will you, while the certain ills you fly to are greater than all the real ones you fly from, will you risk the commission of so fearful a mistake? All profess to be content in the Union if all constitutional rights can be maintained. Is it true, then, that any right plainly written in the Constitution has been denied? I think not. Happily, the human mind is so constituted that no party can reach to the audacity of doing this. Think, if you can, of a single instance in which a plainly written provision of the Constitution has ever been denied. If by the mere force of numbers a majority should deprive a minority of any clearly written constitutional right, it might in a moral point of view justify revolution; certainly would if such right were a vital one. But such is not our case. All the vital rights of minorities and of individuals are so plainly assured to them by affirmations and negations, guaranties and prohibitions, in the Constitution that controversies never arise concerning them. But no organic law can ever be framed with a provision specifically applicable to every question which may occur in practical administration. No foresight can anticipate nor any document of reasonable length contain express provisions for all possible questions. Shall fugitives from labor be surrendered by national or by State authority? The Constitution does not expressly say. May Congress prohibit slavery in the Territories? The Constitution does not expressly say. Must Congress protect slavery in the Territories? The Constitution does not expressly say.

From questions of this class spring all our constitutional controversies, and we divide upon them into majorities and minorities. If the minority will not acquiesce, the majority must, or the Government must cease. There is no other alternative, for continuing the Government is acquiescence on one side or the other. If a minority in such case will secede rather than acquiesce, they make a precedent which in turn will divide and ruin them, for a minority of their own will secede from them whenever a majority refuses to be controlled by such minority. For instance, why may not any portion of a new confederacy a year or two hence arbitrarily secede again, precisely as portions of the present Union now claim to secede from it? All who cherish disunion sentiments are now being educated to the exact temper of doing this. Is there such perfect identity of interests among the States to compose a new union as to produce harmony only and prevent renewed secession? Plainly the central idea of secession is the essence of anarchy. A majority held in restraint by constitutional checks and limitations, and always changing easily with deliberate changes of popular opinions and sentiments, is the only true sovereign of a free people. Whoever rejects it does of necessity fly to anarchy or to despotism. Unanimity is impossible. The rule of a minority, as a permanent arrangement, is wholly inadmissible; so that, rejecting the majority principle, anarchy or despotism in some form is all that is left.

I do not forget the position assumed by some that constitutional questions are to be decided by the Supreme Court, nor do I deny that such decisions must be binding in any case upon the parties to a suit as to the object of that suit, while they are also entitled to very high respect and consideration in all parallel cases by all other departments of the Government. And while it is obviously possible that such decision may be erroneous in any given case, still the evil effect following it, being limited to that particular case, with the chance that it may be overruled and never become a precedent for other cases, can better be borne than could the evils of a different practice. At the same time, the candid citizen must confess that if the policy of the Government upon vital questions affecting the whole people is to be irrevocably fixed by decisions of the Supreme Court, the instant they are made in ordinary litigation between parties in personal actions the people will have ceased to be their own rulers, having to that extent practically resigned their Government into the hands of that eminent tribunal. Nor is there in this view any assault upon the court or the judges. It is a duty from which they may not shrink to decide cases properly brought before them, and it is no fault of theirs if others seek to turn their decisions to political purposes.

One section of our country believes slavery is right and ought to be extended, while the other believes it is wrong and ought not to be extended. This is the only substantial dispute. The fugitive-slave clause of the Constitution and the law for the suppression of the foreign slave trade are each as well enforced, perhaps, as any law can ever be in a community where the moral

prescribed in the instrument itself; and I should, under existing circumstances, favor rather than oppose a fair opportunity being afforded the people to act upon it. I will venture to add that to me the convention mode seems preferable, in that it allows amendments to originate with the people themselves, instead of only permitting them to take or reject propositions originated by others, not especially chosen for the purpose, and which might not be precisely such as they would wish to either accept or refuse. I understand a proposed amendment to the Constitution – which amendment, however, I have not seen – has passed Congress, to the effect that the Federal Government shall never interfere with the domestic institutions of the States, including that of persons held to service. To avoid misconstruction of what I have said, I depart from my purpose not to speak of particular amendments so far as to say that, holding such a provision to now be implied constitutional law, I have no objection to its being made express and irrevocable. The Chief Magistrate derives all his authority from the people, and they have referred none upon him to fix terms for the separation of the States. The people themselves can do this if also they choose, but the Executive as such has nothing to do with it. His duty is to administer the present Government as it came to his hands and to transmit it unimpaired by him to his successor.

Why should there not be a patient confidence in the ultimate justice of the people? Is there any better or equal hope in the world? In our present differences, is either party without faith of being in the right? If the Almighty Ruler of Nations, with His eternal truth and justice, be on your side of the North, or on yours of the South, that truth and that justice will surely prevail by the judgment of this great tribunal of the American people. By the frame of the Government under which we live this same people have wisely given their public servants but little power for mischief, and have with equal wisdom provided for the return of that little to their own hands at very short intervals. While the people retain their virtue and vigilance no Administration by any extreme of wickedness or folly can very seriously injure the Government in the short space of four years. My countrymen, one and all, think calmly and well upon this whole subject. Nothing valuable can be lost by taking time. If there be an object to hurry any of you in hot haste to a step which you would never take deliberately, that object will be frustrated by taking time; but no good object can be frustrated by it. Such of you as are now dissatisfied still have the old Constitution unimpaired, and, on the sensitive point, the laws of your own framing under it; while the new Administration will have no immediate power, if it would, to change either. If it were admitted that you who are dissatisfied hold the right side in the dispute, there still is no single good reason for precipitate action. Intelligence, patriotism, Christianity, and a firm reliance on Him who has never yet forsaken this favored land are still competent to adjust in the best way all our present difficulty. In your hands, my dissatisfied fellow-countrymen, and not in mine, is the momentous issue of civil war. The Government will not assail you. You can have no conflict without being yourselves the aggressors. You have no oath registered in heaven to destroy the Government, while I shall have the most solemn one to 'preserve, protect, and defend it.' I am loath to close. We are not enemies, but friends. We must not be enemies. Though passion may have strained it must not break our bonds of affection. The mystic chords of memory, stretching from every battlefield and patriot grave to every living heart and hearthstone all over this broad land, will yet swell the chorus of the Union, when again touched, as surely they will be, by the better angels of our nature.

Abraham Lincoln:

19 November 1863

The Gettysburg Address

The Battle of Gettysburg, one of the most noted battles of the American Civil War, was fought on 1–3 July 1863. On 19 November of that year the battlefield was dedicated as a national cemetery by President Lincoln. His two-minute speech at the dedication ceremony was to become immortal. At the time of its delivery the speech was relegated to the inside pages of the newspapers, while a two-hour address by Edward Everett, the leading orator of the time, caught the headlines. The following is the text of Lincoln's speech, taken from his own notes.

Fourscore and seven years ago our fathers brought forth on this continent a new nation, conceived in liberty and dedicated to the proposition that all men are created equal. Now we are engaged in a great civil war, testing whether that nation or any nation so conceived and so dedicated can long endure. We are met on a great battlefield of that war. We have come to dedicate a portion of that field as a final resting-place for those who here gave their lives that that nation might live. It is altogether fitting and proper that we should do this. But in a larger sense, we cannot dedicate, we cannot consecrate, we cannot hallow this ground. The brave men, living and dead who struggled here have consecrated it far above our poor power to add or detract. The world will little note nor long remember what we say here, but it can never forget what they did here. It is for us the living rather to be dedicated here to the unfinished work which they who fought here have thus far so nobly advanced. It is rather for us to be here dedicated to the great task remaining before us – that from these honored dead we take increased devotion to that cause for which they gave the last full measure of devotion – that we here highly resolve that these dead shall not have died in vain, that this nation under God shall have a new birth of freedom, and that government of the people, by the people, for the people shall not perish from the earth.

Abraham Lincoln:

4 March 1865

Second Inaugural Address

Lincoln's second inaugural address and his Gettysburg address rank as his two greatest speeches. The *London Spectator* said of his second inaugural address, 'We cannot read it without a renewed conviction that it is the noblest political document known to history, and should have for the nation and the statesmen he left behind him something of a sacred and almost prophetic character.'

At this second appearing to take the oath of the presidential office, there is less occasion for an extended address than there was at the first. Then a statement, somewhat in detail, of a course to be pursued, seemed fitting and proper. Now, at the expiration of four years, during which public declarations have been constantly called forth on every point and phase of the great contest which still absorbs the attention, and engrosses the energies of the nation, little that is new could be presented. The progress of our arms, upon which all else chiefly depends, is as well known to the public as to myself; and it is, I trust, reasonably satisfactory and encouraging to all. With high hope for the future, no prediction in regard to it is ventured.

On the occasion corresponding to this four years ago, all thoughts were anxiously directed to an impending civil war.

All dreaded it – all sought to avert it. While the inaugeral [sic] address was being delivered from this place, devoted altogether to saving the Union without war, insurgent agents were in the city seeking to destroy it without war – seeking to dissole [sic] the Union, and divide effects, by negotiation. Both parties deprecated war; but one of them would make war rather than let the nation survive; and the other would accept war rather than let it perish. And the war came.

One eighth of the whole population were colored slaves, not distributed generally over the Union, but localized in the Southern part of it. These slaves constituted a peculiar and powerful interest. All knew that this interest was, somehow, the cause of the war. To strengthen, perpetuate, and extend this interest was the object for which the insurgents would rend the Union, even by war; while the government claimed no right to do more than to restrict the territorial enlargement of it. Neither party expected for the war, the magnitude, or the duration, which it has already attained. Neither anticipated that the cause of the conflict might cease with, or even before, the conflict itself should cease. Each looked for an easier triumph, and a result less fundamental and astounding. Both read the same Bible, and pray to the same God; and each invokes His aid against the other. It may seem strange that any men should dare to ask a just God's assistance in wringing their bread from the sweat of other men's faces; but let us judge not that we be not judged. The prayers of both could not be answered; that of neither has been answered fully. The Almighty has his own purposes.

'Woe unto the world because of offences! for it must needs be that offences come; but woe to that man by whom the offence cometh!' If we shall suppose that American Slavery is one of those offences which, in the providence of God, must needs come, but which, having continued through His appointed time, He now wills to remove, and that He gives to both North and South, this terrible war, as the woe due to those by whom the offence came, shall we discern therein any departure from those divine attributes which the believers in a Living God always ascribe to Him? Fondly do we hope – fervently do we pray – that this mighty scourge of war may speedily pass away. Yet, if God wills that it continue, until all the wealth piled by the bond-man's two hundred and fifty years of unrequited toil shall be sunk, and until every drop of blood drawn with the lash, shall be paid by another drawn with the sword, as was said three thousand years ago, so still it must be said 'the judgments of the Lord, are true and righteous altogether.'

With malice toward none; with charity for all; with firmness in the right, as God gives us to see the right, let us strive on to finish the work we are in; to bind up the nation's wounds; to care for him who shall have borne the battle, and for his widow, and his orphan – to do all which may achieve and cherish a just and lasting peace, among ourselves, and with all nations.

Abraham Lincoln:

11 April 1865

Speech on Reconstruction

Abraham Lincoln's famous 'Speech on Reconstruction' was delivered in Washington, DC on the day that the Civil War ended.

We meet this evening, not in sorrow, but in gladness of heart. The evacuation of Petersburg and Richmond, and the surrender of the principal insurgent army, give hope of a righteous and speedy peace whose joyous expression can not be restrained. In the midst of this, however, He, from Whom all blessings flow, must not be forgotten. A call for a national thanksgiving is being prepared, and will be duly promulgated. Nor must those whose harder part gives us the cause of rejoicing, be overlooked. Their honors must not be parcelled out with others. I myself, was near the front, and had the high pleasure of transmitting much of the good news to you; but no part of the honor, for plan or execution, is mine. To Gen. Grant, his skillful officers, and brave men, all belongs. The gallant Navy stood ready, but was not in reach to take active part.

By these recent successes the re-inauguration of the national authority – reconstruction – which has had a large share of thought from the first, is pressed much more closely upon our attention. It is fraught with great difficulty. Unlike the case of a war between independent nations, there is no authorized organ for us to treat with. No one man has authority to give up the rebellion for any other man. We simply must begin with, and mould from, disorganized and discordant elements. Nor is it a small additional embarrassment that we, the loyal people, differ among ourselves as to the mode, manner, and means of reconstruction.

As a general rule, I abstain from reading the reports of

attacks upon myself, wishing not to be provoked by that to which I can not properly offer an answer. In spite of this precaution, however, it comes to my knowledge that I am much censured for some supposed agency in setting up, and seeking to sustain, the new State Government of Louisiana. In this I have done just so much as, and no more than, the public knows. In the Annual Message of Dec. 1863 and accompanying Proclamation, I presented a plan of reconstruction (as the phrase goes) which, I promised, if adopted by any State, should be acceptable to, and sustained by, the Executive government of the nation. I distinctly stated that this was not the only plan which might possibly be acceptable; and I also distinctly protested that the Executive claimed no right to say when, or whether members should be admitted to seats in Congress from such States. This plan was, in advance, submitted to the then Cabinet, and distinctly approved by every member of it. One of them suggested that I should then, and in that connection, apply the Emancipation Proclamation to the theretofore excepted parts of Virginia and Louisiana; that I should drop the suggestion about apprenticeship for freed-people, and that I should omit the protest against my own power, in regard to the admission of members to Congress; but even he approved every part and parcel of the plan which has since been employed or touched by the action of Louisiana.

The new constitution of Louisiana, declaring emancipation for the whole State, practically applies the Proclamation to the part previously excepted. It does not adopt apprenticeship for freed-people; and it is silent, as it could not well be otherwise, about the admission of members to Congress. So that, as it applies to Louisiana, every member of the Cabinet fully approved the plan. The Message went to Congress, and I received many commendations of the plan, written and verbal;

and not a single objection to it, from any professed emancipationist, came to my knowledge, until after the news reached Washington that the people of Louisiana had begun to move in accordance with it. From about July 1862, I had corresponded with different persons, supposed to be interested, seeking a reconstruction of a State government for Louisiana. When the Message of 1863, with the plan before mentioned, reached New-Orleans, Gen. Banks wrote me that he was confident the people, with his military co-operation, would reconstruct, substantially on that plan. I wrote him, and some of them to try it; they tried it, and the result is known. Such only has been my agency in getting up the Louisiana government. As to sustaining it, my promise is out, as before stated. But, as bad promises are better broken than kept, I shall treat this as a bad promise, and break it, whenever I shall be convinced that keeping it is adverse to the public interest. But I have not yet been so convinced.

I have been shown a letter on this subject, supposed to be an able one, in which the writer expresses regret that my mind has not seemed to be definitely fixed on the question whether the seceded States, so called, are in the Union or out of it. It would perhaps, add astonishment to his regret, were he to learn that since I have found professed Union men endeavoring to make that question, I have purposely forborne any public expression upon it. As appears to me that question has not been, nor yet is, a practically material one, and that any discussion of it, while it thus remains practically immaterial, could have no effect other than the mischievous one of dividing our friends. As yet, whatever it may hereafter become, that question is bad, as the basis of a controversy, and good for nothing at all – a merely pernicious abstraction.

We all agree that the seceded States, so called, are out of

their proper practical relation with the Union; and that the sole object of the government, civil and military, in regard to those States is to again get them into that proper practical relation. I believe it is not only possible, but in fact, easier, to do this, without deciding, or even considering, whether these states have even been out of the Union, than with it. Finding themselves safely at home, it would be utterly immaterial whether they had ever been abroad. Let us all join in doing the acts necessary to restoring the proper practical relations between these states and the Union; and each forever after, innocently indulge his own opinion whether, in doing the acts, he brought the States from without, into the Union, or only gave them proper assistance, they never having been out of it.

The amount of constituency, so to speak, on which the new Louisiana government rests, would be more satisfactory to all, if it contained fifty, thirty, or even twenty thousand, instead of only about twelve thousand, as it does. It is also unsatisfactory to some that the elective franchise is not given to the colored man. I would myself prefer that it were now conferred on the very intelligent, and on those who serve our cause as soldiers. Still the question is not whether the Louisiana government, as it stands, is quite all that is desirable. The question is 'Will it be wiser to take it as it is, and help to improve it; or to reject, and disperse it?' 'Can Louisiana be brought into proper practical relation with the Union soon by sustaining, or by discarding her new State Government?'

Some twelve thousand voters in the heretofore slave-state of Louisiana have sworn allegiance to the Union, assumed to be the rightful political power of the State, held elections, organized a State government, adopted a free-state constitution, giving the benefit of public schools equally to black and white, and empowering the Legislature to confer the elective franchise upon the colored man. Their Legislature has already voted to ratify the constitutional amendment recently passed by Congress, abolishing slavery throughout the nation. These twelve thousand persons are thus fully committed to the Union, and to perpetual freedom in the state – committed to the very things, and nearly all the things the nation wants – and they ask the nation's recognition, and its assistance to make good their committal. Now, if we reject, and spurn them, we do our utmost to disorganize and disperse them. We in effect say to the white men 'You are worthless, or worse – we will neither help you, nor be helped by you.' To the blacks we say 'This cup of liberty which these, your old masters, hold to your lips, we will dash from you, and leave you to the chances of gathering the spilled and scattered contents in some vague and undefined when, where, and how.'

If this course, discouraging and paralyzing both white and black, has any tendency to bring Louisiana into proper practical relations with the Union, I have, so far, been unable to perceive it. If, on the contrary, we recognize, and sustain the new government of Louisiana the converse of all this is made true. We encourage the hearts, and nerve the arms of the twelve thousand to adhere to their work, and argue for it, and proselyte for it, and fight for it, and feed it, and grow it, and ripen it to a complete success. The colored man too, in seeing all united for him, is inspired with vigilance, and energy, and daring, to the same end. Grant that he desires the elective franchise, will he not attain it sooner by saving the already advanced steps toward it, than by running backward over them? Concede that the new government of Louisiana is only to what it should be as the egg is to the fowl, we shall sooner have the fowl by hatching the egg than by smashing it? Again, if we reject Louisiana, we also reject one vote in favor of the proposed amendment to the national constitution. To meet this proposition, it has been argued that no more than three fourths of those States which have not attempted secession are necessary to validly ratify the amendment. I do not commit myself against this, further than to say that such a ratification would be questionable, and sure to be persistently questioned; while a ratification by three fourths of all the States would be unquestioned and unquestionable.

I repeat the question. 'Can Louisiana be brought into proper practical relation with the Union sooner by sustaining or by discarding her new State Government?' What has been said of Louisiana will apply generally to other States. And yet so great peculiarities pertain to each state; and such important and sudden changes occur in the same state; and, withal, so new and unprecedented is the whole case, that no exclusive, and inflexible plan can safely be prescribed as to details and colatterals. Such an exclusive, and inflexible plan, would surely become a new entanglement. Important principles may, and must, be inflexible.

In the present 'situation' as the phrase goes, it may be my duty to make some new announcement to the people of the South. I am considering, and shall not fail to act, when satisfied that action will be proper.

Phineas D. Gurley:

19 April 1865

The Sermon at Abraham Lincoln's Funeral

Dr Phineas D. Gurley, pastor of the New York Avenue Presbyterian Church, which Lincoln attended when he was President, preached this funeral sermon in the East Room of the White House. Dr Gurley had been at Lincoln's bedside when he died on 15 April.

As we stand here today, mourners around this coffin and around the lifeless remains of our beloved chief magistrate, we recognize and we adore the sovereignty of God. His throne is in the heavens, and His kingdom ruleth over all. He hath done, and He hath permitted to be done, whatsoever He pleased. 'Clouds and darkness are round about Him; righteousness and judgment are the habitation of His throne.' His way is in the sea, and His path in the great waters, and His footsteps are not known. 'Canst thou by searching find out God? Canst thou find out the Almighty unto perfection? It is as high as heaven; what canst thou do? Deeper than hell; what canst thou know? The measure thereof is longer than the earth, and broader than the sea. If He cut off, and shut up, or gather together, then who can hinder Him? For He knoweth vain men; he seeth wickedness also; will He not then consider it?' – We bow before His infinite majesty. We bow, we weep, we worship.

> Where reason fails, with all her powers,
> There faith prevails, and love adores.

It was a cruel, cruel hand, that dark hand of the assassin, which smote our honored, wise, and noble President, and filled the land with sorrow. But above and beyond that hand there is another which we must see and acknowledge. It is the chastening hand of a wise and a faithful Father. He gives us this bitter cup. And the cup that our Father hath given us, shall we not drink it?

> God of the just, Thou gavest us the cup:
> We yield to thy behest, and drink it up.

'Whom the Lord loveth He chasteneth.' O how these blessed words have cheered and strengthened and sustained us through all these long and weary years of civil strife, while our friends and brothers on so many ensanguined fields were falling and dying for the cause of Liberty and Union! Let them cheer, and strengthen, and sustain us to-day. True, this new sorrow and chastening has come in such an hour and in such a way as we thought not, and it bears the impress of a rod that is very heavy, and of a mystery that is very deep. That such a life should be sacrificed, at such a time, by such a foul and diabolical agency; that the man at the head of the nation, whom the people had learned to trust with a confiding and a loving confidence, and upon whom more than upon any other were centered, under God, our best hopes for the true and speedy pacification of the country, the restoration of the Union, and the return of harmony and love; that he should be taken from us, and taken just as the prospect of peace was brightly opening upon our torn and bleeding country, and just as he was beginning to be animated and gladdened with the hope of ere long enjoying with the people the blessed fruit and reward of his and their toil, and care, and patience, and self-sacrificing devotion to the interests of Liberty and the Union – O it is a mysterious and a most afflicting visitation! But it is our Father in heaven, the God of our fathers, and our God, who permits us to be so suddenly and sorely smitten; and we know that His judgments are right, and that in faithfulness He has afflicted us. In the midst of our rejoicings we needed this stroke, this dealing, this discipline; and therefore He has sent it.

Let us remember, our affliction has not come forth out of the dust, and our trouble has not sprung out of the ground. Through and beyond all second causes let us look, and see the sovereign permissive agency of the great First Cause. It is His prerogative to bring light out of darkness and good out of evil. Surely the wrath of man shall praise Him, and the remainder of wrath He will restrain. In the light of a clearer day we may yet see that the wrath which planned and perpetuated the death of the President, was overruled by Him whose judgements are unsearchable, and His ways are past finding out, for the highest welfare of all those interests which are so dear to the Christian patriot and philanthropist, and for which a loyal people have made such an unexampled sacrifice of treasure and of blood. Let us not be faithless, but believing.

Blind unbelief is prone to err,
And scan His work in vain;
God is his own interpreter,
And He will make it plain.

We will wait for his interpretation, and we will wait in faith, nothing doubting. He who has led us so well, and defended and prospered us so wonderfully during the last four years of toil, and struggle, and sorrow, will not forsake us now. He may chasten, but He will not destroy. He may purify us more and more in the furnace of trial, but He will not consume us. No, no! He has chosen us as He did his people of old in the furnace of affliction, and He has said of us as He said of them, 'This people have I formed for myself; they shall show forth My praise.' Let our principal anxiety now be that this new sorrow may be a sanctified sorrow; that it may lead us to deeper repentance, to a more humbling sense of our dependence upon God, and to the more

judgments were calm and accurate, and his purposes were good and pure beyond a question. Always and everywhere he aimed and endeavored to be right and to do right. His integrity was thorough, all-pervading, all-controlling, and incorruptible. It was the same in every place and relation, in the consideration and the control of matters great or small, the same firm and steady principle of power and beauty that shed a clear and crowning lustre upon all his other excellencies of mind and heart, and recommended him to his fellow citizens as the man, who, in a time of unexampled peril, when the very life of the nation was at stake, should be chosen to occupy, in the country and for the country, its highest post of power and responsibility. How wisely and well, how purely and faithfully, how firmly and steadily, how justly and successfully he did occupy that post and meet its grave demands in circumstances of surpassing trial and difficulty, is known to you all, known to the country and the world. He comprehended from the first the perils to which treason has exposed the freest and best Government on the earth, the vast interests of Liberty and humanity that were to be saved or lost forever in the urgent impending conflict; he rose to the dignity and momentousness of the occasion, saw his duty as the Chief Magistrate of a great and imperilled people, and he determined to do his duty, and his whole duty, seeking the guidance and leaning upon the arm of Him of whom it is written, 'He giveth power to the faint, and to them that have no might He increaseth strength.' Yes, he leaned upon His arm. He recognized and received the truth that the 'kingdom is the Lord's, and He is the governor among the nations.' He remembered that 'God is in history,' and he felt that nowhere had His hand and His mercy been so marvelously conspicuous as in the history of this nation. He hoped and he prayed that that same hand would continue to guide us, and that same mercy continue to abound to us in the time of our greatest need.

I speak what I know, and testify what I have often heard him say, when I affirm that that guidance and mercy were the props on which he humbly and habitually leaned; they were the best hope he had for himself and for his country. Hence, when he was leaving his home in Illinois, and coming to this city to take his seat in the executive chair of a disturbed and troubled nation, he said to the old and tried friends who gathered tearfully around him and bade him farewell, 'I leave you with this request: pray for me.' They did pray for him; and millions of other people prayed for him; nor did they pray in vain. Their prayer was heard, and the answer appears in all his subsequent history; it shines forth with a heavenly radiance in the whole course and tenor of his administration, from its commencement to its close. God raised him up for a great and glorious mission, furnished him for his work, and aided him in its accomplishment. Nor was it merely by strength of mind, and honesty of heart, and purity and pertinacity of purpose, that He furnished him; in addition to these things, He gave him a calm and abiding confidence in the overruling providence of God and in the ultimate triumph of truth and righteousness through the power and the blessing of God. This confidence strengthened him in all his hours of anxiety and toil, and inspired him with calm and cheering hope when others were inclining to despondency and gloom. Never shall I forget the emphasis and the deep emotion with which he said in this very room, to a company of clergymen and others, who called to pay him their respects in the darkest days of our civil conflict: 'Gentlemen, my hope of success in this great and terrible struggle rests on that immutable foundation, the justice and goodness of God. And when events are very threatening, and prospects very dark, I still hope that in some way which man can not see all will be well in the end, because our cause is just, and God is on our side.' Such was his sublime and holy faith, and it was an anchor to his soul, both sure and steadfast. It made him firm and strong. It emboldened him in the pathway of duty, however rugged and perilous it might be. It made him valiant for the right; for the cause of God and humanity, and it held him in a steady, patient, and unswerving adherence to a policy of administration which he thought, and which we all now think, both God and humanity required him to adopt.

We admired and loved him on many accounts – for strong and various reasons: we admired his childlike simplicity, his freedom from guile and deceit, his staunch and sterling integrity, his kind and forgiving temper, his industry and patience, his persistent, self-sacrificing devotion to all the duties of his eminent position, from the least to the greatest; his readiness to hear and consider the cause of the poor and humble, the suffering and the oppressed; his charity toward those who questioned the correctness of his opinions and the wisdom of his policy; his wonderful skill in reconciling differences among the friends of the Union, leading them away from abstractions, and inducing them to work together and harmoniously for the common weal; his true and enlarged philanthropy, that knew no distinction of color or race, but regarded all men as brethren, and endowed alike by their Creator 'with certain inalienable rights, among which are life, Liberty, and the pursuit of happiness'; his inflexible purpose that what freedom had gained in our terrible civil strife should never be lost, and that the end of the war should be the end of slavery, and, as a consequence, of rebellion; his readiness to spend and be spent for the attainment of such a triumph – a triumph, the blessed fruits of which shall be as widespreading as the earth and as enduring as the sun: – all these things commanded and fixed our admiration and the admiration of the world, and stamped upon his character and life the unmistakable impress of greatness. But more sublime than any or all of these, more holy and influential, more beautiful, and strong, and sustaining, was his abiding confidence in God and in the final triumph of truth and righteousness through Him and for His sake.

This was his noblest virtue, his grandest principle, the secret alike of his strength, his patience, and his success. And this, it seems to me, after being near him steadily, and with him often, for more than four years, is the principle by which, more than by any other, 'he, being dead, yet speaketh.' Yes; by his steady enduring confidence in God, and in the complete ultimate success of the cause of God, which is the cause of humanity, more than by any other way, does he now speak to us and to the nation he loved and served so well. By this he speaks to his successor in office, and charges him to 'have faith in God.' By this he speaks to the members of his cabinet, the men with whom he counselled so often and was associated so long, and he charges them to 'have faith in God.' By this he speaks to the officers and men of our noble army and navy, and, as they stand at their posts of duty and peril, he charges them to 'have faith in God.' By this he speaks to all who occupy positions of influence and authority in these sad and troublous times, and he charges them all to 'have faith in God.' By this he speaks to this great people as they sit in sackcloth to-day, and weep for him with a bitter wailing, and refuse to be comforted, and he charges them to 'have faith in God.' And by this he will speak through the ages and to all rulers and peoples in every land, and his message to them will be, 'Cling to Liberty and right; battle for them; bleed for them; die for them, if need be; and have confidence in God.' O that the voice of this testimony may sink down into our hearts today and every day, and into the heart of the nation, and exert its appropriate influence upon our feelings, our faith, our patience, and our devotion to the cause of freedom and humanity – a cause dearer to us now than ever before, because consecrated by the blood of its most conspicuous defender, its wisest and most fondly-trusted friend.

He is dead; but the God in whom he trusted lives, and He can guide and strengthen his successor, as He guided and strengthened him. He is dead; but the memory of his virtues, of his wise and patriotic counsels and labors, of his calm and steady faith in God lives, is precious, and will be a power for good in the country quite down to the end of time. He is dead; but the cause he so ardently loved, so ably, patiently, faithfully represented and defended – not for himself only, not for us only, but for all people in all their coming generations, till time shall be no more – that cause survives his fall, and will survive it. The light of its brightening prospects flashes cheeringly to-day athwart the gloom occasioned by his death, and the language of God's united providences is telling us that, though the friends of Liberty die, Liberty itself is immortal. There is no assassin strong enough and no weapon deadly enough to quench its inextinguishable life, or arrest its onward march to the conquest and empire of the world. This is our confidence, and this is our consolation, as we weep and mourn to-day. Though our beloved President is slain, our beloved country is saved. And so we sing of mercy as well as of judgment. Tears of gratitude mingle with those of sorrow. While there is darkness, there is also the dawning of a brighter, happier day upon our stricken and weary land. God be praised that our fallen Chief lived long enough to see the day dawn and the daystar of joy and peace arise upon the nation. He saw it, and he was glad. Alas! alas! He only saw the dawn. When the sun has risen, full-orbed and glorious, and a happy reunited people are rejoicing in its light – alas! alas! it will shine upon his grave. But that grave will be a precious and a consecrated spot.

The friends of Liberty and of the Union will repair to it in years and ages to come, to pronounce the memory of its occupant blessed, and, gathering from his very ashes, and from the rehearsal of his deeds and virtues, fresh incentives to patriotism, they will there renew their vows of fidelity to their country and their God.

And now I know not that I can more appropriately conclude this discourse, which is but a sincere and simple utterance of the heart, than by addressing to our departed President, with some slight modification, the language which Tacitus, in his life of Agricola, addresses to his venerable and departed father-in-law:

> With you we may now congratulate; you are blessed, not only because your life was a career of glory, but because you were released, when, your country safe, it was happiness to die. We have lost a parent, and, in our distress, it is now an addition to our heartfelt sorrow that we had it not in our power to commune with you on the bed of languishing, and receive your last embrace. Your dying words would have been ever dear to us; your commands we should have treasured up, and graved them on our hearts. This sad comfort we have lost, and the wound for that reason, pierces deeper. From the world of spirits behold your desolate family and people; exalt our minds from fond regret and unavailing grief to contemplation of your virtues. Those we must not lament; it were impiety to sully them with a tear. To cherish their memory, to embalm them with our praises, and, so far as we can, to emulate your bright example, will be the truest mark of our respect, the best tribute we can offer. Your wife will thus preserve the memory of the best of husbands, and thus your children will prove their filial piety. By dwelling

constantly on your words and actions, they will have an illustrious character before their eyes, and, not content with the bare image of your mortal frame, they will have what is more valuable – the form and features of your mind. Busts and statues, like their originals, are frail and perishable. The soul is formed of finer elements, and its inward form is not to be expressed by the hand of an artist with unconscious matter – our manners and our morals may in some degree trace the resemblance. All of you that gained our love and raised our admiration still subsists, and will ever subsist, preserved in the minds of men, the register of ages, and the records of fame. Others, who had figured on the stage of life and were the worthies of a former day, will sink, for want of a faithful historian, into the common lot of oblivion, inglorious and unremembered; but you, our lamented friend and head, delineated with truth, and fairly consigned to posterity, will survive yourself, and triumph over the injuries of time.

Karl Marx:

20–21 September 1871

Political Action and the Working Class

These notes were originally taken down in French from two speeches which Marx made at the London Conference of the Communist Party (Protocols of the Sessions of 20–21 September 1871).

September 20

Citizen Lorenzo reminds us to stick to the Rules, and Citizen Bastelica followed his example. In both the original Statutes and the Inaugural Address I read that the General Council is obligated to prepare an agenda for the Congresses for discussion. The programme which the General Council prepared for the Conference deals with the organization of the Association, and Vaillant proposal relates directly to this point. Hence the objection of Lorenzo and Bastelica is unfounded.

[Note: This day, French delegate Edouard Vaillant proposed a resolution stressing the inseparability of politics and economics, they are inherently intertwined, so he urged workers to unite political activities. Proudhonists in the International objected.]

In virtually all countries, certain members of the International, invoking the mutilated conception of the Statutes adopted at the Geneva Congress, have made propaganda in favour of abstention from politics; and the governments have been quite careful not to impede this restraint. In Germany, Schweitzer and others in the pay of Bismarck even attempted to harness the cart to government policy. In France, this criminal abstention allowed Favre, Picard, and others, to seize power on September 4; this abstention made it possible, on March 18, to set up a dictatorial committee composed largely of Bonapartists and intrigants, who, in the first days, lost the Revolution by inactivity, days which they should have devoted to strengthening the Revolution.

In America, a recently held workers' congress [National Labor Union, August 7–10, 1871, Baltimore] resolved to occupy itself with political questions and to replace professional politicians with workers like themselves, who were authorized to defend the interests of their class. In England, it is not so easy for a worker to get to Parliament. Since members of Parliament do not receive any compensation, and the worker has to work to support himself, Parliament becomes unattainable for him, and the bourgeoisie knows very well that its stubborn refusal to allow salaries for members of Parliament is a means of preventing the working class from being represented in it.

One should never believe that it is of small significance to have workers in Parliament. If one stifles their voices, as in the case of De Potter and Castian, or if one ejects them, as in the case of Manuel – the reprisals and oppressions exercise a deep effect on the people. If, on the other hand, they can speak from the parliamentary tribune, as do Bebel and Liebknecht, the whole world listens to them. In the one case or the other, great publicity is provided for our principles. To give but one example: when during the [Franco-Prussian] war, which was fought in France, Bebel and Liebknecht undertook to point out the responsibility of the working class in the face of those events, all of Germany was shaken; and even in Munich, the city where revolutions take place only over the price of beet, great demonstrations took place demanding an end to the war. The governments are hostile to us, one must respond to them with all the means at our disposal. To get workers into Parliament is synonymous with a victory over the governments, but one must choose the right men, not Tolains.

Marx supports the proposal of Citizen Vaillant, as well as Frankel's amendment, to state it as a premise, and thus strengthen it, that the Association has always demanded, and not merely from today, that the workers must occupy themselves with politics.

September 21

Marx said he had already spoken yesterday in favour of Vaillant's motion, and therefore he would not oppose him today. He replied to Bastelica that at the beginning of the Conference it was already decided that it would take up exclusively the question of organization and not the question of principles. In regard to the reference to the Rules, he calls attention to the fact that the Statutes and the Inaugural Address, which he has re-read, are to be read as a whole.

He explained the history of abstention from politics and said that one ought not to let himself be irritated by this question. The men who propagated this doctrine were well-meaning utopians, but those who want to take such a road today are not. They reject politics until after a violent struggle, and thereby drive the people into a formal, bourgeois opposition, which we must battle against at the same time we fight against the governments. We must unmask Gambetta, so that the people are no longer hoodwinked. Marx shares Vaillant's opinion. We must reply with a challenge to all the governments that are subjecting the International to persecutions.

Reaction exists on the whole Continent; it is general and permanent – even in the United States and England – in one form or another.

We must announce to the governments: We know you are the armed power which is directed against the proletarians; we will move against you in peaceful ways where it is possible, and with arms if it should become necessary.

Marx is of the opinion that Vaillant's proposal requires some changes, and he therefore supports Outine's motion.

[Note: Outine proposed Vaillant's motion, the amendments by Serraillier and Frankel, be passed to the General Council for further study, under the subject 'The Political Efficacy of the Working Class' – Outine's motion passed.]

Victoria C. Woodhall:

20 November 1871

'And the truth shall make you free'

Victoria Woodhall made this speech on the principles of social freedom at Steinway Hall, New York, to a 3,000-strong audience.

It has been said by a very wise person that there is a trinity in all things, the perfect unity of the trinity or a tri-unity being necessary to make a complete objective realization. Thus we have the theological Trinity: The Father, the Son and the Holy Ghost; or Cause, Effect and the Process of Evolution. Also the political Trinity: Freedom, Equality, Justice or Individuality, Unity, Adjustment; the first term of which is also resolvable into these parts, thus: Religious freedom, political freedom and social freedom, while Religion, Politics and Socialism are the Tri-unity of Humanity. There are also the beginning, the end and the intermediate space, time and motion, to all experiences of space, time and motion, and the diameter, circumference and area, or length, breadth and depth to all form.

Attention has been called to these scientific facts, for the purpose of showing that for any tri-unity to lack one of its terms is for it to be incomplete; and that in the order of natural evolution, if two terms exist, the third must also exist.

Religious freedom does, in a measure, exist in this country, but not yet perfectly; that is to say, a person is not entirely independent of public opinion regarding matters of conscience. Though since Political freedom has existed in theory, every person has the right to entertain any religious theory he or she may conceive to be true, and government can take no cognizance thereof – he is only amenable to society – despotism. The necessary corollary to Religious and Political freedom is

Social freedom, which is the third term of the trinity; that is to say, if Religious and Political freedom exist, perfected, Social freedom is at that very moment guaranteed, since Social freedom is the fruit of that condition.

We find the principle of Individual freedom was quite dormant until it began to speak against the right of religious despots, to determine what views should be advocated regarding the relations of the creature to the Creator. Persons began to find ideas creeping into their souls at variance with the teachings of the clergy; which ideas became so strongly fixed that they were compelled to protest against Religious Despotism. Thus, in the sixteenth century, was begun the battle for Individual freedom. The claim that rulers had no right to control the consciences of the people was boldly made, and right nobly did the fight continue until the absolute right to individual opinion was wrung from the despots, and even the common people found themselves entitled to not only entertain but also to promulgate any belief or theory of which they could conceive.

With yielding the control over the consciences of individuals, the despots had no thought of giving up any right to their persons. But Religious freedom naturally led the people to question the right of this control, and in the eighteenth century a new protest found expression in the French Revolution, and it was baptized by a deluge of blood yielded by thousands of lives. But not until an enlightened people freed themselves from English tyranny was the right to self-government acknowledged in theory, and not yet even is it fully accorded in practice, as a legitimate result of that theory.

It may seem to be a strange proposition to make, that there is no such thing yet existent in the world as self-government, in its political aspects. But such is the fact. If self-government be the rule, every self must be its subject. If a person govern, not only himself but others, that is despotic government, and it matters not if that control be over one or over a thousand individuals, or over a nation; in each case it, would be the same principle of power exerted outside of self and over others, and this is despotism, whether it is exercised by one person over his subjects, or by twenty persons over a nation, or by one-half the people of a nation over the other half thereof. There is no escaping the fact that the principle by which the male citizens of these United States assume to rule the female citizens is not that of self-government, but that of despotism; and so the fact is that poets have sung songs of freedom, and anthems of liberty have resounded for an empty shadow.

King George III, and his Parliament denied our forefathers the right to make their own laws; they rebelled, and being successful, inaugurated this government. But men do not seem to comprehend that they are now pursuing toward women the same despotic course that King George pursued toward the American colonies.

But what is freedom? The press and our male governors are very much exercised about this question, since a certain set of resolutions were launched upon the public by Paulina Wright Davis at Apollo Hall, May 12, 1871. They are as follows:

> Resolved, That the basis of order is freedom from bondage; not, indeed, of such 'order' as resigned in Warsaw, which grew out of the bondage; but of such order as reigns in Heaven, which grows out of that developed manhood and womanhood in which each becomes 'a law unto himself'.
>
> Resolved, That freedom is a principle, and that as such it may be trusted to ultimate in harmonious social results, as in America, it has resulted in harmonious and

beneficent political results; that it has not hitherto been adequately trusted in the social domain, and that the woman's movement means no less than the complete social as well as the political enfranchisement of mankind.

Resolved, That the evils, sufferings and disabilities of women, as well as of men, are social still more than they are political, and that a statement of woman's rights which ignores the rights of self-ownership as the first of all rights is insufficient to meet the demand, and is ceasing to enlist the enthusiasm and even the common interest of the most intelligent portion of the community.

Resolved, That the principle of freedom is one principle, and not a collection of many different and unrelated principles; that there is not at bottom one principle of freedom of conscience as in Protestantism, and another principle of freedom from slavery as in Abolitionism, another of freedom of locomotion as in our dispensing in America with the passport system of Europe, another of the freedom of the press as in Great Britain and America, and still another of social freedom at large; but that freedom is on and indivisible; and that slavery is so also; that freedom and bondage or restriction is the alternative and the issue, alike, in every case; and that if freedom is good in one case it is good in all; that we in America have builded on freedom, politically, and that we cannot consistently recoil from that expansion of freedom which shall make it the basis of all our institutions; and finally, that so far as we have trusted it, it has proved, in the main, safe and profitable.

Now, is there anything so terrible in the language of these

resolutions as to threaten the foundations of society? They asset that every individual has a better right to herself or himself than any other person can have. No living soul, who does not desire to have control over, or ownership in, another person, can have any valid objection to anything expressed in these resolutions. Those who are not willing to give up control over others; who desire to own somebody beside themselves; who are constitutionally predisposed against self-government and the giving of the same freedom to others that they demand for themselves, will of course object to them, and such are the people with whom we shall have to contend in this new struggle for a greater liberty.

Now, the individual is either self-owned and self-possessed or is not so self-possessed. If he be self-owned, he is so because he has an inherent right to self, which right cannot be delegated to any second person; a right – as the American Declaration of Independence has it – which is 'inalienable'. The individual must be responsible to self and God for his acts. If he be owned and possessed by some second person, then there is no such thing as individuality: and that for which the world has been striving these thousands of years is the merest myth.

But against this irrational, illogical, inconsequent and irreverent theory I boldly oppose the spirit of the age-that spirit which will not admit all civilization to be a failure, and all past experience to count for nothing; against that demagogism, I oppose the plain principle of freedom in its fullest, purest, broadest, deepest application and significance – the freedom which we see exemplified in the starry firmament, where whirl innumerable worlds, and never one of which is made to lose its individuality, but each performs its part in the grand economy of the universe, giving and receiving its natural repulsions and attractions; we also see it exemplified in every department of nature about us: in the sunbeam and the dewdrop; in the storm-cloud and the spring shower; in the driving snow and the congealing rain – all of which speak more eloquently than can human tongue of the heavenly beauty, symmetry and purity of the spirit of freedom which in them reigns untrammeled.

Our government is based upon the proposition that: All men and women are born free and equal and entitled to certain inalienable rights, among which are life, liberty and the pursuit of happiness. Now what we, who demand social freedom, ask, is simply that the government of this country shall be administered in accordance with the spirit of this proposition. Nothing more, nothing less. If that proposition means anything, it means just what it says, without qualification, limitation or equivocation. It means that every person who comes into the world of outward existence is of equal right as an individual, and is free as an individual, and that he or she is entitled to pursue happiness in whatever direction he or she may choose. Now this is absolutely true of all men and all women. But just here the wiseacres stop and tell us that everybody must not pursue happiness in his or her own way; since to do so absolutely, would be to have no protection against the action of individual. These good and well-meaning people only see one-half of what is involved in the proposition. They look at a single individual and for the time lose sight of all others. They do not take into their consideration that every other individual beside the one whom they contemplate is equally with him entitled to the same freedom; and that each is free within the area of his or her individual sphere; and not free within the sphere of any other individual whatever. They do not seem to recognize the fact that the moment one person gets out of his sphere into the sphere of another, that other must protect him or herself against such invasion of rights. They do not seem to be able to comprehend that the moment one person encroaches upon another person's rights he or she ceases to be a free man or woman and becomes a despot. To all such persons we assert: that it is freedom and not despotism which we advocate and demand; and we will as rigorously demand that individuals be restricted to their freedom as any person dare to demand; and as rigorously demand that people who are predisposed to be tyrants instead of free men or women shall, by the government, be so restrained as to make the exercise of their proclivities impossible.

If life, liberty and the pursuit of happiness are inalienable rights in the individual, and government is based upon that inalienability, then it must follow as a legitimate sequence that the functions of that government are to guard and protect the right to life, liberty and the pursuit of happiness, to the end that every person may have the most perfect exercise of them. And the most perfect exercise of such rights is only attained when every individual is not only fully protected in his rights, but also strictly restrained to the exercise of them within his own sphere, and positively prevented from proceeding beyond its limits, so as to encroach upon the sphere of another: unless that other first agree thereto.

From these generalizations certain specializations are deducible, by which all questions of rights must be determined:

1. Every living person has certain rights of which no law can rightfully deprive him.

2. Aggregates of persons form communities, who erect governments to secure regularity and order.

3. Order and harmony can alone be secured in a community where every individual of whom it is composed is fully protected in the exercise of all individual rights.

4. Any government which enacts laws to deprive individuals of the free exercise of their right to life, liberty and the pursuit of

happiness is despotic, and such laws are not binding upon the people who protest against them, whether they be a majority or a minority.

5. When every individual is secure in the possession and exercise of all his rights, then every one is also secure from the interference of all other parties.

6. All inharmony and disorder arise from the attempts of individuals to interfere with the rights of other individuals, or from the protests of individuals against governments for depriving them of their inalienable rights.

These propositions are all self-evident, and must be accepted by every person who subscribes to our theory of government, based upon the sovereignty of the individual; consequently any law in force which conflicts with any of them is not in accord with that theory and is therefore unconstitutional.

A fatal error into which most people fall, is, that rights are conceded to governments, while they are only possessed of the right to perform duties, as a farther analysis will show:

In the absence of any arrangement by the members of a community to secure order, each individual is a law unto himself, so far as he is capable of maintaining it against all other individuals; but at the mercy of all such who are bent on conquest. Such a condition is anarchy.

But if in individual freedom the whole number of individuals unite to secure equality and protection to themselves, they thereby surrender no individual rights to the community, but they simply invest the community with the power to perform certain specified duties, which are set forth in the law of their combination. Hence a government erected by the people is invested, not with the rights of the people, but with the duty of protecting and maintaining their rights intact; and any government is a failure or a success just so far as it fails or succeeds in this duty; and these are the legitimate functions of government.

I have before said that every person has the right to, and can, determine for himself what he will do, even to taking the life of another. But it is equally true that the attacked person has the right to defend his life against such assault. If the person succeed in taking the life, he thereby demonstrates that he is a tyrant who is at all times liable to invade the right to life, and that every individual of the community is put in jeopardy by the freedom of this person. Hence it is the duty of the government to so restrict the freedom of this person as to make it impossible for him to ever again practice such tyranny. Here the duty of the community ceases. It has no right to take the life of the individual. That is his own, inalienably vested in him, both by God and the Constitution.

A person may also appropriate the property of another if he so choose, and there is no way to prevent it; but once having thus invaded the rights of another, the whole community is in danger from the propensity of this person. It is therefore the duty of government to so restrain the liberty of the person as to prevent him from invading the spheres of other persons in a manner against which he himself demands, and is entitled to, protection.

The same rule applies to that class of persons who have a propensity to steal or to destroy the character of others. This class of encroachers upon others' rights, in some senses, are more reprehensible than any other, save only those who invade the rights of life; since for persons to be made to appear what they are not may, perhaps, be to place them in such relations with third persons as to destroy their means of pursuing happiness. Those who thus invade the pursuit of happiness by others, should be held to be the worst enemies of society; proportion-

neither right nor duty beyond the uniting – the contracting – individuals. So neither can there be an appeal to a third party to settle any difference which may arise between such parties. All such contracts have their legitimate basis and security in the honor and purposes of the contracting parties. It seems to me that, admitting our theory of government, no proposition can be plainer than is this, notwithstanding the practice is entirely different. But I am now discussing the abstract principles of the rights of freedom, which no practice that may be in vogue must be permitted to deter us from following to legitimate conclusions.

In all general contracts, people have the protection of government in contracting for an hour, a day, a week, a year, a decade, or a life, and neither the government nor any other third party or persons, or aggregates of persons ever think of making a scale of respectability, graduated by the length of time for which the contracts are made and maintained. Least of all does the government require that any of these contracts shall be entered into for life. Why should the social relations of the sexes be made subject to a different theory? All enacted laws that are for the purpose of perpetuating conditions which are themselves the results of evolution are so many obstructions in the path of progress; since if an effect attained to-day is made the ultimate, progress stops. 'Thus far shalt thou go, and no farther,' is not the adage of a progressive age like the present. Besides, there can be no general law made to determine what individual cases demand, since a variety of conditions cannot be subject to one and the same rule of operation. Here we arrive at the most important of all facts relating to human needs and experiences: That while every human being has a distinct individuality, and is entitled to all the rights of a sovereign over it, it is not taken into the consideration that no two of these individualities are made up of the self-same powers and experiences, and therefore cannot be governed by the same law to the same purposes.

I would recall the attention of all objecting egotists, Pharisees and would-be regulators of society to the true functions of government – to protect the complete exercise of individual rights, and what they are no living soul except the individual has any business to determine or to meddle with, in any way whatever, unless his own rights are first infringed.

If a person believe that a certain theory is a truth, and consequently the right thing to advocate and practice, but from its being unpopular or against established public opinion does not have the moral courage to advocate or practice it, that person is a moral coward and traitor to his own conscience, which God gave for a guide and guard.

What I believe to be the truth I endeavor to practice, and, in advocating it, permit me to say I shall speak so plainly that none may complain that I did not make myself understood.

The world has come up to the present time through the outworking of religious, political, philosophical and scientific principles, and today we stand upon the threshold of greater in more important things than have ever interested the intellect of man. We have arrived where the very foundation of all that has been must be analyzed and understood – and this foundation is the relation of the sexes. These are the bases of society – the very last to secure attention, because the most comprehensive of subjects.

All other departments of inquiry which have their fountain in society have been formulated into special sciences, and made legitimate and popular subjects for investigation; but the science of society itself has been, and still is, held to be too sacred a thing for science to lay its rude hands upon. But of the relations of science to society we may say the same that has been said of the relations of science to religion: 'That religion has always wanted to do good, and now science is going to tell it how to do it.'

Over the sexual relations, marriages have endeavored to preserve sway and to hold the people in subjection to what has been considered a standard of moral purity. Whether this has been successful or not may be determined from the fact that there are scores of thousand of women who are denominated prostitutes, and who are supported by hundreds of thousands of men who should, for like reasons, also be denominated prostitutes, since what will change a woman into a prostitute must also necessarily change a man into the same.

This condition, called prostitution, seems to be the great evil at which religion and public morality hurl their special weapons of condemnation, as the sum total of all diabolism; since for a woman to be a prostitute is to deny her not only all Christian, but also all humanitarian rights.

But let us inquire into this matter, to see just what it is; not in the vulgar or popular, or even legal sense, but in a purely scientific and truly moral sense.

It must be remembered that we are seeking after such for the sake of the truth, and in utter disregard of everything except the truth; that is to say, we are seeking for the truth, 'let it be what it may and lead where it may.' To illustrate, I would say the extremest thing possible. If blank materialism were true, it would be best for the world to know it.

If there be any who are not in harmony with this desire, then such have nothing to do with what I have to say, for it will be said regardless of antiquate forms or fossilized dogmas, but in the simplest and least offending language that I can choose.

If there is anything in the whole universe that should enlist the earnest attention of everybody, and their support and advocacy to secure it, it is that upon which the true Welfare and happiness of everybody depends. Now to what more than to anything else do humanity owe their welfare and happiness? Most clearly to being born into earthly existence with a sound and perfect physical, mental and moral beginning of life, with no taint or disease attaching to them, either mentally, morally or physically. To be so born involves the harmony of conditions which will produce such results. To have such conditions involves the existence of such relations of the sexes as will in themselves produce them.

Now I will put the question direct. Are not these eminently proper subjects for inquiry and discussion, not in that manner of maudlin sentimentality in which it has been the habit, but in a dignified, open, lowest and fearless way, in which subjects of so great importance should be inquired into and discussed?

An exhaustive treatment of these subjects would involve the inquiry what should be the chief end to be gained by entering into sexual relations. This I must simply answer by saying, 'Good children, who will not need to be regenerated,' and pass to the consideration of the relations themselves.

All the relations between the sexes that are recognized as legitimate are denominated marriage. But of what does marriage consist? This very pertinent question requires settlement before any real progress can be made as to what Social Freedom and Prostitution mean. It is admitted by everybody that marriage is a union of the opposite in sex, but is it a principle of nature outside of all law, or is it a law outside of all nature? Where is the point before reaching which it is not marriage, but having reached which it is marriage? Is it where two meet and realize that the love elements of their nature are harmonious, and that they blend into and make one purpose of life? or is it where a soulless form is pronounced over two who know no commingling of life's hopes?

Or are both these processes required – first, the marriage union without the law, to be afterward solemnized by the law? If both terms are required, does the marriage continue after the first departs? or if the restrictions of the law are removed and the love continues, does marriage continue? or if the law unite two who hate each other, is that marriage? Thus are presented all the possible aspects of the case.

The courts hold if the law solemnly pronounce two married, that they are married, whether love is present or not. But is this really such a marriage as this enlightened age should demand? No! It is a stupidly arbitrary law, which can find no analogies in nature. Nature proclaims in broadest terms, and all her subjects re-echo the same grand truth, that sexual unions, which result in reproduction, are marriage. And sex exists wherever there is reproduction.

By analogy, the same law ascends into the sphere of and applies among men and women; for are not they a part and parcel of nature in which this law exists as a principle? This law of nature by which men and women are united by love is God's marriage law, the enactments of men to the contrary notwithstanding. And the precise results of this marriage will be determined by the character of those united; all the experiences evolved from the marriage being the legitimate sequences thereof.

Marriage must consist either of love or of law, since it may exist in form with either term absent; that is to say, people may be married by law and all love be lacking; and they may also be married by love and lack all sanction of law. True marriage must in reality consist entirely either of law or love, since there can be no compromise between the law of nature and statute law by which the former shall yield to the latter.

Law cannot change what nature has already determined. Neither will love obey if law command. Law cannot compel two

marriage is performed without special mental volition upon the part of either, although the intellect may approve what the affections determine; thus is to say, they marry because they love, and they love because they can neither prevent nor assist it. Suppose after this marriage has continued an indefinite time, the unity between them departs, could they any more prevent it than they can prevent the love? It came without their bidding, may it not also go without their bidding? And if it go, does not the marriage cease, and should any third persons or parties, either as individuals or government, attempt to compel the continuance of a unity wherein none of the elements of the union remain?

At no point in the process designated has there been any other than an exercise of the right of the two individuals to pursue happiness in their own way, which has neither crossed nor interfered with any one else's right to the same pursuit; therefore, there is no call for a law to change, modify, protect or punish this exercise. It must be concluded, then, if individuals have the Constitutional right to pursue happiness in their own way, that all compelling laws of marriage and divorce are despotic, being remnants of the barbaric ages in which they were originated, and utterly unfitted for an age so advanced upon that, and so enlightened in the general principles of freedom and equality, as is this.

It must be remembered that it is the sphere of government to perform the duties which are required of it by the people, and that it has, in itself, no rights to exercise. These belong exclusively to the people whom it represents. It is one of the rights of a citizen to have a voice in determining what the duties of government shall be, and also provide how that right may be exercised; but government should not prohibit any right.

To love is a right higher than Constitutions or laws. It is a right which Constitutions and laws can neither give nor take, and with which they have nothing whatever to do, since in its very nature it is forever independent of both Constitutions and laws, and exists – comes and goes – in spite of them. Governments might just as well assume to determine how people shall exercise their right to think or to say that they shall not think at all, as to assume to determine that they shall not love, or how they may love, or that they shall love.

The proper sphere of government in regard to the relations of the sexes, is to enact such laws as in the present conditions of society are necessary to protect each individual in the free exercise of his or her right to love, and also to protect each individual from the forced interference of every other person, that would compel him or her to submit to any action which is against their wish and will. If the law do this it fulfills its duty. If the law do not afford this protection, and worse still, if it sanction this interference with the rights of an individual, then it is infamous law and worthy only of the old-time despotism; since individual tyranny forms no part of the guarantee of, or the right to, individual freedom.

It is therefore a strictly legitimate conclusion that where there is no love as a basis of marriage there should be no marriage, and if that which was the basis of a marriage is taken away that the marriage also ceases from the time, statute laws to the contrary notwithstanding.

Such is the character of the law that permeates nature from simplest organic forms – units of nucleated protoplasm to the most complex aggregation thereof – the human form. Having determined that marriage consists of a union resulting from love, without any regard whatever to the sanction of law, and consequently that the sexual relations resulting therefrom are strictly legitimate and natural, it is a very simple matter to determine what part of the sexual relations which are maintained are prostitutions of the relations.

It is certain by this Higher Law, that marriages of convenience, and, still more, marriages characterized by mutual or partial repugnance, are adulterous. And it does not matter whether the repugnance arises before or subsequently to the marriage ceremony. Compulsion, whether of the law or of a false public opinion, is detestable, as an element even, in the regulation of the most tender and important of all human relations.

I do not care where it is that sexual commerce results from the dominant power of one sex over the other, compelling him or her to submission against the instincts of love, and where hate or disgust is present, whether it be in the gilded palaces of Fifth avenue or in the lowest purlieus of Greene Street, there is prostitution, and all the law that a thousand State Assemblies may pass cannot make it otherwise.

I know whereof I speak; I have seen the most damning misery resulting from legalized prostitution. Misery such as the most degraded of those against whom society has shut her doors never know. Thousands of poor, weak, unresisting wives are yearly murdered, who stand in spirit-life looking down upon the sickly, half made-up children left behind, imploring humanity for the sake of honor and virtue to look into this matter, to look into it to the very bottom, and bring out into the fair daylight all the blackened, sickening deformities that have so long been hidden by the screen of public opinion and a sham morality.

It does not matter how much it may still be attempted to gloss these things over and to label them sound and pure; you, each and every one of you, know that what I say is truth, and if you question your own souls you dare not reply: it is not so. If these things to which I refer, but of which I shudder to think, are not abuses of the sexual relations, what are?

You may or may not think there is help for them, but I say Heaven help us if such barbarism cannot be cured.

I would not be understood to say that there are no good conditions in the present marriage state. By no means do I say this; on the contrary, a very large proportion of present social relations are commendable – are as good as the present status of society makes possible. But what I do assert, and, that most positively, is, that all which is good and commendable, now existing, would continue to exist if all marriage laws were repealed to-morrow. Do you not perceive that law has nothing to do in continuing the relations which are based upon continuous love? These are not results of the law to which, perhaps, their subjects yielded a willing or unwilling obedience. Such relations exist in spite of the law; would have existed had there been no law, and would continue to exist were the law annulled.

It is not of the good there is in the present condition of marriage that I complain, but of the ill, nearly the whole of which is the direct result of the law which continues the relations in which it exists. It seems to be the general argument that if the law of marriage were annulled it would follow that everybody must necessarily separate, and that all present family relations would be sundered, and complete anarchy result therefrom. Now, whoever makes that argument either does so thoughtlessly or else he is dishonest; since if he make it after having given any consideration thereto, he must know it to be false. And if he have given it no consideration then is he no proper judge. I give it as my opinion, founded upon an extensive knowledge of, and intimate acquaintance with, married people, if marriage laws were repealed that less than a fourth of those now married would immediately separate, and that one-half of these would return to their allegiance voluntarily within one year; only those who, under every consideration of virtue and good, should be separate, would permanently remain separated. And objectors as well as I know it would be so. I assert that it is false to assume that chaos would result from the abrogation of marriage laws, and on the contrary affirm that from that very hour the chaos was existing would begin to turn into order and harmony. What then creates social disorder? Very clearly, the attempt to exercise powers over human rights which are not warrantable upon the hypothesis of the existence of human rights which are inalienable in, and sacred to, the individual.

It is true there is no enacted law compelling people to marry, and it is therefore argued that if they do marry they should always be compelled to abide thereby. But there is a law higher than any human enactments which does compel marriage – the law of nature – the law of God. There being this law in the constitution of humanity, which, operating freely, guarantees marriage, why should men enforce arbitrary rules and forms? These, though having no virtue in themselves, if not complied with by men and women, they in the meantime obeying the law of their nature, bring down upon them the condemnations of an interfering community. Should people, then, voluntarily entering legal marriage be held thereby 'till death do them part'? Most emphatically no, if the desire to do so do not remain. How can people who enter upon marriage in utter ignorance of that which is to render the union happy or miserable be able to say that they will always 'love and live together.' They may take these vows upon them in perfect good faith and repent of them in sackcloth and ashes within a twelve-month.

I think it will be generally conceded that without love there should be no marriage. In the constitution of things nothing can be more certain. This basic fact is fatal to the theory of marriage for life: since if love is what determines marriage, so, also, should it determine its continuance. If it be primarily right of men and women to take on the marriage relation of their own free will and accord, so, too, does it remain their right to determine how long it shall continue and when it shall cease. But to be respectable people must comply with the law, and thousands do comply therewith, while in their hearts they protest against it as an unwarrantable interference and proscription of their rights. Marriage laws that would be consistent with the theory of individual rights would be such as would regulate these relations, such as regulate all other associations of people. They should only be obliged to file marriage articles, containing whatever provisions may be agreed upon, as to their personal rights, rights of property, of children, or whatever else they may deem proper for them to agree upon. And whatever these articles might be, they should in all cases be equally entitled to public respect and protection. Should separation afterward come, nothing more should be required than the simple filing of counter articles.

There are hundreds of lawyers who subsist by inventing schemes by which people may obtain divorces, and the people desiring divorces resort to all sorts of tricks and crimes to get them. And all this exists because there are laws which would compel the oneness of those to whom unity is beyond the realm of possibility. There are another class of persons who, while virtually divorced, endeavor to maintain a respectable position in society, by agreeing to disagree, each following his and her individual ways, behind the cloak of legal marriage. Thus there are hundreds of men and women who to external appearances are husband and wife, but in reality are husband or wife to quite different persons.

If the conditions of society were completely analyzed, it would be found that all persons whom the law holds married against their wishes find some way to evade the law and to live the life they desire. Of what use, then, is the law except to make hypocrites and pretenders of a sham respectability?

But, exclaims a very fastidious person, then you would have all women become prostitutes! By no means would I have any woman become a prostitute. But if by nature women are so, all the virtue they possess being of the legal kind, and not that which should exist with or without law, then I say they will not become prostitutes because the law is repealed, since at heart they are already so. If there is no virtue, no honesty, no purity, no trust among women except as created by the law, I say heaven help our morality, for nothing human can help it.

It seems to me that no grosser insult could be offered to woman than to insinuate that she is honest and virtuous only because the law compels her to be so; and little do men and women realize the obloquy thus cast upon society, and still less do women realize what they admit of their sex by such assertions. I honor and worship that purity which exists in the soul of every noble man or woman, while I pity the woman who is virtuous simply because a law compels her.

But, says another objector, though the repeal of marriage laws might operate well enough in all those cases where a mutual love or hate would determine continuous marriage or immediate divorce, how can a third class of cases be justified, in which but one of the parties desire the separation, while the other clings to the unity?

I assume, in the first place, when there is not mutual love there is no union to continue and nothing to justify, and it has already been determined that, as marriage should have love as a basis, if love depart marriage also departs. But laying this aside, see if there can any real good or happiness possibly result from an enforced continuance of marriage upon the part of one party thereto. Let all persons take this question home to their own souls, and there determine if they could find happiness in holding unwilling hearts in bondage. It is against the nature of things that any satisfaction can result from such a state of things except it be the satisfaction of knowing that you have succeeded in virtually imprisoning the person whom you profess to love, and that would be demoniacal.

Again. It must be remembered that the individual affairs of two persons are not the subject of interference by any third party, and if one of them chose to separate, there is no power outside of the two which can rightly interfere to prevent. Beside, who is to determine whether there will be more happiness sacrificed by a continuation or a separation. If a person is fully determined to separate, it is proof positive that another feeling stronger than all his or her sentiments of duty determine it. And here, again, who but the individual is to determine which course will secure the most good? Suppose that a separation is desired because one of the two loves and is loved elsewhere. In this case, if the union be maintained by force, at least two of three, and, probably, all three persons will be made unhappy thereby; whereas if separation come and the other union be consummated, there will be but one, unhappy. So even here, if the greatest good of the greatest number is to rule, separation is not only legitimate, but desirable. In all other things except marriage it is always held to be the right thing to do to break a bad bargain or promise just as soon as possible, and I hold that of all things in which this rule should apply, it should first apply to marriages.

Now, let me ask, would it not rather be the Christian way, in such cases, to say to the disaffected party: 'Since you no longer love me, go your way and be happy, and make those to whom you go happy also.' I know of no higher, holier love than that described, and of no more beautiful expression of it than was given in the columns of the Woman's Journal, of Boston, whose conductors have felt called upon to endeavor to convince the people that it has no affiliation with those who hold to no more radical doctrine of Free Love than they proclaim as follows:

> The love that I cannot command is not mine; let me not disturb myself about it, nor attempt to filch it from its rightful owner. A heart that I supposed mine has drifted and gone. Shall I go in pursuit? Shall I forcibly capture the truant and transfix it with the barb of my selfish affections, pin it to the wall of my chamber? God forbid! Rather let me leave my doors and windows open, intent only on living so nobly that the best cannot fail to be drawn to me by an irresistible attraction.

To me it is impossible to frame words into sentences more holy, pure and true than are these. I would ever carry them in my soul as my guide and guard, feeling that in living by them happiness would certainly be mine. To the loving wife who mourns a lost heart, let me recommend them as a panacea. To the loving husband whose soul is desolate, let me offer these as words of healing balm. They will live in history, to make their writer the loved and revered of unborn generations.

The tenth commandment of the Decalogue says: 'Thou shalt not covet thy neighbor's wife.' And Jesus, in the beautiful parable of the Samaritan who fell among thieves, asks: 'Who is thy neighbor?' and answers his own question in a way to lift the conception wholly out of the category of mere local proximity into a sublime spiritual conception. In other words, he spiritualizes the word and sublimates the morality of the commandment. In the same spirit I ask now, Who is a wife? And I answer, not the woman who, ignorant of her own feelings, or with lying lips, has promised, in hollow ceremonial, and before the law, to love, but she who really loves most, and most truly, the man who commands her affections, and who in turn loves her, with or without the ceremony of marriage; and the man who holds the heart of such a woman in such a relation is 'thy neighbor', and that woman is 'thy neighbor's wife' meant in the commandment; and whosoever, though he should have been a hundred times married to her by the law, shall claim, or covet even, the possession of that woman as against her true lover and husband in the spirit, sins against the commandment.

We know positively that Jesus would have answered in that way. He has defined for us 'the neighbor', not in the paltry and commonplace sense, but spiritually. He has said. 'He that looketh on a woman to lust after her hath committed adultery with her already in his heart.' So, therefore, he spiritualized the idea of adultery. In the kingdom of heaven, to be prayed for daily, to come on earth, there is to be no 'marrying or giving in marriage', that is to say, formally and legally; but spiritual marriage must always exist, and had Jesus been called on to define a wife, can anybody doubt that he would, in the same spirit, the spiritualizing tendency and character of all his doctrine, have spiritualized the marriage relation as absolutely as he did the breach of it? that he would, in other words, have said in meaning precisely what I now say? And when Christian ministers are no longer afraid or ashamed to be Christians they will embrace this doctrine. Free Love will be an integral part of the religion of the future.

It can now be asked: What is the legitimate sequence of Social Freedom? To which I unhesitatingly reply: Free Love, or freedom of the affections. 'And are you a Free Lover?' is the almost incredulous query.

I repeat a frequent reply: 'I am; and I can honestly, in the fullness of my soul, raise on my voice to my Marker, and thank Him that I am, and that I have had the strength and the devotion to truth to stand before this traducing and vilifying community in a manner representative of that which shall come with healing on its wings for the bruised hearts and crushed affections of humanity.'

And to those who denounce me for this I reply: 'Yes, I am a Free Lover. I have an inalienable, constitutional and natural right to love whom I may, to love as long or as short a period as I can; to change that love every day if I please, and with that right neither you nor any law you can frame have any right to interfere. And I have the further right to demand a free and unrestricted exercise of that right, and it is your duty not only to accord it, but, as a community, to see that I am protected in it. I trust that I am fully understood, for I mean just that, and nothing less!'

To speak thus plainly and pointedly is a duty I owe to myself. The press have stigmatized me to the world as an advocate, theoretically and practically, of the doctrine of Free Love, upon which they have placed their stamp of moral deformity; the vulgar and inconsequent definition which they hold makes the theory an abomination. And though this conclusion is a no more legitimate and reasonable one than that would be which should call the Golden Rule a general license to all sorts of debauch, since Free Love bears the same relations to the moral deformities of which it stands accused as does the Golden Rule to the Law of the Despot, yet it obtains among many intelligent people. But they claim, in the language of one of these exponents, that 'Words belong to the people; they are the common property of the mob. Now the common use, among the mob, of the term Free Love, is a synonym for promiscuity.' Against this absurd proposition I oppose the assertion that words do not belong to the mob, but to that which they represent. Words are the exponents and interpretations of ideas. If I use a word which exactly interprets and represents what I would be understood to mean, shall I go to the mob and ask of them what interpretation they choose to place upon it? If lexicographers, when they prepare their dictionaries, were to go to the mob for the rendition of words, what kind of language would we have?

I claim that freedom means to be free, let the mob claim to the contrary as strenuously as they may. And I claim that love means an exhibition of the affections, let the mob claim what they may. And therefore, in compounding these words into Free Love, I claim that united they mean, and should be used to convey, their united definitions, the mob to the contrary notwithstanding. And when the term Free Love finds a place in dictionaries, it will prove my claim to have been correct, and that the mob have not received the attention of the lexicographers, since it will not be set down to signify sexual debauchery, and that only, or in any governing sense.

It is not only usual but also just, when people adopt a new theory, or promulgate a new doctrine, that they give it a name significant of its character. There are, however, exceptional cases to be found in all ages. The Jews coined the name of Christians, and, with withering contempt, hurled it upon the early followers of Christ. It was the most opprobrious epithet they could invent to express their detestation of those humble but honest and brave people. That name has now come to be considered as a synonym of all that is good, true and beautiful in the highest departments of our natures, and is revered in all civilized nations.

In precisely the same manner the Pharisees of to-day, who hold themselves to be representative of all there is that is good ad pure, as did the Pharisees of old, have coined the word Free-Love, and flung it upon all who believe not alone in Religious and Political Freedom, but in that larger Freedom, which includes both these, Social Freedom.

For my part, I am extremely obliged to our thoughtful Pharisaical neighbors for the kindness shown us in the invention of so appropriate a name. If there is a more beautiful word in the English language than love, that word is freedom, and that these two words, which, with us, attach or belong to everything that is pure and good, should have been joined by our enemies, and handed over to us already coined, is certainly a high consideration, for which we should never cease to be thankful. And when we shall be accused of all sorts of wickedness and vileness by our enemies, who in this have been so just, may I not hope that, remembering how much they have done for us, we may be able to say, 'Father, forgive them, for they know not what they do,' and to forgive them ourselves with or whole hearts.

Of the love that says: 'Bless me, darling'; of the love so called, which is nothing but selfishness, the appropriation of another soul as the means of one's own happiness merely, there is abundance in the world; and the still more animal, the mere desire for temporary gratification, with little worthy the name of love, also abounds. Even these are best left free, since as evils they will thus be best cured; but of that celestial love which say: 'Bless you, darling,' and which strives continually to confer blessing; of that genuine love whose office it is to bless others or another, there cannot be too much in the world, and when it shall be fully understood that this is the love which we mean and commend there will be no objection to the term Free Love, and none to the thing signified.

We not only accept our name, but we contend that none other could so well signify the real character of that which it designates – to be free and to love. But our enemies must be reminded that the fact of the existence and advocacy of such a doctrine cannot immediately elevate to high condition the great number who have been kept in degradation and misery by previous false systems. They must not expect at this early day of the new doctrine, that all debauchery has been cleaned out of men and women. In the haunts where it retreats, the benign influence of its magic presence has not yet penetrated. They must not expect that brutish men and debased women have as yet been touched by its wand of hope, and that they have already obeyed the bidding to come up higher. They must not expect that ignorance and fleshly lust have already been lifted to the region of intellect and moral purity. They must not expect that Free Love, before it is more than barely announced to the world, can perform what Christianity in eighteen hundred years has failed to do.

They must not expect any of these things have already been accomplished, but I will tell you what they may expect. They may expect more good to result from the perfect freedom which we advocate in one century than has resulted in a hundred centuries from all other causes, since the results will be in exact proportion to the extended application of the freedom. We have a legitimate right to predicate such results, since all freedom that has been practiced in all ages of the world has been beneficial just in proportion to the extent of human nature it covered.

Will any of you dare to stand up and assert that Religious Freedom ever produced a single bad result? or that Political Freedom ever injured a single soul who embraced and practiced it? If you can do so, then you may legitimately assert that Social Freedom may also produce equally bad results, but you cannot do otherwise, and be either conscientious or honest.

It is too late in the age for intelligent people to cry out thief, unless they have first been robbed, and it is equally late for them to succeed in crying down anything as of the devil to which name attaches that angels love. It may be very proper and legitimate, and withal perfectly consistent, for philosophers of the Tribune school to bundle all the murderers, robbers and rascals together, and hand them over to our camp, labeled as Free Lovers. We will only object that they ought to hand the whole of humanity over, good, bad and indifferent, and not assort its worst representatives.

My friends, you see this thing we call Freedom is a large word, implying a deal more than people have ever yet been able to recognize. It reaches out its all-embracing arms, and while encircling our good friends and neighbors, does not neglect to also include their less worthy brothers and sisters, every one of whom is just as much entitled to the use of this freedom as is either one of us.

But objectors tell us that freedom is a dangerous thing to have, and that they must be its conservators, dealing it out to such people, and upon such matters, as they shall appoint. Having coined our name, they straightway proceed to define it, and to give force to their definition, set about citing illustrations to prove not only their definition to be a true one, but also that its application is just.

Among the cases cited as evidences of the evil tendencies of Free Love are those of Richardson and Crittenden. The celebrated McFarland-Richardson case was heralded world-wide as a case of this sort. So far as Richardson and Mrs McFarland were concerned, I have every reason to believe it was a genuine one, in so far as the preventing obstacles framed by the 'conservators' would permit. But when they assert that the murder of Richardson by McFarland was the legitimate result of Free Love, then I deny it in toto. McFarland murdered Richardson because he believed that the law had sold Abby Sage soul and body to him, and, consequently, that he owned her, and that no other person had any right to her favor, and that she had no right to bestow her love upon any other person, unless that ownership was first satisfied. The murder of Richardson, then, is not chargeable to his love or her love, but to the fact of the supposed ownership, which right of possession the law of marriage conferred on McFarland.

If anything further is needed to make the reputation of that charge clear, I will give it by illustration. Suppose that a pagan should be converted to Christianity through the efforts of some Christian minister, and that the remaining pagans should kill that minister for what he had done, would the crime be chargeable upon the Christian religion? Will any of you make that assertion? If not, neither can you charge that the death of Richardson should be charged to Free Love. But a more recent case is still clearer proof of the correctness of my position. Mrs Fair killed Crittenden. Why? Because she believed in the spirit of the marriage law; that she had a better right to him than had Mrs Crittenden, to whom the law had granted him; and rather than to give him up to her, to whom he evidently desired to go, and where, following his right to freedom, he did go, she killed him. Could a more perfect case of the spirit of the marriage law be formulate? Most assuredly, no!

Now, from the standpoint of marriage, reverse this case to that of Free Love, and see what would have been the result had all those parties been believers in and practicers of that theory. When Mr Crittenden evinced a desire to return to Mrs Crittenden, Mrs Fair, in practicing the doctrine of Free Love, would have said, 'I have no right to you, other than you freely give; you loved me and exercised your right of freedom in so doing. You now desire to return to Mrs Crittenden, which is equally your right, and which I must respect. Go, and in peace, and my blessing shall follow, and if it can return you to happiness, then will you be happy.'

Would not that have been the better the Christian course, and would not every soul in the broad land capable of a noble impulse, and having knowledge of all the relevant facts, have honored Mrs Fair for it? Instead of a murder, with the probability of another to complement it, would not all parties have been happy in having done right? Would not Mrs Crittenden have even loved Mrs Fair for such an example of nobility, and could she not safely have received her even into her own heart and home, and have been a sister to her, instead of the means of her conviction of murder?

I tell you, my friends and my foes, that you have taken hold of the wrong end of this business. You are shouldering upon Free Love the results that flow from precisely its antithesis, which is the spirit, if not the letter, of your marriage theory, which is slavery, and not freedom.

I have a better right to speak, as one having authority in this matter, than most of you have, since it has been my province to study it in all its various lights and shades. When I practiced clairvoyance, hundreds, aye thousands, of desolate, heart-broken men, as well as women, came to me for advice. And they were from all walks of life, from the humblest daily laborer to the haughtiest dame of wealth. The tales of horror, of wrongs inflicted and endured, which were poured into my ears, first awakened me to a realization of the hollowness and the rottenness of society, and compelled me to consider whether laws which were prolific of so much crime and misery as I found to exist should be continued; and to ask the question whether it were not better to let the bond go free. In time I was fully convinced that marriage laws were productive of precisely the reverse of that for which they are supposed to have been framed, and I came to recommend the grant of entire freedom to those who were complained of an inconstant; and the frank asking for it by those who desired it. My invariable advice was: 'Withdraw lovingly, but completely, all claim and all complaint as an injured and deserted husband or wife. You need not perhaps disguise the fact that you suffer keenly from it, but take on yourself all the fault that you have not been able to command a more continuous love; that you have not proved to be all that you once seemed to be. Show magnanimity, and in order to show it, try to feel it. Cultivate that kind of love which loves the happiness and well-being of your partner most, his or her person next, and yourself last. Be kind to, and sympathize with, the new attraction rather than waspish and indignant. Know for a certainty that love cannot be clutched or gained by being fought for; while it is not impossible that it may be won back by the nobility of one's own deportment. If it cannot be, then it is gone forever, and you must make the best of it and reconcile yourself to it, and do the next thing – you may perhaps continue to hold on to a slave, but you have lost a lover.'

Some may indeed think if I can keep the semblance of a husband or wife, even if it be not a lover, better still that it be so. Such is not my philosophy or my faith, and for such I have no advice to give. I address myself to such as have souls, and whose souls are in question; if you belong to the other sort, take advice of a Tombs lawyer and not of me. I have seen a few instances of the most magnanimous action among the persons involved in a knot of love, and with the most angelic results. I believe that the love which goes forth to bless, and if it be to surrender in order to bless, is love in the true sense, and that it tends greatly to beget love, and that the love which is demanding thinking only of self, is not love.

I have learned that the first great error married people commit is in endeavoring to hide from each other the little irregularities into which all are liable to fall. Nothing is so conducive to continuous happiness as mutual confidence. In whom, if not in the husband or the wife, should be one confide? Should they not be each other's best friends, never failing in time of anxiety, trouble and temptation to give disinterested and unselfish counsel? From such a perfect confidence as I would have men and women cultivate, it is impossible that bad or wrong should flow. On the contrary, it is the only condition in which love and happiness can go hand in hand. It is the only practice that can insure continuous respect, without which love withers and dies out. Can you not see that in mutual confidence and freedom the very strongest bonds of love are forged? It is more blessed to grant favors than to demand them, and the blessing is large and prolific of happiness, or small and insignificant in results, just in proportion as the favor granted is large or small. Tried by this rule, the greater the blessing or happiness you can confer on your partners, in which your own selfish feelings are not consulted, the greater the satisfaction that will redound to yourself. Think of this mode of adjusting your difficulties, and see what a clear way opens before you. There are none who have once felt the influence of a high order of love, so callous, but that they intuitively recognize the true grandeur and nobility of such a line of conduct. It must always be remembered that you can never do right until you are first free to do wrong; since the doing of a thing under compulsion is evidence neither of good nor bad intent; and if under compulsion, who shall decide what would be the substituted rule of action under full freedom?

In freedom alone is there safety and happiness, and when people learn this great fact, they will have just begun to know how to live. Instead then of being the destroying angel of the household, I would become the angel of purification to purge out all insincerity, all deception, all baseness and all vice, and to replace them by honor, confidence and truth.

I know very well that much of the material upon which the work must begin is very bad and far gone in decay. But I would have everybody perfectly free to do either right or wrong according to the highest standard, and if there are those so unfortunate as not to know how to do that which can alone bring happiness, I would treat them as we treat those who are intellectual without culture – who are ignorant and illiterate.

There are none so ignorant but they may be taught. So, too, are there none so unfortunate in their understanding of the true and high relation of the sexes as not to be amenable to the right kind of instruction. First of all, however, the would-be teachers of humanity must become truly Christian, meek and lowly in spirit, forgiving and kind in action, and ever ready to do as did Christ to the Magdalen. We are not so greatly different from what the accusing multitude were in that time. But Christians, forgetting the teaching of Christ, condemn and say, 'Go on in your sin.' Christians must learn to claim nothing for themselves that they are unwilling to accord others. They must remember that all people endeavor, so far as lies in their power, and so far as it is possible for them to judge, to exercise their human right, or determine what their action shall be, that will bring them most happiness; and instead of being condemned and cast out of society therefor, they should be protected therein, so long as others' rights are not infringed upon. We think they do not do the best thing; it is our duty to endeavor to show them the better and the higher, and to induce them to walk therein. But because a person chooses to perform an act that we think a bad one, we have no right to put the brand of excommunication upon him. It is our Christian and brotherly duty to persuade him instead that it is more to his good to do something better next time, at the same time, however, assuring him he only did what he had a right to do.

If our sisters who inhabit Greene Street and other filthy localities choose to remain in debauch, and if our brothers choose to visit them there, they are only exercising the same right that we exercise in remaining away, and we have no more right to abuse and condemn them for exercising their rights that way, than they have to abuse and condemn us for exercising our rights our way. But we have a duty, and that is by our love, kindness and sympathy to endeavor to prevail upon them to desert those ways which we feel are so damaging to all that is high and pure and true in the relations of the sexes.

If these are the stray sheep from the fold of truth and purity, should we not go out and gather them in, rather than remain within the fold and hold the door shut, lest they should enter in and defile the fold? Nay, my friends, we have only an assumed right to thus sit in judgment over our unfortunate sisters, which is the same right of which men have made use to prevent women from participation in government.

The sin of all time has been the exercise of assumed powers. This is the essence of tyranny. Liberty is a great lesson to learn. It is a great step to vindicate our own freedom. It is more, far more, to learn to leave others free, and free to do just what we perhaps may deem wholly wrong. We must recognize that others have consciences and judgment and rights as well as we, and religiously abstain from the effort to make them better by the use of any means to which we have no right to resort, and to which we cannot resort without abridging the great doctrine, the charter of all our liberties, the doctrine of Human Rights.

But the public press, either in real or affected ignorance or what they speak, denounce Free Love as the justification of, and apologist for, all manner and kind of sexual debauchery, and thus, instead of being the teachers of the people, as they should be, are the power which inculcates falsehood and wrong. The teachings of Christ, whom so many now profess to imitate, were direct and simple upon this point. He was not too good to acknowledge all men as brothers and all women as sisters; it mattered not whether they were highly advanced in knowledge and morals, or if they were of low intellectual and moral culture.

It is seriously to be doubted if any of Christ's disciples, or men equally as good as were they, could gain fellowship in any of your Fifth avenue church palaces, since they were nothing more than the humblest of fishermen, of no social or mental standing. Nevertheless, they were quite good enough for Christ to associate with, and fit to be appointed by Him to be 'fishers of men'. The Church seems to have forgotten that good does sometimes come out of the Nazareths of the world, and that wisdom may fall from the mouths of 'babes and sucklings'. Quite too much of the old pharisaical spirit exists in society today to warrant its members' claims, that they are the representatives and followers of Christ. For they are the I-am-holier-than-thou kind of people, who affect to, and to a great extent do, prescribe the standards of public opinion, and who ostracize everybody who will not bow to their mandates.

Talk of Freedom, of equality, of justice! I tell you there is scarcely a thought put in practice that is worthy to be the offspring of those noble words. The veriest systems of despotism still reign in all matters pertaining to social life. Caste stands as boldly out in this country as it does in political life in the kingdoms of Europe.

It is true that we are obliged to accept the situation just as it is. If we accord freedom to all persons we must expect them to make their own best use thereof, and, as I have already said, must protect them in such use until they learn to put it to better uses. But in our predication we must be consistent, and now ask who among you would be worse men and women all social laws repealed?

Would you necessarily dissolve your present relations, desert your dependent husbands – for there are even some of them – and wives and children simply because you have the right so to do? You are all trying to deceive yourselves about this matter. Let me ask of husbands if they think there would be fifty thousand women of the town supported by them if their wives were ambitious to have an equal number of men of the town to support, and for the same purposes? I tell you, nay! It is because men are held innocent of this support, and all the vengeance is visited upon the victims, that they have come to have an immunity in their practices.

Until women come to hold men to equal account as they do the women with whom they consort; or until they regard these women as just as respectable as the men who support them, society will remain in its present scale of moral excellence. A man who is well known to have been the constant visitor to these women is accepted into society, and if he be rich is eagerly sought both by mothers having marriageable daughters and by the daughters themselves. But the women with whom they have consorted are too vile to be even acknowledged as worthy of Christian burial, to say nothing of common Christian treatment. I have heard women reply when this difficulty was pressed upon them, 'We cannot ostracize men as we are compelled to women, since we are dependent on them for support.' Ah! here's the rub. But do you not see that these other sisters are also dependent upon men for their support, and mainly so because you render it next to impossible for them to follow any legitimate means of livelihood? And are only those who have been fortunate enough to secure legal support entitled to live?

When I hear that argument advanced, my heart sinks within me at the degraded condition of my sisters. They submit to a degradation simply because they see no alternative except self-support, and they see no means for that. To put on the semblance of holiness they cry out against those who, for like reasons, submit to like degradation; the only difference between the two being in a licensed ceremony, and a slip of printed paper costing twenty-five cents and upward.

The good women of one of the interior cities of New York some two years since organized a movement to put down prostitution. They were, by stratagem, to find out who visited houses of prostitution, and then were to ostracize them. They pushed the matter until they found their own husbands, brothers and sons involved, and then suddenly desisted, and nothing has since been heard of the eradication of prostitution in that city. If the same experiment were to be tried in New York the result would be the same. The supporters of prostitution would be found to be those whom women cannot ostracize. The same disability excuses the presence of women in the very home, and I need not tell you that Mormonism is practiced in other places beside Utah. But what is the logic of these things? Why, simply this, A woman, be she wife or mistress, who consorts with a man who consorts with other women, is equally, with them and him, morally responsible, since the receiver is held to be as culpable as the thief.

The false and hollow relations of the sexes are thus resolved into the mere question of the dependence of women upon men for support, and women, whether married or single, are supported by men because they are women and their opposites in sex. I can see no moral difference between a woman who marries and lives with a man because he can provide for her wants, and the woman who is not married, but who is provided for at the same price. There is a legal difference, to be sure, upon one side of which is set the seal of respectability, but there is no virtue in law. In the fact of law, however, is the evidence of the lack of virtue, since if the law be required to enforce virtue, its real presence is wanting; and women need to comprehend this truth.

The sexual relation, must be rescued from this insidious form of slavery. Women must rise from their position as ministers to the passions of men to be their equals. Their entire system of education must be changed. They must be trained to be like men, permanent and independent individualities, and not their mere appendages or adjuncts, with them forming but one member of society. They must be the companions of men from choice, never from necessity.

It is a label upon nature and God to say this world is not calculated to make women, equally with men, self-reliant and self-supporting individuals. In present customs, however, this is apparently impossible. There must come a change, and one of the direct steps to it will be found in the newly claimed political equality of women with men. This attained, one degree of subjugation will be removed. Next will come, following equality of right, equality of duty, which includes the duty of self-hood, or independence as an individual. Nature is male and female throughout, and each sex is equally dependent upon nature for sustenance. It is an infamous thing to say a condition of society which requires women to enter into and maintain sexual relations with men is their legitimate method of protecting life. Sexual relations should be the result of entirely different motives that for the purpose of physical support. The spirit of the present theory is, that they are entered upon and maintained as a means of physical gratification, regardless of the consequences which may result therefrom, and are administered by the dictum of the husband, which is often in direct opposition to the will and wish of the wife. She has no control over her own person, having been taught to 'submit herself to her husband.'

I protest against this form of slavery, I protest against the custom which compels women to give the control of their maternal functions over to anybody. It should be theirs to determine when, and under what circumstances, the greatest of all constructive processes – the formation of an immortal soul –

should be begun. It is a fearful responsibility with which women are intrusted by nature, and the very last thing that they should be compelled to do is to perform the office of that responsibility against their will, under improper conditions or by disgusting means.

What can be more terrible than for a delicate, sensitively organized woman to be compelled to endure the presence of a beast in the shape of a man, who knows nothing beyond the blind passion with which he is filled, and to which is often added to delirium of intoxication? You do not need to be informed that there are many persons who, during the acquaintance preceding marriage, preserve a delicacy, tenderness and regard for womanly sensitiveness and modest refinement which are characteristic of true women, thus winning and drawing out their love-nature to the extreme, but who, when the decree has been pronounced which makes them indissolubly theirs, cast all these aside and reveal themselves in their true character, as without regard, human or divine, for aught save their own desires. I know I speak the truth, and you too know I speak the truth, when I say that thousands of the most noble, loving-natured women by whom the world was ever blessed, prepared for, and desirous of pouring their whole life into the bond of union, prophesied by marriage, have had all these generous and warm impulses thrust back upon them by the rude monster into which the previous gentleman developed. To these natures thus frosted and stultified in their fresh youth and vigor, life becomes a burden almost too terrible to be borne, and thousands of pallid checks, sunken eyes, distorted imaginations and diseased functions testify too directly and truly to leave a shade of doubt as to their real cause. Yet women, in the first instance, and men through them as their mothers, with an ignorant persistence worthy only of the most savage despotism, seem determined that it shall not be investigated; and so upon this voluntary ignorance and willful persistence society builds. It is high time, however, that they should be investigated, high time that your sisters and daughters should no longer be led to the altar like sheep to the shambles, in ignorance of the uncertainties they must inevitably encounter. For it is no slight thing to hazard a life's happiness upon a single act.

I deem it a false and perverse modesty that shuts off discussion, and consequently knowledge, upon these subjects. They are vital, and I never performed a duty which I felt more called upon to perform than I now do in denouncing as barbarous the ignorance which is allowed to prevail among young women about to enter those relations which, under present customs, as often bring a life-long misery as happiness.

Mistakes made in this most important duty of life can never be rectified; a commentary upon the system which of itself is sufficient in the sight of common sense to forever condemn it. In marriage, however, common sense is dispensed with, and a usage substituted therefor which barbarism has bequeathed us, and which becomes more barbarous as the spiritual natures of women gain the ascendancy over the mere material. The former slaves, before realizing that freedom was their God-appointed right, did not feel the horrors of their condition. But when, here and there, some among them began to have an interior knowledge that they were held in obedience by an unrighteous power, they then began to rebel in their souls. So, too, is it with women. So long as they knew nothing beyond a blind and servile obedience and perfect self-abnegation to the will and wish of men, they did not rebel; but the time has arrived wherein, here and there, a soul is awakened by some terrible ordeal, or some divine inspiration, to the fact that women as much as men are personalities, responsible to themselves for the use which they permit to be made of themselves, and they rebel demanding freedom, to hold their own lives and bodies from the demoralizing influence of sexual relations that are not founded in and maintained by love. And this rebellion will continue, too, until love, unshackled, shall be free to go to bless the object that can call it forth, and until, when called forth, it shall be respected as holy, pure and true. Every day farther and wider does it spread, and bolder does it speak. None too soon will the yoke fall by which the unwilling are made to render a hypocritical obedience to the despotism of public opinion, which, distorted and blinded by a sham sentimentality, is a false standard of morals and virtue, and which is utterly destructive to true morality and to real virtue, which can only be fostered and cultivated by freedom of the affections.

Free Love, then, is the law by which men and women of all grades and kinds are attracted to or repelled from each other, and does not describe the results accomplished by either; these results depend upon the condition and development of the individual subjects. It is the natural operation of the affectional motives of the sexes, unbiased by any enacted law or standard of public opinion. It is the opportunity which gives the opposites in sex the conditions in which the law of chemical affinities raised into the domain of the affections can have unrestricted sway, as it has in all departments of nature except in enforced sexual relations among men and women.

It is an impossibility to compel incompatible elements of matter to unite. So also is it impossible to compel incompatible elements of human nature to unite. The sphere of chemical science is to bring together such elements as will produce harmonious compounds. The sphere of social science is to accomplish the same thing in humanity. Anything that stands in the way of this accomplishment in either department is an obstruction to the natural order of the universe. There would be just as much common sense for the chemist to write a law commanding that two incompatible elements should unite, or that two, once united, should so remain, even if a third, having a stronger affinity for one of them than they have for each other, should be introduced, as it is for chemists of society to attempt to do the same by individuals; for both are impossible. If in chemistry two properties are united by which the environment is not profited, it is the same law of affinity which operates as where a compound is made that is of the greatest service to society. This law holds in social chemistry; the results obtained from social compounds will be just such as their respective properties determine.

Thus I might go on almost infinitely to illustrate the difference which must be recognized between the operations of a law and the law itself. Now the whole difficulty in marriage law is that it endeavors to compel unity between elements in which it is impossible; consequently there is an attempt made to subvert not only the general order of the universe, but also the special intentions of nature, which are those of God. The results, then, flowing from operations of the law of Free Love will be high, pure and lasting, or low, debauched and promiscuous, just in the degree that those loving, are high or low in the scale of sexual progress; while each and all are strictly natural, and therefore legitimate in their respective spheres.

Promiscuity in sexuality is simply the anarchical stage of development wherein the passions rule supreme. When spirituality comes in and rescues the real man or woman from the domain of the purely material, promiscuity is simply impossible. As promiscuity is the analogue to anarchy, so is spirituality to scientific selection and adjustment. Therefore I am fully persuaded that the very highest sexual unions are those that are monogamic, and that these are perfect in proportion as they are lasting. Now if to this be added the fact that the highest kind of love is that which is utterly freed from and devoid of selfishness, and whose highest gratification comes from rendering its object the greatest amount of happiness, let that happiness depend upon whatever it may, then you have my ideal of the highest order of love and the most perfect degree of order to which humanity can attain. An affection that does not desire to bless its object, instead of appropriating it by a selfish possession to its own uses, is not worthy the name of love. Love is that which exists to do good, not merely to get good, which is constantly giving instead of desiring.

A Caesar is admired by humanity, but a Christ is revered. These persons who have lived and sacrificed themselves most for the good of humanity, without thought of recompense, are held in greatest respect. Christian believes that Christ died to save the world, giving His life as a ransom therefor. That was the greatest gift He could make to show His love for mankind.

The general test of love to-day is entirely different from that which Christ gave. That is now deemed the greatest love which has the strongest and most uncontrollable wish to be made happy, by the appropriation, and if need be the sacrifice, of all the preferences of its objects. It says: 'Be mine. Whatever may be your wish, yield it up to me.' How different would the world be were this sort of selfishness supplanted by the Christ love, which says: Let this cup pass from me. Nevertheless, not my will but thine be done. Were the relations of the sexes thus regulated, misery, crime and vice would be banished, and the pale, wan face of female humanity replaced by one glowing with radiant delight and healthful bloom, and the heart of humanity beat with a heightened vigor and renewed strength, and its intellect cleared of all shadows, sorrows and blights. Contemplate this, and then denounce me for advocating Freedom if you can, and I will bear your curse with a better resignation.

Oh! my brothers and sisters, let me entreat you to have more faith in the self-regulating efficacy of freedom. Do you not see how beautifully it works among us in other respects? In America everybody is free to worship God according to the dictates of his own conscience, or even not to worship anything, notwithstanding you or I may think that very wicked or wrong. The respect for freedom we make paramount over our individual opinions, and the result is peace and harmony, when the people of other countries are still throttling and destroying each other to enforce their individual opinions on others. Free Love is only the appreciation of this beautiful principle of freedom. One step further I entreat you to trust it still, and though you may see a thousand dangers, I see peace and happiness and steady improvement as the result.

To more specifically define Free Love I would say that I prefer to use the word love with lust as its antithesis, love representing the spiritual and lust the animal; the perfect and harmonious interrelations of the two being the perfected human. This use has its justification in other pairs of words; as good and evil; heat and cold; light and dark; up and down; north and south; which in principle are the same, but in practice we are obliged to judge of them as relatively different. The point from which judgment is made is that which we occupy, or are related to, individually, at any given time. Thus what would be up to one person might be down to another differently situated, along the line which up and down described. So also is it of good and evil. What is good to one low down the ladder may not only be, but actually is, evil to one further ascended; nevertheless it is the same ladder up which both climb. It is the comprehension of this scientific fact that guarantees the best religion. And it is the non-comprehension of it that sets us as judges of our brothers and sisters, who are below us in the scale of development, to whom we should reach down the kind and loving hand of assistance, rather than force them to retreat farther away from us by unkindness, denunciation and hate.

In fine, and to resume: We have found that humanity is composed of men and women of all grades of developments, from the most hideous human monster up to the highest perfected saint: that all of them, under our theory of government, are entitled to worship God after the dictates of their several consciences; that God is worshiped just as essentially in political and social thought and action as He is in religious thought and action; that no second person or persons have any right to interfere with the action of the individual unless he interfere with others' rights, and then only to protect such rights; that the thoughts and actions of all individuals, whether high and pure, or low and debauched, are equally entitled to the protection of the laws, and, through them, to that of all members of the community. Religious thought and action already receive the equal protection of the laws. Political thought and action are about to secure the equal protection of the laws. What social thought and action demand of the laws and their administrators is the same protection which Religion has, and Politics is about to have.

I know full well how strong is the appeal that can be made in behalf of marriage, an appeal based on the sanctions of usage and inherited respect, and on the sanctions of religion reinforced by the sanctions of law. I know how much can be said, and how forcibly it can be said, on the ground that women, and especially that the children born of the union of the sexes, must be protected, and must, therefore, have the solemn contract of the husband and father to that effect. I know how long and how powerfully the ideality and sentiment of mankind have clustered, as it were in a halo, around this time-honored institution of marriage. And yet I solemnly believe that all that belongs to a dispensation of force and contract, and of a law and unworthy sense of mutual ownership, which is passing, and which is destined rapidly to pass, completely away; not to leave us without love, nor without the happiness and beauty of the most tender relation of human souls; nor without security for woman, and ample protection for children; but to lift us to a higher level in the enjoyment of every blessing. I believe in love with liberty; in protection without slavery; in the care and culture of offspring by new and better methods, and without the tragedy of self-immolation on the part of parents. I believe in the family, spiritually constituted, expanded, amplified, and scientifically and artistically organized, as a unitary home. I believe in the most wonderful transformation of human society as about to come, as even now at the very door, through general progress, science and the influential intervention of the spirit world. I be-lieve in more than all that the millennium has ever signified to the most religious mind; and I believe that in order to prepare minds to contemplate and desire and enact the new and better life, it is necessary that the old and still prevalent superstitious veneration for the legal marriage tie be relaxed and weakened; not to pander to immorality, but as introductory to a nobler manhood and a more glorified womanhood; as, indeed, the veritable gateway to a paradise regained.

Do not criticize me, therefore, from a commonplace point of view. Question me, first, of the grounds of my faith. Conceive, if you can, the outlook for that humanity which comes trooping through the long, bright vista of futurity, as seen by the eyes of a devout spiritualist and a transcendental socialist. My whole nature is prophetic. I do not and cannot live merely in the present. Credit, first, the burden of my prophecy; and from the new standing-ground so projected forth into the future, look back upon our times, and so judge of my doctrine; and if, still, you cannot concede either the premises or the conclusion, you may, perhaps, think more kindly of me personally, as an amiable enthusiast, than if you deemed me deliberately wicked in seeking to disturb the foundations of our existing social order.

I prize dearly the good opinion of my fellow-beings. I would, so gladly, have you think well of me, and not ill. It is because I love you all, and love your well-being still more than I love you, that I tell you my vision of the future, and that I would willingly disturb your confidence, so long cherished, in the old dead or dying-out past. Believe me honest, my dear friends, and so forgive and think of me lovingly in turn, even if you are compelled still to regard me as deceived. I repeat, that I love you all; that I love every human creature, and their well being; and that I believe, with the profoundest conviction, that what I have urged in this discourse is conducive to that end.

Thus have I explained to you what Social Freedom or, as some choose to denominate it, Free Love, is, and what its advocates demand. Society says, to grant it is to precipitate itself into anarchy. I oppose to this arbitrary assumption the logic of general freedom, and aver that order and harmony will be secured where anarchy now reigns. The order of nature will soon determine whether society is or I am right. Let that be as it may, I repeat: 'The love that I cannot command is not mine; let me not disturb myself about it, nor attempt to filch it from its rightful owner. A heart that I supposed mine has drifted and gone. Shall I go in pursuit? Shall I forcibly capture the truant and transfix it with the barb of my selfish affection, and pin it to the wall of my character? Rather let me leave my doors and windows open, intent only on living so nobly that the best cannot fail to be drawn to me by an irresistible attraction.'

Susan B. Anthony:

1873

On Women's Right to Vote

Since nineteenth-century American women did not have the right to vote, Susan B. Anthony became a strong advocate of women's suffrage. In 1872, after casting an 'illegal' vote in the presidential election, she was arrested. She was fined $100 but refused to pay.

Friends and fellow citizens: I stand before you tonight under indictment for the alleged crime of having voted at the last presidential election, without having a lawful right to vote. It shall be my work this evening to prove to you that in thus voting, I not only committed no crime, but, instead, simply exercised my citizen's rights, guaranteed to me and all United States citizens by the National Constitution, beyond the power of any state to deny.

The preamble of the Federal Constitution says: 'We, the people of the United States, in order to form a more perfect union, establish justice, insure domestic tranquillity, provide for the common defense, promote the general welfare, and secure the blessings of liberty to ourselves and our posterity, do ordain and establish this Constitution for the United States of America.'

It was we, the people; not we, the white male citizens; nor yet we, the male citizens; but we, the whole people, who formed the Union. And we formed it, not to give the blessings of liberty, but to secure them; not to the half of ourselves and the half of our posterity, but to the whole people – women as well as men. And it is a downright mockery to talk to women of their enjoyment of the blessings of liberty while they are denied the use of the only means of securing them provided by this democratic republican government – the ballot.

For any state to make sex a qualification that must ever result in the disfranchisement of one entire half of the people is to pass a bill of attainder, or an *ex post facto* law, and is therefore a violation of the supreme law of the land. By it the blessings of liberty are forever withheld from women and their female posterity.

To them this government has no just powers derived from the consent of the governed. To them this government is not a democracy. It is not a republic. It is an odious aristocracy; a hateful oligarchy of sex; the most hateful aristocracy ever established on the face of the globe; an oligarchy of wealth, where the rich govern the poor. An oligarchy of learning, where the educated govern the ignorant, or even an oligarchy of race, where the Saxon rules the African, might be endured; but this oligarchy of sex, which makes father, brothers, husband, sons, the oligarchs over the mother and sisters, the wife and daughters, of every household – which ordains all men sovereigns, all women subjects, carries dissension, discord, and rebellion into every home of the nation.

Webster, Worcester, and Bouvier all define a citizen to be a person in the United States, entitled to vote and hold office. The only question left to be settled now is: Are women persons? And I hardly believe any of our opponents will have the hardihood to say they are not. Being persons, then, women are citizens; and no state has a right to make any law, or to enforce any old law, that shall abridge their privileges or immunities. Hence, every discrimination against women in the constitutions and laws of the several states is today null and void, precisely as is every one against Negroes.

Walt Whitman:
28 January 1877

In Memory of Thomas Paine

Walt Whitman (1819–92), one of America's most celebrated poets, became a strong advocate of individual freedom and dignity, democracy and human brotherhood. He delivered this speech at Lincoln Hall, Philadelphia, for the one hundred and fortieth anniversary of Thomas Paine's birthday.

Some thirty-five years ago, in New York city, at Tammany Hall, of which place I was then a frequenter, I happen'd to become quite well acquainted with Thomas Paine's perhaps most intimate chum, and certainly his later years' very frequent companion, a remarkably fine old man, Col. Fellows, who may yet be remember'd by some stray relics of that period and spot. If you will allow me, I will first give a description of the Colonel himself. He was tall, of military bearing, aged about 78, I should think, hair white as snow, clean-shaved on the face, dress'd very neatly, a tail-coat of blue cloth with metal buttons, buff vest, pantaloons of drab color, and his neck, breast and wrists showing the whitest of linen. Under all circumstances, fine manners; a good but not profuse talker, his wits still fully about him, balanced and live and undimm'd as ever. He kept pretty fair health, though so old. For employment – for he was poor – he had a post as constable of some of the upper courts. I used to think him very picturesque on the fringe of a crowd holding a tall staff, with his erect form, and his superb, bare, thick-hair'd, closely-cropt white head. The judges and young lawyers, with whom he was ever a favorite, and the subject of respect, used to call him Aristides. It was the general opinion among them that if manly rectitude and the instincts of absolute justice remain'd vital anywhere about New York City Hall, or Tammany, they were to be found in Col. Fellows. He liked young men, and enjoy'd to leisurely talk with them over a social glass of toddy, after his day's work, (he on these occasions never drank but one glass,) and it was at reiterated meetings of this kind in old Tammany's back parlor of those days, that he told me much about Thomas Paine. At one of our interviews he gave me a minute account of Paine's sickness and death. In short, from those talks, I was and am satisfied that my old friend, with his mark'd advantages, had mentally, morally and emotionally gauged the author of 'Common Sense', and besides giving me a good portrait of his appearance and manners, had taken the true measure of his interior character.

Paine's practical demeanor, and much of his theoretical belief, was a mixture of the French and English schools of a century ago, and the best of both. Like most old fashion'd people, he drank a glass or two every day, but was no tippler, nor intemperate, let alone being a drunkard. He lived simply and economically, but quite well – was always cheery and courteous, perhaps occasionally a little blunt, having very positive opinions upon politics, religion, and so forth. That he labor'd well and wisely for the States in the trying of their parturition, and in the seeds of their character, there seems to me no question. I dare not say how much of what our Union is owning and enjoying to-day – its independence – its ardent belief in, and substantial practice of radical human rights – and the severance of its government from all ecclesiastical and superstitious dominion – I dare not say how much of all this is owing to Thomas Paine, but I am inclined to think a good portion of it decidedly is.

But I was not going either into an analysis or eulogium of the man. I wanted to carry you back a generation or two, and give you by indirection a moment's glance – and also to ventilate a very earnest and I believe authentic opinion, nay conviction, of that time, the fruit of the interviews I have mention'd, and of questioning and cross-questioning, clench'd by my best information since, that Thomas Paine had a noble personality, as exhibited in presence, face, voice, dress, manner, and what may be call'd his atmosphere and magnetism, especially the later years of his life. I am sure of it. Of the foul and foolish fictions yet told about the circumstances of his decease, the absolute fact is that as he lived a good life, after its kind, he died calmly and philosophically, as became him. He served the embryo Union with most precious service – a service that every man, woman and child in our thirty-eight States is to some extent receiving the benefit of today – and I for one here cheerfully, reverently throw my pebble on the cairn of his memory. As we all know, the season demands – or rather, will it ever be out of season? – that America learn to better dwell on her choicest possession, the legacy of her good and faithful men – that she well preserve their fame, if unquestion'd – or, if need be, that she fail not to dissipate what clouds have intruded on that fame, and burnish it newer, truer and brighter, continually.

Mark Twain:

17 December 1877

Pleasant Reminiscences Concerning Literary Folk

Under his pen name of Mark Twain, Samuel L. Clemens (1835–1910) became an exceptionally popular author during his lifetime, and is still regarded as one of America's best writers. He delivered this address at Boston at a dinner given by the publishers of *The Atlantic Monthly* to celebrate the seventieth anniversary of the birth of John Greenleaf Whittier.

This is an occasion peculiarly meet for the digging up of pleasant reminiscences concerning literary folk; therefore I will drop lightly into history myself. Standing here on the shore of the Atlantic and contemplating certain of its largest literary billows, I am reminded of a thing which happened to me thirteen years ago, when I had just succeeded in stirring up a little Nevadian literary puddle myself, whose spume-flakes were beginning to blow thinly Californiaward. I started an inspection tramp through the southern mines of California. I was callow and conceited, and I resolved to try the virtue of my nom de guerre.

I very soon had an opportunity. I knocked at a miner's lonely log cabin in the foot-hills of the Sierras just at nightfall. It was snowing at the time. A jaded, melancholy man of fifty, barefooted, opened the door to me. When he heard my *nom de guerre* he looked more dejected than before. He let me in – pretty reluctantly, I thought – and after the customary bacon and beans, black coffee and hot whiskey, I took a pipe. This sorrowful man had not said three words up to this time. Now he spoke up and said, in the voice of one who is secretly suffering, 'You're the fourth – I'm going to move.'

'The fourth what?' said I.

'The fourth littery man that has been here in twenty-four hours – I'm going to move.'

'You don't tell me!' said I; 'who were the others?'

'Mr Longfellow, Mr Emerson, and Mr Oliver Wendell Holmes – confound the lot!'

You can easily believe I was interested. I supplicated – three hot whiskeys did the rest – and finally the melancholy miner began. Said he: 'They came here just at dark yesterday evening, and I let them in of course. Said they were going to the Yosemite. They were a rough lot, but that's nothing; everybody looks rough that travels afoot. Mr Emerson was a seedy little bit of a chap, red-headed. Mr Holmes was as fat as a balloon; he weighed as much as three hundred, and had double chins all the way down to his stomach. Mr Longfellow was built like a prize-fighter. His head was cropped and bristly, like as if he had a wig made of hair-brushes. His nose lay straight down his face, like a finger with the end joint tilted up. They had been drinking, I could see that. And what queer talk they used! Mr Holmes inspected this cabin, then he took me by the buttonhole, and says he:

"Through the deep caves of thought
I hear a voice that sings,
Build thee more stately mansions,
O my soul!"

'Says I, "I can't afford it, Mr Holmes, and moreover I don't want to." Blamed if I liked it pretty well, either, coming from a stranger, that way. However, I started to get out my bacon and beans, when Mr Emerson came and looked on awhile, and then he takes me aside by the buttonhole and says:

"Give me agates for my meat;
Give me cantharids to eat;
From air and ocean bring me foods,
From all zones and altitudes."

'Says I, "Mr Emerson, if you'll excuse me, this ain't no hotel." You see it sort of riled me – I warn't used to the ways of literary swells. But I went on a-sweating over my work, and next comes Mr Longfellow and buttonholes me, and interrupts me. Says he:

"Honor be to Mudjekeewis!
You shall hear how Pau-Puk-Keewis –"

'But I broke in, and says I, "Beg your pardon, Mr Longfellow, if you'll be so kind as to hold your yawp for about five minutes and let me get this grub ready, you'll do me proud." Well, sir, after they'd filled up I set out the jug. Mr Holmes looks at it, and then he fires up all of a sudden and yells:

"Flash out a stream of blood-red wine!
For I would drink to other days."

'By George, I was getting kind of worked up. I don't deny it, I was getting kind of worked up. I turns to Mr Holmes, and says I, "Looky here, my fat friend, I'm a-running this shanty, and if the court knows herself, you'll take whiskey straight or you'll go dry."

'Them's the very words I said to him. Now I don't want to sass such famous literary people, but you see they kind of forced me. There ain't nothing unreasonable 'bout me; I don't mind a passel of guests a-treadin' on my tail three or four times, but when it comes to standing on it it's different, "and if the court knows herself," I says, "you'll take whiskey straight or you'll go dry." Well, between drinks they'd swell around the cabin and strike attitudes and spout; and pretty soon they got out a greasy old deck and went to playing euchre at ten cents a corner – on trust. I began to notice some pretty suspicious things. Mr Emerson dealt, looked at his hand, shook his head, says: "I am the doubter and the doubt" – and ca'mly bunched the hands and went to shuffling for a new layout. Says he:

"They reckon ill who leave me out;
They know not well the subtle ways I keep.
I pass and deal again!"

'Hang'd if he didn't go ahead and do it, too! Oh, he was a cool one! Well, in about a minute things were running pretty tight, but all of a sudden I see by Mr Emerson's eye he judged he had 'em. He had already corralled two tricks, and each of the others one. So now he kind of lifts a little in his chair and says:

> "I tire of globes and aces! –
> Too long the game is played!"

– and down he fetched a right bower. Mr Longfellow smiles as sweet as pie and says:

> "Thanks, thanks to thee, my worthy friend,
> For the lesson thou hast taught,"

– and blamed if he didn't down with another right bower! Emerson claps his hand on his bowie, Longfellow claps his on his revolver, and I went under a bunk. There was going to be trouble; but that monstrous Holmes rose up, wobbling his double chins, and says he, "Order, gentlemen; the first man that draws, I'll lay down on him and smother him!" All quiet on the Potomac, you bet!

'They were pretty how-come-you-so by now, and they begun to blow. Emerson says, "The nobbiest thing I ever wrote was 'Barbara Frietchie'." Says Longfellow, "It don't begin with my 'Biglow Papers'." Says Holmes, "My 'Thanatopis' lays over 'em both." They mighty near ended in a fight. Then they wished they had some more company – and Mr Emerson pointed to me and says:
"Is yonder squalid peasant all
That this proud nursery could breed?"

'He was a-whetting his bowie on his boot – so I let it pass. Well, sir, next they took it into their heads that they would like some music; so they made me stand up and sing "When Johnny Comes Marching Home" till I dropped – at thirteen minutes past four this morning. That's what I've been through, my friend. When I woke at seven, they were leaving, thank goodness, and Mr Longfellow had my only boots on, and his'n under his arm. Says I, "Hold on, there, Evangeline, what are you going to do with them?" He says, "Going to make tracks with 'em; because:

> Lives of great men all remind us
> We can make our lives sublime;
> And, departing, leave behind us
> Footprints on the sands of time."

'As I said, Mr Twain, you are the fourth in twenty-four hours – and I'm going to move; I ain't suited to a littery atmosphere.'

I said to the miner, 'Why, my dear sir, these were not the gracious singers to whom we and the world pay loving reverence and homage; these were impostors.'

The miner investigated me with a calm eye for a while; then said he, 'Ah! impostors, were they? Are you?'

I did not pursue the subject, and since then I have not travelled on my nom de guerre enough to hurt. Such was the reminiscence I was moved to contribute, Mr Chairman. In my enthusiasm I may have exaggerated the details a little, but you will easily forgive me that fault, since I believe it is the first time I have ever deflected from perpendicular fact on an occasion like this.

Chief Joseph:
1877

'Looking Glass is dead'

Chief Joseph of the Nez Perce (1840?–1904), known as 'Thunder Traveling to the Loftier Mountain Heights', led his people in an unsuccessful attempt to resist the takeover of their lands in the Oregon Territory by white settlers. They were finally forced to surrender to the US Army on 5 October 1877. These are the words that Chief Joseph said on that occasion.

Tell General Howard I know his heart. What he told me before, I have it in my heart. I am tired of fighting. Our Chiefs are killed; Looking Glass is dead, Ta Hool Hool Shute is dead. The old men are all dead. It is the young men who say yes or no. He who led on the young men is dead. It is cold, and we have no blankets; the little children are freezing to death. My people, some of them, have run away to the hills, and have no blankets, no food. No one knows where they are – perhaps freezing to death. I want to have time to look for my children, and see how many of them I can find. Maybe I shall find them among the dead. Hear me, my Chiefs! I am tired; my heart is sick and sad. From where the sun now stands I will fight no more forever.

Henry W. Grady:

22 December 1886

The New South

This speech was delivered before the New England Society of New York. Twenty-five years after the Civil War, it was the first time that a Southerner had been invited to address this assembly.

'There was a South of slavery and secession – that South is dead. There is a South of union and freedom – that South, thank God, is living, breathing, growing every hour.' These words, delivered from the immortal lips of Benjamin H. Hill, at Tammany Hall in 1866, true then, and truer now, I shall make my text to-night.

Mr President and Gentlemen: Let me express to you my appreciation of the kindness by which I am permitted to address you. I make this abrupt acknowledgment advisedly, for I feel that if, when I raise my provincial voice in this ancient and August presence, I could find courage for no more than the opening sentence, it would be well if, in that sentence, I had met in a rough sense my obligation as a guest, and had perished, so to speak, with courtesy on my lips and grace in my heart. [*Laughter.*] Permitted through your kindness to catch my second wind, let me say that I appreciate the significance of being the first Southerner to speak at this board, which bears the substance, if it surpasses the semblance, of original New England hospitality [*Applause*], and honors a sentiment that in turn honors you, but in which my personality is lost, and the compliment to my people made plain. [*Laughter.*]

I bespeak the utmost stretch of your courtesy to-night. I am not troubled about those from whom I come. You remember the man whose wife sent him to a neighbor with a pitcher of milk, and who, tripping on the top step, fell, with such casual interruptions as the landing afforded, into the basement; and while picking himself up had the pleasure of hearing his wife call out: 'John, did you break the pitcher?'

'No, I didn't,' said John, 'but I be dinged if I don't!' [*Laughter.*] So, while those who call to me from behind may inspire me with energy if not with courage, I ask an indulgent hearing from you. I beg that you will bring your full faith in American fairness and frankness of judgment upon what I shall say. There was an old preacher once who told some boys of the Bible lesson he was going to read in the morning. The boys finding the place, glued together the connecting ages. [*Laughter.*] The next morning he read on the bottom of one page: 'When Noah was one hundred and twenty years old he took unto himself a wife, who was' – then turning the page – 'one hundred and forty cubits long [*Laughter*], forty cubits wide, built of gopher-wood [*Laughter*], and covered with pitch inside and out.' [*Loud and continued laughter.*] He was naturally puzzled at this. He read it again, verified it, and then said: 'My friends, this is the first time I ever met this in the Bible, but I accept it as an evidence of the assertion that we are fearfully and wonderfully made.' [*Immense laughter.*] If I could get you to hold such faith to-night I could proceed cheerfully to the task I otherwise approach with a sense of consecration.

Pardon me one word, Mr President, spoken for the sole purpose of getting into the volumes that go out annually freighted with the rich eloquence of your speakers – the fact that the Cavalier as well as the Puritan was on the continent in its early days, and that he was 'up and able to be about'. [*Laughter.*] I have read your books carefully and I find no mention of that fact, which seems to me an important one for preserving a sort of historical equilibrium if for nothing else.

Let me remind you that the Virginia Cavalier first challenged France on this continent – that Cavalier John Smith gave New England its very name, and was so pleased with the job that he has been handing his own name around ever since – and that while Miles Standish was cutting off men's ears for courting a girl without her parents' consent, and forbade men to kiss their wives on Sunday, the Cavalier was courting everything in sight, and that the Almighty had vouchsafed great increase to the Cavalier colonies, the huts in the wilderness being full as the nests in the woods.

But having incorporated the Cavalier as a fact in your charming little books I shall let him work out his own salvation, as he has always done with engaging gallantry, and we will hold no controversy as to his merits. Why should we? Neither Puritan nor Cavalier long survived as such. The virtues and traditions of both happily still live for the inspiration of their sons and the saving of the old fashion. [*Applause.*] But both Puritan and Cavalier were lost in the storm of the first Revolution; and the American citizen, supplanting both and stronger than either, took possession of the Republic bought by their common blood and fashioned to wisdom, and charged himself with teaching men government and establishing the voice of the people as the voice of God. [*Applause.*]

My friend Dr Talmage has told you that the typical American has yet to come. Let me tell you that he has already come. [*Applause.*] Great types like valuable plants are slow to flower and fruit. But from the union of these colonist Puritans and Cavaliers, from the straightening of their purposes and the crossing of their blood, slow perfecting through a century, came he who stands as the first typical American, the first who comprehended within himself all the strength and gentleness, all the majesty and grace of this Republic – Abraham Lincoln. [*Loud and continued applause.*] He was the sum of Puritan and Cavalier, for in his ardent nature were fused the virtues of both, and in the depths of his great soul the faults of both were lost. [*Renewed applause.*] He was greater than Puritan, greater than Cavalier, in that he was American [*Renewed applause.*] and that in his homely form were first gathered the vast and thrilling forces of his ideal government – charging it with such tremendous meaning and so elevating it above human suffering that martyrdom, though infamously aimed, came as a fitting crown to a life consecrated from the cradle to human liberty. [*Loud and prolonged cheering.*] Let us, each cherishing the traditions and honoring his fathers, build with reverent hands to the type of this simple but sublime life, in which all types are honored; and in our common glory as Americans there will be plenty and to spare for your forefathers and for mine. [*Renewed cheering.*]

In speaking to the toast with which you have honored me, I accept the term, 'The New South', as in no sense disparaging to the Old. Dear to me, sir, is the home of my childhood and the traditions of my people. I would not, if I could, dim the glory they won in peace and war, or by word or deed take aught from the splendor and grace of their civilization – never equaled and, perhaps, never to be equaled in its chivalric strength and grace. There is a New South, not through protest against the Old, but because of new conditions, new adjustments and, if you please, new ideas and aspirations. It is to this that I address myself, and to the consideration of which I hasten lest it become the Old South before I get to it. Age does not endow all things with strength and virtue, nor are all new things to be despised. The shoemaker who put over his door 'John Smith's shop. Founded in 1760', was more than matched by his young rival across the street who hung out this sign: 'Bill Jones. Established 1886. No old stock kept in this shop.'

Dr Talmage has drawn for you, with a master's hand, the picture of your returning armies. He has told you how, in the pomp and circumstance of war, they came back to you, marching with proud and victorious tread, reading their glory in a nation's eyes! Will you bear with me while I tell you of another army that sought its home at the close of the late war – an army that marched home in defeat and not in victory – in pathos and not in splendor, but in glory that equaled yours, and to hearts as loving as ever welcomed heroes home. Let me picture to you the footsore Confederate soldier, as, buttoning up in his faded gray jacket the parole which was to bear testimony to his children of his fidelity and faith, he turned his face southward from Appomattox in April, 1865. Think of him as ragged, half-starved, heavy-hearted, enfeebled by want and wounds; having fought to exhaustion, he surrenders his gun, wrings the hands of his comrades in silence, and lifting his tear-stained and pallid face for the last time to the graves that dot the old Virginia hills, pulls his gray cap over his brow and begins the slow and painful journey. What does he find – let me ask you, who went to your homes eager to find in the welcome you had justly earned, full payment for four years' sacrifice – what does he find when, having followed the battle-stained cross against overwhelming odds, dreading death not half so much as surrender, he reaches the home he left so prosperous and beautiful? He finds his house in ruins, his farm devastated, his slaves free, his stock killed, his barns empty, his trade destroyed, his money worthless; his social system, feudal in its magnificence, swept away; his people without law or legal status, his comrades slain, and the burdens of others heavy on his shoulders. Crushed by defeat, his very traditions are gone; without money, credit, employment, material or training; and, besides all this, confronted with the gravest problem that ever met human intelligence – the establishing of a status for the vast body of his liberated slaves.

What does he do – this hero in gray with a heart of gold?

Does he sit down in sullenness and despair? Not for a day. Surely God, who had stripped him of his prosperity, inspired him in his adversity. As ruin was never before so overwhelming, never was restoration swifter. The soldier stepped from the trenches into the furrow; horses that had charged Federal guns march before the plow, and fields that ran red with human blood in April were green with the harvest in June; women reared in luxury cut up their dresses and made breeches for their husbands, and, with a patience and heroism that fit women always as a garment, gave their hands to work. There was little bitterness in all this. Cheerfulness and frankness prevailed. 'Bill Arp' struck the keynote when he said: 'Well, I killed as many of them as they did of me, and now I am going to work.' [*Laughter and applause.*] Or the soldier returning home after defeat and roasting some corn on the roadside, who made the remark to his comrades: 'You may leave the South if you want to, but I am going to Sandersville, kiss my wife and raise a crop, and if the Yankees fool with me any more I will whip 'em again.' [*Renewed applause.*] I want to say to General Sherman – who is considered an able man in our hearts, though some people think he is a kind of careless man about fire – that from the ashes he left us in 1864 we have raised a brave and beautiful city; that somehow or other we have caught the sunshine in the bricks and mortar of our homes, and have builded therein not one ignoble prejudice or memory. [*Applause.*]

But in all this what have we accomplished? What is the sum of our work? We have found out that in the general summary the free Negro counts more than he did as a slave. We have planted the schoolhouse on the hilltop and made it free to white and black. We have sowed towns and cities in the place of theories and put business above politics. [*Applause.*] We have challenged your spinners in Massachusetts and your iron-makers in Pennsylvania. We have learned that the $400,000,000 annually received from our cotton crop will make us rich, when the supplies that make it are home-raised. We have reduced the commercial rate of interest from twenty-four to six per cent, and are floating four per cent bonds. We have learned that one Northern immigrant is worth fifty foreigners, and have smoothed the path to southward, wiped out the place where Mason and Dixon's line used to be, and hung our latch-string out to you and yours. [*Prolonged cheers.*] We have reached the point that marks perfect harmony in every household, when the husband confesses that the pies which his wife cooks are as good as those his mother used to bake; and we admit that the sun shines as brightly and the moon as softly as it did 'before the war'. [*Laughter.*] We have established thrift in city and country. We have fallen in love with work. We have restored comfort to homes from which culture and elegance never departed. We have let economy take root and spread among us as rank as the crabgrass which sprang from Sherman's cavalry camps, until we are ready to lay odds on the Georgia Yankee, as he manufactures relics of the battlefield in a one-story shanty and squeezes pure olive oil out of his cotton-seed, against any downeaster that ever swapped wooden nutmegs for flannel sausages in the valleys of Vermont. [*Loud and continuous laughter.*] Above all, we know that we have achieved in these 'piping times of peace' a fuller independence for the South than that which our fathers sought to win in the forum by their eloquence or compel on the field by their swords. [*Loud applause.*]

It is a rare privilege, sir, to have had part, however humble, in this work. Never was nobler duty confided to human hands than the uplifting and upbuilding of the prostrate and bleeding South, misguided perhaps, but beautiful in her suffering, and honest, brave and generous always. [*Applause.*] In the record of her social, industrial, and political institutions we await with confidence the verdict of the world.

But what of the Negro? Have we solved the problem he presents or progressed in honor and equity towards the solution? Let the record speak to the point. No section shows a more prosperous laboring population than the Negroes of the South; none in fuller sympathy with the employing and land-owning class. He shares our school fund, has the fullest protection of our laws and the friendship of our people. Self-interest, as well as honor, demand that he should have this. Our future, our very existence depend upon our working out this problem in full and exact justice. We understand that when Lincoln signed the Emancipation Proclamation, your victory was assured; for he then committed you to the cause of human liberty, against which the arms of man cannot prevail [*Applause*]; while those of our statesmen who trusted to make slavery the cornerstone of the Confederacy doomed us to defeat as far as they could, committing us to a cause that reason could not defend or the sword maintain in the sight of advancing civilization. [*Renewed applause.*] Had Mr Toombs said, which he did not say, that he would call the roll of his slaves at the foot of Bunker Hill, he would have been foolish, for he might have known that whenever slavery became entangled in war it must perish, and that the chattel in human flesh ended forever in New England when your fathers – not to be blamed for parting with what didn't pay – sold their slaves to our fathers – not to be praised for knowing a paying thing when they saw it. [*Laughter.*]

The relations of the Southern people with the Negro are close and cordial. We remember with what fidelity for four years he guarded our defenceless women and children, whose husbands and fathers were fighting against his freedom. To his eternal credit be it said that whenever he struck a blow for his own liberty he fought in open battle, and when at last he raised his black and humble hands that the shackles might be struck off, those hands were innocent of wrong against his helpless charges, and worthy to be taken in loving grasp by every man who honors loyalty and devotion. [*Applause.*] Ruffians have maltreated him, rascals have misled him, philanthropists established a bank for him, but the South, with the North, protects against injustice to this simple and sincere people. To liberty and enfranchisement is as far as law can carry the Negro. The rest must be left to conscience and common sense. It should be left to those among whom his lot is cast, with whom he is indissolubly connected and whose prosperity depends upon their possessing his intelligent sympathy and confidence. Faith has been kept with him in spite of calumnious assertions to the contrary by those who assume to speak for us or by frank opponents. Faith will be kept with him in the future, if the South holds her reason and integrity. [*Applause.*]

But have we kept faith with you? In the fullest sense, yes. When Lee surrendered – I don't say when Johnston surrendered, because I understand he still alludes to the time when he met General Sherman last as the time when he 'determined to abandon any further prosecution of the struggle' – when Lee surrendered, I say, and Johnston quit, the South became, and has since been, loyal to this Union. We fought hard enough to know that we were whipped, and in perfect frankness accepted as final the arbitrament of the sword to which we had appealed. The South found her jewel in the toad's head of defeat. The shackles that had held her in narrow limitations fell forever when the shackles of the Negro slave were broken. [*Applause.*] Under the old regime the Negroes were slaves to the South, the South was a slave to the system. The old plantation, with its simple police regulation and its feudal habit, was the only type possible under slavery. Thus we gathered in the hands of a splendid and chivalric oligarchy the substance that should have been diffused among the people, as the rich blood, under certain artificial conditions, is gathered at the heart, filling that with affluent rapture, but leaving the body chill and colorless. [*Applause.*]

The Old South rested everything on slavery and agriculture, unconscious that these could neither give nor maintain healthy growth. The New South presents a perfect democracy, the oligarchs leading in the popular movements social system compact and closely knitted, less splendid on the surface but stronger at the core – a hundred farms for every plantation, fifty homes for every palace, and a diversified industry that meets the complex needs of this complex age.

The New South is enamored of her new work. Her soul is stirred with the breath of a new life. The light of a grander day is falling fair on her face. She is thrilling with the consciousness of growing power and prosperity. As she stands upright, full-statured and equal among the people of the earth, breathing the keen air and looking out upon the expanding horizon, she understands that her emancipation came because in the inscrutable wisdom of God her honest purpose was crossed and her brave armies were beaten. [*Applause.*]

This is said in no spirit of time-serving or apology. The South has nothing for which to apologize. She believes that the late struggle between the States was war and not rebellion, revolution and not conspiracy, and that her convictions were as honest as yours. I should be unjust to the dauntless spirit of the South and to my own convictions if I did not make this plain in this presence. The South has nothing to take back. In my native town of Athens is a monument that crowns its central hills – a plain, white shaft. Deep cut into its shining side is a name dear to me above the names of men, that of a brave and simple man who died in brave and simple faith. Not for all the glories of New England – from Plymouth Rock all the way – would I exchange the heritage he left me in his soldier's death. To the foot of that shaft I shall send my children's children to reverence him who ennobled their name with his heroic blood. But, sir, speaking from the shadow of that memory, which I honor as I do nothing else on earth, I say that the cause in which he suffered and for which he gave his life was adjudged by higher and fuller wisdom than his or mine, and I am glad that the omniscient God held the balance of battle in His Almighty hand, and that human slavery was swept forever from American soil – the American Union saved from the wreck of war. [*Loud applause.*]

This message, Mr President, comes to you from consecrated ground. Every foot of the soil about the city in which I live is sacred as a battleground of the Republic. Every hill that invests it is hallowed to you by the blood of your brothers, who died for your victory, and doubly hallowed to us by the blood of those who died hopeless, but undaunted, in defeat – sacred soil to all of us rich with memories that make us purer and stronger and better, silent but stanch witnesses in its red desolation of the matchless valor of American hearts and the deathless glory of American arms – speaking an eloquent witness in its white peace and prosperity to the indissoluble union of American States and the imperishable brotherhood of the American people. [*Immense cheering.*]

Now, what answer has New England to this message? Will she permit the prejudices of war to remain in the hearts of the conquerors, when it has died in the hearts of the conquered? [*Cries of 'No! No!'*] Will she transmit this prejudice to the next generation, that in their hearts, which never felt the generous ardor of conflict, it may perpetuate itself? [*'No! No!'*] Will she withhold, save in strained courtesy, the hand which straight from his soldier's heart Grant offered to Lee at Appomattox? Will she make the vision of a restored and happy people, which gathered above the couch of your dying captain, filling his heart with grace, touching his lips with praise and glorifying his path to the grave; will she make this vision on which the last sight of his expiring soul breathed a benediction, a cheat and a delusion? [*Tumultuous cheering and shouts of 'No! No!'*] If she does, the South, never abject in asking for comradeship, must accept with dignity its refusal; but if she does not; if she accepts in frankness and sincerity this message of goodwill and friendship, then will the prophecy of Webster, delivered in this very Society forty years ago amid tremendous applause, be verified in its fullest and final sense, when he said: 'Standing hand to hand and clasping hands, we should remain united as we have been for sixty years, citizens of the same country, members of the same government, united, all united now and united forever.' There have been difficulties, contentions, and controversies, but I tell you that in my judgment:

> Those opposed eyes,
> Which like the meteors of a troubled heaven,
> All of one nature, of one substance bred,
> Did lately meet in th'intestine shock,
> Shall now, in mutual well-beseeming ranks,
> March all one way.

[*Prolonged applause.*]

Josephine E. Butler:
1888

Appeal to the Women of America

Josephine E. Butler (1828–1906) addressed this appeal to the International Council of Women.

Dear ladies: Being prevented by domestic circumstances from attending your assemblies personally, I am glad to entrust a few words of greeting to my dear and honored friend, Mrs Steward, who has consented to cross the Atlantic, at my earnest request, as a delegate from our Ladies' National Association. That Association was formed in the winter of 1869, having for its definite aim the obtaining of the repeal of the Acts of Parliament of 1866–9 for the State regulation of vice; or, in other words, for the provisioning of the army and navy (not in Great Britain alone, but in our Indian Empire and all our colonies) with selected and superintended and healthy women. A celibate soldiery, it was said by our heathen legislators of that day, required such a provision as urgently and as regularly as they required daily rations.

Now, I have no reason to suppose that this special subject (always a mournful and repellant one) will be formally brought forward in your convention, although the kindred and closely allied subject of personal and social purity will surely be so. It would, however, be impossible for me either to appear at or write to your convention in the aim of furnishing a contribution to your deliberations except in connection with my own life-work, and the deep convictions which instigated that life-work, and which have become even more and more profound as I continued in it.

The Committee of our Ladies' National Association, therefore, strongly desired that a delegate should be selected from our midst who had been associated in that work from an early period; and such an one is Mrs Steward, who has been an indefatigable worker, not only in England, but in Belgium, in pursuit of and for the saving of the English girl victims who were bought, stolen and destroyed under this diabolical system of State-protected vice in that country. There is now a crowd of younger workers who are bravely preaching the purity crusade and doing excellent vigilance work; but there are few of the veterans left who inaugurated in 1869 the fierce contest with our Government, the Houses of Lords and Commons, the medical boards, the press, and the upper classes generally, in order to gain the abolition of the vice-protecting laws, and to assert the equality of the moral law for the two sexes, as well as the dignity and sacredness of womanhood. Among those veteran workers were included the names of Florence Nightingale, Harriet Martineau, Mary Somerville, Mary Carpenter, and others. Some are gone to their rest, others are aged and worn, and waiting for their call home. Those who remain hold together and work together still, bound to each other by strong affection, and by the memory of past suffering and conflict shared together. Of this group Mrs Steward is one, and I commend her to your sisterly kindness and hospitality.

It may not be out of place here, in order to set forth the motives which drove us to devote ourselves to this crusade before all others, to quote some words of mine which were drawn from me at a great meeting in Leeds in July, 1870. Some of us had been long working for the 'Higher Education of Women'. A council for that end had been formed, embracing members from all the northern parts of England.

I was for three years the President of that Council. But in 1870, feeling impelled to resign the Presidentship, I thought it right to give my reasons for doing so. I venture to give words spoken on that occasion:

The President said 'there were gentlemen present who would give some account of the educational movement now going on in our country in its different branches'. She proposed to give a short sketch of the educational efforts now being made on the Continent under the auspices of the International Association of Women. They had arrived at a period of the world's history when the injunction, 'Look not every one to his own things, but to the things of others also,' had become applicable to nations as well as to individuals. In fact, England could not safely live any longer for itself only, nor could any country; and she thought there was an exclusiveness peculiar to our insular character as a nation, which required correction before we could hope to give and receive all the benefit we might, and to get rid of war and other disturbances of progress and happiness.

The objects of this International Association were the amelioration of the social position of women, and their moral and intellectual elevation through education, and the granting of the various rights which they claimed.

Mrs Butler detailed the practical steps which have been taken in the direction of this education, both at home and in Switzerland, Italy, Germany, Russia, France, and Constantinople; and in proceeding to consider the relation of this educational movement to a more general and a very great social movement, including innumerable interests, a movement which she trusted would result sooner or later in a purer and juster state of society, she said:

> I proposed at our meeting yesterday to resign the office of President of this Council as soon as may be convenient to this Council to allow me to do so. It is not

because I am not deeply interested in the cause which this Council represents. I may say I am more deeply interested than ever, for I see in the education of women one of the most necessary means of freeing poorer women from the awful slavery of which I have seen so much lately; nor do I undervalue the higher culture of the individual as a means towards the attainment of the highest personal happiness. The strangely Providential guidance of all our schemes has lately been deeply impressed on my mind.

We started our educational schemes, I believe, in an honest and humble spirit, and they appeared to us the readiest path towards aiding our fellow-women, the distressed, the needy, and the wronged; and I believe our labor has not been in vain. But in this, as in all our work on earth, we need further enlightening and teaching. Looking back on my own experience of the past year, it appears to me as if God in his goodness had said to me, 'I approve your motive and your work; but you are trying to lay on the topmost stones while there is an earthquake shaking your foundations. You must first descend to the lowest depths before you can safely build up,' and then He showed us a plague spot. He showed us a deadly poison working through the wholesale, systematic and now legalized degradation of women to the service of vice. He showed us the ready elements for a speedy destruction of society, which the highest education itself would not be able to stem. Not that our work in the cause of education has in any sense been a failure; far from it; but we need a still larger infusion into these noble schemes for educating the masses, of the spirit of self-sacrifice, even of martyrdom. We need to have our hearts more deeply penetrated with pity, and to be more resolutely bent on making all our practical efforts tend to the revival of justice and of a pure and equal moral standard and equal laws.

While, therefore, I continue to regard the cause of education as a most sacred cause, I come to the present meeting with a saddened heart, and I only propose to relinquish the office I now hold because I feel that God has called me to a more painful one. All members have not the same office; all are not called to descend to the depths of woe, to clear out moral sewers and to cast in their lot among wretched slave gangs in order to help the slaves to carry the weight of their chains if not to break them away. This work, I think, is mine, but there is other work not less holy, and which aims not less directly at a future emancipation; so while I feel all the deeper gratitude to you, my fellow-workers in this Council for the work you are doing in the cause of humanity, I am obliged to confess to you that, for my own part, I fear I may not in future be able to give the needful time to this work which it demands. I wish to leave it in abler and freer hands. It has my deepest sympathy. It points to one of the most important of all the means by which we hope to undo the heavy burdens and let the oppressed go free and inaugurate a purer and sounder national life. To keep pace, however, with this portion of the great work, one requires to have the head and heart free, and that cannot be the case with one who is called to deal with the most miserable, to walk side by side, hand in hand, with the outcast, the victim of our social sins, whose names one scarcely dares to name in refined society. I am full of hope for the education cause,

> and for the anti-slavery cause, in which we are engaged. Nevertheless my very soul grows faint before the facts of 1870, and though that faintness of soul may complete one's fitness to be a fellow-sufferer with the slave, it does not increase one's capacity for a work which requires intellectual energy.

It is impossible, and would not be right, that I should trouble you with a report of the arduous work which our Women's Abolitionist Society accomplished between 1869 and 1874. Suffice it to say that we shook the Government and aroused the whole nation. Mountains were removed by the energy imparted by a gigantic faith.

In 1874 a 'new departure' was inaugurated. The battle was carried across the channel to France – where, under the First Napoleon, this abominable and impure tyranny had first been instituted in the end of the eighteenth century – to Italy, to Switzerland, to Germany, and to the Netherlands. It afterwards spread to Spain, Holland, Denmark, Austria, Hungary, and Sweden and Norway. We now have friends in Russia, but no association is yet formed there. In the first report of the Continental work the movement was described by our Financial Secretary, Professor Stuart MP:

> It was indeed a wise intuition which led the women of England to carry into its original strongholds the campaign against the system of regulated vice, against whose encroachments we are contending in this country. That move will benefit the agitation for repeal in this country not only by the vast strengthening and encouragement which the knowledge of the sympathy and co-operation of persons of all tongues and

> countries has brought to so many of our workers here, but also because it has opened up an attack upon the whole vicious system in its rear; and, drying up the sources and roots, so to speak, will cause the system to fall more easily in this country, and not least because it has called forth in many countries the co-operation of new workers who may, confident of success, and with united force and power, carry on the work against profligacy itself throughout a Christendom united for that end.
>
> Not only have we seen, during the year of work just concluded, refuges for the fallen established throughout many cities of Europe, and men and women of many languages joining together to call for and work for the abolition of regulated prostitution, and to aim through that at the abolition finally of prostitution itself; but we have seen whole cities shaken as it were with the wind of a new revival, recognizing the crime that they have committed before God in regulating and licensing the destruction of His image; we have seen through the length and breadth of nations societies formed, actively working in a cause which had before laid dormant; and we have seen the whole great nation of Italy, called as it were by the voice of God through His poor and weak servants, recognizing that virtue and purity alone can be the basis of future greatness.

In a brief time we had won the public adhesion to our cause of many of the most distinguished persons on the Continent, among whom we counted Joseph Mazzini and Garibaldi, in Italy; Jules Favre, Jules Simon, and Victor Hugo, in France;

the Count Agenor de Gasparin and the Countess de Gasparin, of Geneva; Baron de Bunsen and Count Ungern Sternberg, in Germany; M. Emile de Laveleye, the well known writer and economist, of Belgium, and many others. But it is not so much to the adhesion of the great men that we hold as to the active concurrence of the thousands of women on the Continent of Europe who have been awakened on this question, and who have formed numerous and ever-increasing associations for working out our aims, more especially in Switzerland, Holland, France, and the Scandinavian Peninsula.

Our Continental Secretary, M. Humbert, writing on this subject after 14 years' experience, says: 'Happy are those nations in which women themselves have taken the initiative in this great movement, for in such cases the movement will never die; whereas in countries where the work is left entirely to men, although some reforms may be achieved, the movement is fitful and never possesses the same life.'

This brings to me the most recent expansion of our work in the Colonies and in India. It is in allusion to this new expansion that M. Humbert writes the letter just quoted. He continues: 'How are we to proceed successfully for the emancipation of women from the hateful thraldom imposed on them by the civilization of conquering races (the thraldom of compulsory and State regulated prostitution) among Buddhists, Brahmins, Mahometans, or Pagans where the fate of women in this world, at least, depends absolutely on the will of man, their master? This is a difficult question to answer. We see occasionally a spark kindled amongst those nations, but the light is short lived, and it continually requires to be rekindled.' In spite of these difficulties, however, we are pushing forward our work in Egypt and in the French Colonies of North Africa, as well as in other directions.

We believe that the question is coming rapidly to the front in India. The present mission of Mr Dyer to India is producing an awakening there that will be productive of very decided results from a parliamentary and governmental point of view. We as women are more especially concerned with the awakening of the women of India on the subject of this imperially imposed degradation of their race and to kindred questions vitally concerning womanhood. On this side we are full of hope. It is affecting to see the petitions which are now in the hands of some of our Members of Parliament this session. These petitions are from Anglo-Indian and native women, and many are signed in Hindoo characters. The prayer of the petition is for relief from this degrading law. We receive also privately very touching appeals from Indian ladies, and to these our Association responds with eager sympathy. The following quotation from one of the replies sent from the Leeds branch of our Abolition Society will show you the spirit with which the women of the world are communicating with each other on this subject:

> Do let us assure you, dear Indian friends, that we have found that so long as our motives are pure, no evil knowledge can hurt us. We have seen, on the contrary, that work of this kind undertaken in the spirit of consecration (and in no other spirit can anyone endure to continue the work) may lead to a higher and purer knowledge of life and the human heart. That many have found (as all must do sooner or later) that intellectual force alone cannot guard against the horror of this evil and have thus been driven to seek more spiritual means of warfare and so have passed into a higher life.
>
> Do be sure, dear friends, that whatever your enemies may say of you, in the invisible Kingdom of Righteousness

> you can but be purified by this labor of love.
>
> And when you most greatly doubt success, when the power and will of the enemy seem indeed to be too powerful for the feebleness of your hands, we feel sure you will find, as we have found, that from quarters least expected, from the darkest parts of your sky, from the weakest parts of your army, help and light and strength will come to you. Our victories do not often come to us in the manner or at the time that we expect, any more than do our defeats.
>
> We cannot direct the whole order of the conduct of life; we can only fight in our own place, obeying the nearest word that reaches us, knowing that no army can be beaten of which each individual soldier refuses to accept defeat.

Thus the women of the world are reaching out their hands to each other, and banding themselves together so that when councils, rulers, and lords of science endeavor by decrees or by social tyranny to give a continuance to the most degrading institution which has defiled the history of the human race, they will have the power to say: 'You shall not slay us or our sisters.' They have struck a note for which the ages have been waiting, and which even the Church itself in its organized ecclesiastical forms has never yet intoned.

There is a point on which I have sometimes thought (possibly without reason) that American women feel less strongly than we do. I allude to the physical treatment forcibly imposed, the personal outrage on women which lies at the root of the practical working of the whole system of the state regulation of vice. You have happily not had in America the practical experience which we, in the Old World, have had of the degrading effects of this outrage. It is the final and most complete expression of the foul idea of woman as a chattel, a slave, an instrument, a mere vessel, officially dedicated to the vilest uses.

At our last International Congress, held at Lausanne in September, 1887, some of our less-instructed followers had been occupying too much of our time in an attempt to defend up to a certain point the State's action in tyrannizing over women. Thinking that the moment had come for a decided word on the part of women themselves, I gave utterance to the thoughts which were in my mind, and in doing so I proclaimed in the name of all women that whatever subtlety of argument might weigh with certain doctors, legislators, etc., this was nothing to us, and we women solemnly declared again the principle of our own dignity, and our determination never to sanction the enslavement of any woman by the outrage perpetrated under this system. At the close of my few words Mme. de Morsier, of Paris, rose, and with uplifted hand asked earnestly that every woman present who agreed with and re-echoed from the depths of her heart the words of Mrs Butler should stand up. The large hall was crowded with women as well as men. The men continued sitting, but every woman rose, and with right hand uplifted high, followed the action of Mme. de Morsier and Mme. de Gingins, responding to the solemn words uttered by her: 'In the name of God, amen.' There was a significant silence of a few moments. Some of the gentlemen were surprised, most were deeply moved, and to every woman present, I feel convinced, it was a ratification of our principles never to be forgotten. The sound of it went far abroad beyond the mere hall of meeting itself.

I mention this incident merely as an illustration of the spirit of our women in their jealous guardianship of the sacredness of womanhood even in the persons of the most degraded of their sisters. I myself believe this spirit to be thoroughly in accord with that of our Master, Christ.

As an inevitable and necessary accompaniment of the establishment of licensed houses of ill-fame under Government patronage all over the world there exists, as you all know, the most extensive slave traffic in the interest of vice. This fact has become so fully acknowledged during the last few years as to have given rise to that admirable and much-needed Society, the 'International Association of Friends of Girls', originating in Switzerland and now spreading all over and far beyond Europe. That Society has been greatly strengthened in England since the Congress held in London in 1886; and this fact is brought home to us by the reassuring sight at various railway stations and landing places of the warnings and friendly placards so diligently distributed and put up by the English branch of the Society, informing all girls and women of where they may find friends, and of what dangers they must beware. Our Federation has collected carefully many facts and statistics concerning this worldwide slave traffic.

People in Europe speak with indignation of the traffic in negroes. It would be just as well if they would open their eyes to what is going on much nearer throughout the whole of Europe, especially in Germany and Austria, where the exportation of white slaves is carried on on a large scale. A terrible picture is presented to us of the enforced movement to and fro upon the face of the earth of these youthful victims of human cruelty. Numbers are embarked at Hamburg, whose destination is South America, Bahia, and Rio de Janeiro. The greater number are probably engaged for Montevideo and Buenos Ayres; others are sent by the Straits of Magellan to Valparaiso. Other cargoes are sent to North America, some being forwarded to England, others direct. The competition which the traders meet with when they land sometimes constrains them to go further ahead; they are found, therefore, descending the Mississippi with their cargoes to New Orleans and Texas. Others are taken on to California.

In the market of California they are sorted and thence taken to provision the different localities on the coast as far as Panama. Others are sent from the New Orleans market to Cuba, the Antilles, and Mexico. Others are taken from Bohemia, Germany, and Switzerland across the Alps to Italy, and thence further south to Alexandria and Suez, and eastward to Bombay, Calcutta, Singapore, Hong Kong, and Shanghai. The Russian official houses of vice draw their slaves in a great measure from Eastern Prussia, Pomerania, and Poland. The most important Russian station is Riga; it is there that the traders of St Petersburg and Moscow sort and get ready their cargoes for Nijni-Novgorod, and from this latter place cargoes are sent on to the more distant towns of Siberia. At Tschita a young German was found who had been sold and resold in this manner.

You in America are happily free from the State regulation of vice; but undoubtedly there is an extensive traffic in white slaves in your midst, and a constant importation of poor foreigners to your shores who are destined to moral and spiritual destruction. I trust you will, from your Congress, put out strong hands for the abolition of this traffic.

It may be that I am writing to some who have been accustomed to think of the poor outcasts of society as beings different from others, in some way tainted from their birth, creatures apart, without the tenderness and capacities for good possessed by your own cherished daughters.

You may have imagined them to be for the most part reckless and willful sinners, or, if in the first instance betrayed or forced into sin, now at least so utterly destroyed and corrupted as to have become something unmentionable in polite society. Now, all who have had a practical acquaintance with the lives of poor and tempted women, know how mistaken is such a judgment, how cruelly false in most cases. But granting for the moment that women who have fallen from virtue have become so degraded as to be repulsive or uninteresting to you, what have you to say concerning outraged children? And thousands of these are but children in age and in knowledge.

Who will dare to say that any child is determinedly, willfully wicked and degraded; that any child in the world is further from God's kingdom than we grown-up people are, however virtuous we may be? Nay, but 'of such is the Kingdom of Heaven.' One who never errs has said it. We are not told that He selected an exceptionally pure and holy child when He set a little child in the midst of the multitude and said that, except we become as such a little child we shall in nowise enter the Kingdom of Heaven. Verily, 'their angels do always behold the face of my Father which is in Heaven, and woe be to that man, to that nation, to those mothers of men and of nations, who, seeing that little child fallen among thieves, robbed, wounded, murdered, dying, shall calmly pass by on the other side!' A day is coming in which it will not avail any of us to say we knew it not; for now we know it. The means of knowing it, and the means of helping to redress this wrong, are within our reach, at our very hand. I cherish the hope and the belief that the time is at hand when all women who are indeed at heart mothers and worthy of the name, will give up the chilling reserve which seems too much like acquiescence in evil, and will come forward to the rescue, not only for the sake of the innocent and betrayed, but for the sake of their sons and of our national life.

This letter is sent forth with earnest prayer that while pardoning the imperfections of my poor appeal, God would make use of it to fan the holy and purifying fire which I feel sure is already kindled in your hearts. When I kneel in my chamber to plead for the deliverance of these little ones for whom Christ died, I seem to see the childish faces gathering in crowds around me, filling the space on every side – the faces of the slaughtered dead as well as of the living. These victims, voiceless and unable to plead their own cause, seem to make their ceaseless and mute appeal from their scattered, unknown graves and from out those dark habitations of cruelty where they are now helplessly imprisoned.

But their weeping has been heard in Heaven, and judgment is at hand. Of their destroyers it may be said: 'They murder the fatherless; yet they say the Lord shall not see it.' Of you, O friends, let it be said, and let the Saviour Himself speak the words 'Inasmuch as ye have done it unto one of the least of these, ye have done it to me.'

I am yours in the service of God and of humanity.

Josephine E. Butler

PART V

The Twentieth Century

Emmeline Pankhurst:

24 March 1908

'If women had the vote'

Emmeline Pankhurst led the British suffragettes and only resorted to militant campaigning for the vote for women after having her views constantly rejected. She made this speech at the Portman Rooms in London in March 1908. Later that year she was arrested outside the House of Commons and was imprisoned for three months. British women won the right to vote in 1918, ten years before Pankhurst's death.

Men politicians are in the habit of talking to women as if there were no that affect women. 'The fact is,' they say, 'the home is the place for women. Their interests are the rearing and training of children. These are the things that interest women. Politics have nothing to do with these things, and therefore politics do not concern women.' Yet the laws decide how women are to live in marriage, how their children are to be trained and educated, and what the future of their children is to be. All that is decided by Act of Parliament. Let us take a few of laws, and see what there is to say about them from the women's point of view.

First of all, let us take the marriage laws. They are made by men for women. Let us consider whether they are equal, whether they are just, whether they are wise. What security of maintenance has the married woman? Many a married woman having given up her economic independence in order to marry, how is she compensated for that loss? What security does she get in that marriage for which she gave up economic independence? Take the case of a woman who has been earning a good income. She is told that she ought to give up her employment when she becomes a wife and a mother. What does she get in return? All that a married man is obliged by law to do for his wife is to provide for her shelter of some kind, food of some kind, and clothing of some kind. It is left to his good pleasure to decide what the shelter shall be, what the food shall be, what the clothing shall be. It is left to him to decide what money shall be spent on the home, and how it shall be spent; the wife has no voice legally in deciding any of these things. She has no legal claim upon any definite portion of his income. If he is a good man, a conscientious man, he does the right thing. If he is not, if he chooses almost to starve his wife, she has no remedy. What he thinks sufficient is what she has to be content with.

I quite agree, in all these illustrations, that the majority of men are considerably better than the law compels them to be, so the majority of women do not suffer as much as they might suffer if men were all as bad as they might be, but since there are some bad men, some unjust men, don't you agree with me that the law ought to be altered so that those men could be dealt with? ...

Now let us look at [the woman's] position if she had been very unfortunate in marriage, so unfortunate as to get a bad husband, an immoral husband, a vicious husband, a husband unfit to be the father of little children. We turn to the Divine Court. How is she to get rid of such a man? If a man has got married to a bad wife, and he wants to be rid of her, he has but to prove against her one act of infidelity. But if a woman who is married to a vicious husband wants to get rid of him, not one act nor a thousand acts of infidelity entitle her to a divorce; she must prove either bigamy, desertion, or gross cruelty, in addition to immorality before she can get rid of that man.

Let us consider her position as a mother. We have repeated this so often at our meetings that I think the echo of what we have said must have reached many. By English law no married woman exists as the mother of the child she brings into the world. In the eyes of the law she is not the parent of her child. The child, according to our marriage laws, has only one parent, who can decide the future of the child, who can decide where it shall live, how it shall live, how much shall be spent upon it, how it shall be educated, and what religion it shall profess. That parent is the father.

These are examples of some of the laws that men have made, laws that concern women. I ask you, if women had had the vote, should we had such laws? If women had had the vote, as men has the vote, we should have had equal laws. We should have had equal laws for divorce, and the law would have said that as Nature has given to children two parents, so the law should recognize that they have two parents.

I have spoken to you about the position of the married women who does not exist legally as a parent, the parent of her own child. In marriage, children have one parent. Out of marriage children have also one parent. That parent is the mother – the unfortunate mother. She alone is responsible for the future of her child; she alone is punished if her child is neglected and suffers from neglect. But let me give you one illustration. I was in Herefordshire during the by-election. While I was there, an unmarried mother was brought before the bench of magistrates charged with having neglected her illegitimate child. She was a domestic servant, and had put the child out to nurse. The magistrates – there were colonels and landowners on that bench – did not ask what wages the mother got; they did not ask who the father was or whether he contributed to the support of the child. They sent that woman to prison for three months for having neglected her child. I ask you women here tonight, if women had had some share in the making of the laws, don't you think they would have found a way of making all fathers of such children equally responsible with the mothers for the welfare of those children?

Mahatma Gandhi:

23 March 1922

'Non-cooperation with evil is as much a duty as is cooperation with good'

Gandhi introduced his programme of non-violent non-cooperation (Satyagraha) at the Indian National Congress in 1920 and travelled the length and breadth of India promoting it. He was arrested in 1922 and accused of sedition in some articles he had written in his magazine Youth India. The following extract is taken from Gandhi's trial at Ahmadabad, at which he was sentenced to six years' imprisonment.

Non-violence is the first article of my faith. It is the last article of my faith. But I had to make my choice. I had either to submit to a system which I considered had done an irreparable harm to my country or incur the risk of the mad fury of my people bursting forth when they understood the truth from my lips. I know that my people have sometimes gone mad. I am deeply sorry for it; and I am therefore, here, to submit not a light penalty but to the highest penalty. I do not ask for mercy. I do not plead any extenuating act. I am here, therefore, to invite and submit to the highest penalty that can be inflicted upon me for what in law is a deliberate crime and what appears to me to be the highest duty of a citizen. The only course open to you, Mr Judge, is, as I am just going to say in my statement, either to resign your post or inflict on me the severest penalty if you believe that the system and law you are assisting to administer are good for the people. But by the time I have finished with my statement you will, perhaps, have a glimpse of what is raging within my breast to run this maddest risk which a sane man can run.

have emasculated the people and induced in them the habit of simulation. This awful habit had added to the ignorance and the self-deception of the administrators. Section 124-A under which I am happily charged is perhaps the prince among the political sections of the Indian Penal Code designed to suppress the liberty of the citizen. Affection cannot be manufactured or regulated by law. If one has no affection for a person or thing one should be free to give the fullest expression of his disaffection so long as he does not contemplate, promote or incite to violence. But the section under which Mr Banker and I are charged is one under which mere promotion of disaffection is a crime. I have studied some of the cases tried under it, and I know that some of the most loved of India's patriots have been convicted under it. I consider it a privilege, therefore, to be charged under it. I have endeavoured to give in their briefest outline the reasons for my disaffection. I have no personal ill-will against any single administrator, much less can I have any disaffection towards the King's person. But I hold it to be a virtue to be disaffected towards a government which in its totality has done more harm to India than any previous system. India is less manly under the British rule than she ever was before. Holding such a belief, I consider it to be a sign to have affection for the system. And it has been a precious privilege for me to be able to write what I have in the various articles tendered in evidence against me.

In fact I believe that I have rendered a service to India and England by showing in non-cooperation the way out of the unnatural state in which both are living. In my humble opinion, non-cooperation with evil is as much a duty as is cooperation with good. But in the past, non-cooperation has been deliberately expressed in violence to the evildoer. I am endeavouring to show to my countrymen that violent non-cooperation only multiplies evil and that as evil can only be sustained by violence, withdrawal of support of evil requires complete abstention from violence. Non-violence implies voluntary submission to the penalty for non-cooperation with evil. I am here, therefore, to invite and submit cheerfully to the highest penalty that can be inflicted upon me for what in law is deliberate crime and what appears to me to be the highest duty of a citizen. The only course open to you, the Judge and the Assessors, is either to resign your posts and thus dissociate yourselves from evil if you feel that the law you are called upon to administer is an evil and that in reality I am innocent, or to inflict on me the severest penalty if you believe that the system and the law you are assisting to administer are good for the people of this country and that my activity is therefore injurious to the public weal.

Adolf Hitler:

30 January 1939

'The annihilation of the Jewish race in Europe!'

In this speech to the German Reichstag (Parliament) commemorating the sixth anniversary of his coming to power, Hitler publicly threatened the Jews.

In the course of my life I have very often been a prophet, and have usually been ridiculed for it. During the time of my struggle for power it was in the first instance the Jewish race which only received my prophecies with laughter when I said that I would one day take over the leadership of the State, and with it that of the whole nation, and that I would then among other things settle the Jewish problem. Their laughter was uproarious, but I think that for some time now they have been laughing on the other side of their face. Today I will once more be a prophet:

if the international Jewish financiers in and outside Europe should succeed in plunging the nations once more into a world war, then the result will not be the Bolshevization of the earth, and thus the victory of Jewry, but the annihilation of the Jewish race in Europe!

Winston Churchill:

4 June 1940

'We shall defend our island whatever the cost'

This speech was made by the British Prime Minister in the House of Commons just after the evacuation from Dunkirk – one of the most depressing moments in the Second World War. Churchill had to tell the hushed House that 30,000 British troops were either killed, wounded or missing. Nevertheless, he encouraged the resolve of the British people and made an eloquent appeal for total support from America.

From the moment when the defences at Sedan on the Meuse were broken at the end of the second week in May only a rapid retreat to Amiens and the south could have saved the British-French armies who had entered Belgium at the appeal of the Belgian King.

This strategic fact was not immediately realized. The French High Command hoped it would be able to close the gap. The armies of the north were under their orders. Moreover, a retirement of that kind would have involved almost certainly the destruction of a fine Belgian Army of twenty divisions and abandonment of the whole of Belgium.

Therefore, when the force and scope of the German penetration was realized and when the new French Generalissimo,

General [Maxime] Weygand, assumed command in place of General Gamelin, an effort was made by the French and British Armies in Belgium to keep holding the right hand of the Belgians and give their own right hand to the newly created French Army which was to advance across the Somme in great strength.

However, the German eruption swept like a sharp scythe south of Amiens to the rear of the armies in the north – eight or nine armoured divisions, each with about 400 armoured vehicles of different kinds divisible into small self-contained units.

This force cut off all communications between us and the main French Army. It severed our communications for food and ammunition. It ran first through Amiens, afterward through Abbeville, and along the coast to Boulogne and Calais, almost to Dunkerque.

Behind this armoured and mechanized onslaught came a number of German divisions in lorries, and behind them, again, plodded comparatively slowly the dull, brute mass of the ordinary German Army and German people, always ready to be led to the trampling down in other lands of liberties and comforts they never have known in their own.

I said this armoured scythe stroke almost reached Dunkerque – almost but not quite. Boulogne and Calais were scenes of desperate fighting. The guards defended Boulogne for a while and were then withdrawn by orders from this country.

The rifle brigade of the Sixtieth Rifles (Queen Victoria's Rifles), with a battalion of British tanks and 1,000 Frenchmen, in all about 4,000 strong, defended Calais to the last. The British brigadier was given an hour to surrender. He spurned the offer. Four days of intense street fighting passed before the silence reigned in Calais which marked the end of a memorable resistance.

Only thirty unwounded survivors were brought off by the

navy, and we do not know the fate of their comrades. Their sacrifice was not, however, in vain. At least two armoured divisions which otherwise would have been turned against the BEF had to be sent to overcome them. They have added another page to the glories of the light division.

The time gained enabled the Gravelines water line to be flooded and held by French troops. Thus the port of Dunkerque was held open. When it was found impossible for the armies of the north to reopen their communications through Amiens with the main French armies, only one choice remained. It seemed, indeed, forlorn hope. The Belgian and French armies were almost surrounded. Their sole line of retreat was to a single port and its neighbouring beaches. They were pressed on every side by heavy attacks and were far outnumbered in the air.

When a week ago today I asked the House to fix this afternoon for the occasion of a statement, I feared it would be my hard lot to announce from this box the greatest military disaster of our long history.

I thought, and there were good judges who agreed with me, that perhaps 20,000 or 30,000 men might be re-embarked, but it certainly seemed that the whole French First Army and the whole BEF, north of the Amiens-Abbeville gap would be broken up in open field or else have to capitulate for lack of food and ammunition.

These were the hard and heavy tidings I called on the House and nation to prepare themselves for.

The whole root and core and brain of the British armies of later years, seemed due to perish upon the field. That was the prospect a week ago, but another blow which might have proved final was still to fall upon us.

The King of Belgians called upon us to come to his aid. Had not this ruler and his government severed themselves from the

Allies who rescued their country from extinction in the late war, and had they not sought refuge in what has been proved to be fatal neutrality, then the French and British armies at the outset might well have saved not only Belgium but perhaps even Holland.

At the last moment, when Belgium was already invaded, King Leopold called upon us to come to his aid, and even at the last moment we came. He and his brave and efficient army of nearly half a million strong guarded our eastern flank; this kept open our only retreat to the sea.

Suddenly, without any prior consultation and with the least possible notice, without the advice of his ministers and on his own personal act, he sent a plenipotentiary to the German Command surrendering his army and exposing our flank and the means of retreat.

I asked the House a week ago to suspend its judgment because the facts were not clear. I do not think there is now any reason why we should not form our own opinions upon this pitiful episode. The surrender of the Belgian Army compelled the British Army at the shortest notice to cover a flank to the sea of more than thirty miles' length which otherwise would have been cut off.

In doing this and closing this flank, contact was lost inevitably between the British and two of three corps forming the First French Army who were then further from the coast than we were. It seemed impossible that large numbers of Allied troops could reach the coast. The enemy attacked on all sides in great strength and fierceness, and their main power, air force, was thrown into the battle.

The enemy began to fire cannon along the beaches by which alone shipping could approach or depart. They sowed magnetic mines in the channels and seas and sent repeated waves of hostile aircraft, sometimes more than 100 strong, to cast bombs on a single pier that remained and on the sand dunes.

Their U-boats, one of which was sunk, and motor launches took their toll of the vast traffic which now began. For four or five days the intense struggle raged. All armoured divisions, or what was left of them, together with great masses of German infantry and artillery, hurled themselves on the ever narrowing and contracting appendix within which the British and French armies fought.

Meanwhile the Royal Navy, with the willing help of countless merchant seamen and hosts of volunteers, strained every nerve and every effort and every craft to embark the British and Allied troops.

Over 220 light warships and more than 650 other vessels were engaged. They had to approach this difficult coast, often in adverse weather, under an almost ceaseless hail of bombs and increasing concentration of artillery fire. Nor were the seas themselves free from mines and torpedoes.

It was in conditions such as these that our men carried on with little or no rest for days and nights, moving troops across dangerous waters and bringing with them always the men whom they had rescued. The numbers they brought back are the measure of their devotion and their courage.

Hospital ships, which were plainly marked, were the special target for Nazi bombs, but the men and women aboard them never faltered in their duty.

Meanwhile the RAF, who already had been intervening in the battle so far as its range would allow it to go from home bases, now used a part of its main metropolitan fighter strength to strike at German bombers.

The struggle was protracted and fierce. Suddenly the scene has cleared. The crash and thunder has momentarily, but only for the moment, died away. The miracle of deliverance achieved by the valour and perseverance, perfect discipline, faultless service, skill and unconquerable vitality is a manifesto to us all.

The enemy was hurled back by the British and French troops. He was so roughly handled that he dare not molest their departure seriously. The air force decisively defeated the main strength of the German Air Force and inflicted on them a loss of at least four to one.

The navy, using nearly 1,000 ships of all kinds, carried over 335,000 men, French and British, from the jaws of death back to their native land and to the tasks which lie immediately before them.

We must be very careful not to assign to this deliverance attributes of a victory. Wars are not won by evacuations, but there was a victory inside this deliverance which must be noted.

Many of our soldiers coming back have not seen the air force at work. They only saw the bombers which escaped their protective attack. This was a great trial of strength between the British and German Air Forces.

Can you conceive of a greater objective for the power of Germany in the air than to make all evacuations from these beaches impossible and to sink all of the ships, numbering almost 1,000? Could there have been an incentive of greater military importance and significance to the whole purpose of the war?

They tried hard and were beaten back. They were frustrated in their task; we have got the armies away and they have paid fourfold for any losses sustained. Very large formations of German aeroplanes were turned on several occasions from the attack by a quarter their number of RAF planes and dispersed in different directions. Twelve aeroplanes have been hunted by two. One aeroplane was driven into the water and cast away by the charge of a British aeroplane which had no more ammunition.

All of our types and our pilots have been vindicated. The Hurricane, Spitfire and Defiance have been vindicated. When I consider how much greater would be our advantage in defending the air above this island against overseas attacks, I find in these facts a sure basis on which practical and reassuring thoughts may rest, and I will pay my tribute to these young airmen.

May it not be that the cause of civilization itself will be defended by the skill and devotion of a few thousand airmen? There never has been, I suppose, in all the history of the world such opportunity for youth.

The Knights of the Round Table and Crusaders have fallen back into distant days, not only distant but prosaic; but these young men are going forth every morning, going forth holding in their hands an instrument of colossal shattering power, of whom it may be said that every morn brought forth a noble chance and every chance brought forth a noble deed. These young men deserve our gratitude, as all brave men who in so many ways and so many occasions are ready and will con-tin-ueto be ready to give their life and their all to their native land.

I return to the army. In a long series of very fierce battles, now on this front, now on that, fighting on three fronts at once, battles fought by two or three divisions against an equal or sometimes larger number of the enemy, and fought very fiercely on old ground so many of us knew so well, our losses in men exceed 30,000 killed, wounded and missing. I take this occasion for expressing the sympathy of the House with those who have suffered bereavement or are still anxious.

The President of the Board of Trade (Sir Andrew Duncan) is not here today. His son has been killed, and many here have felt private affliction of the sharpest form, but I would say about the missing – we have had a large number of wounded come home safely to this country – there may be very many reported missing who will come back home some day.

In the confusion of departure it is inevitable that many should be cut off. Against this loss of over 30,000 men we may set the far heavier loss certainly inflicted on the enemy, but our losses in material are enormous. We have perhaps lost one-third of the men we lost in the opening days of the battle on March 21, 1918, but we have lost nearly as many guns – nearly 1,000 – and all our transport and all the armoured vehicles that were with the army of the north.

These losses will impose further delay on the expansion of our military strength. That expansion has not been proceeding as fast as we had hoped. The best of all we had to give has been given to the BEF, and although they had not the number of tanks and some articles of equipment which were desirable they were a very well and finely equipped army. They had the first fruits of all our industry had to give. That has gone and now here is further delay.

How long it will be, how long it will last depends upon the exertions which we make on this island. An effort, the like of which has never been seen in our records, is now being made. Work is proceeding night and day. Sundays and week days. Capital and labour have cast aside their interests, rights and customs and put everything into the common stock. Already the flow of munitions has leaped forward. There is no reason why we should not in a few months overtake the sudden and serious loss that has come upon us without retarding the development of our general programme.

Nevertheless, our thankfulness at the escape of our army with so many men, and the thankfulness of their loved ones, who passed through an agonizing week, must not blind us to the fact that what happened in France and Belgium is a colossal military disaster.

The French Army has been weakened, the Belgian Army has been lost and a large part of those fortified lines upon which so much faith was reposed has gone, and many valuable mining districts and factories have passed into the enemy's possession.

The whole of the Channel ports are in his hands, with all the strategic consequences that follow from that, and we must expect another blow to be struck almost immediately at us or at France.

We were told that Hitler has plans for invading the British Isles. This has often been thought of before. When Napoleon lay at Boulogne for a year with his flat-bottomed boats and his Grand Army, some one told him there were bitter weeds in England. There certainly were and a good many more of them have since been returned. The whole question of defence against invasion is powerfully affected by the fact that we have for the time being in this island incomparably more military forces than we had in the last war. But this will not continue. We shall not be content with a defensive war. We have our duty to our Allies.

We have to reconstitute and build up the BEF once again under its gallant Commander in Chief, Lord Gort. All this is entrain. But now I feel we must put our defence in this island into such a high state of organization that the fewest possible numbers will be required to give effectual security and that the largest possible potential offensive effort may be released.

On this we are now engaged. It would be very convenient to enter upon this subject in secret sessions. The government would not necessarily be able to reveal any great military secrets, but we should like to have our discussions free and without the restraint imposed by the fact that they would be read the next day by the enemy.

The government would benefit by the views expressed by the House. I understand that some request is to be made on this subject, which will be readily acceded to by the government. We have found it necessary to take measures of increasing stringency, not only against enemy aliens and suspicious characters of other nationalities but also against British subjects who may become a danger or a nuisance should the war be transported to the United Kingdom.

I know there are a great many people affected by the orders which we have made who are passionate enemies of Nazi Germany. I am very sorry for them, but we cannot, under the present circumstances, draw all the distinctions we should like to do. If parachute landings were attempted and fierce nights followed, those unfortunate people would be far better out of the way for their own sake as well as ours.

There is, however, another class for which I feel not the slightest sympathy. Parliament has given us powers to put down fifth column activities with the strongest hand, and we shall use those powers subject to the supervision and correcting of the House without hesitation until we are satisfied and more than satisfied that this malignancy in our midst has been effectually stamped out.

Turning once again to the question of invasion, there has, I will observe, never been a period in all those long centuries of which we boast when an absolute guarantee against invasion, still less against serious raids, could have been given to our people. In the days of Napoleon the same wind which might have carried his transports across the Channel might have driven away a blockading fleet. There is always the chance, and it is that chance which has excited and befooled the imaginations of many continental tyrants.

We are assured that novel methods will be adopted, and when we see the originality, malice and ingenuity of aggression which our enemy displays we may certainly prepare ourselves for every kind of novel stratagem and every kind of brutal and treacherous manoeuvre. I think no idea is so outlandish that it should not be considered and viewed with a watchful, but at the same time steady, eye.

We must never forget the solid assurances of sea power and those which belong to air power if they can be locally exercised. I have myself full confidence that if all do their duty and if the best arrangements are made, as they are being made, we shall prove ourselves once again able to defend our island home, ride out the storms of war, outlive the menace of tyranny, if necessary, for years, if necessary, alone.

At any rate, that is what we are going to try to do. That is the resolve of His Majesty's Government, every man of them. That is the will of Parliament and the nation. The British Empire and the French Republic, linked together in their cause and their need, will defend to the death their native soils, aiding each other like good comrades to the utmost of their strength, even though a large tract of Europe and many old and famous States have fallen or may fall into the grip of the Gestapo and all the odious apparatus of Nazi rule.

We shall not flag nor fail. We shall go on to the end. We shall fight in France and on the seas and oceans; we shall fight with growing confidence and growing strength in the air. We shall defend our island whatever the cost may be; we shall fight on beaches, landing grounds, in fields, in streets and on the hills. We shall never surrender and even if, which I do not for the moment believe, this island or a large part of it were subjugated and starving, then our empire beyond the seas, armed and guarded by the British Fleet, will carry on the struggle until in God's good time the New World with all its power and might, sets forth to the liberation and rescue of the Old.

Martin Luther King:

28 August 1963

'I have a dream'

Martin Luther King (1929–68), African-American clergyman and civil-rights leader, first gained national prominence by advocating passive resistance to segregation and by leading a year-long boycott (1955–6) against the segregated bus lines in Montgomery, Alabama. He subsequently set up the Southern Christian Leadership Conference as a base for non-violent marches, protests and demonstrations for African-American rights, such as the 1963 March on Washington at which he delivered his most famous speech, 'I have a dream.' London's *Guardian* newspaper voted this speech as the greatest speech of the century.

Five score years ago, a great American, in whose symbolic shadow we stand, signed the Emancipation Proclamation. This momentous decree came as a great beacon light of hope to millions of Negro slaves who had been seared in the flames of withering injustice. It came as a joyous daybreak to end the long night of captivity.

But one hundred years later, we must face the tragic fact that the Negro is still not free. One hundred years later, the life of the Negro is still sadly crippled by the manacles of segregation and the chains of discrimination. One hundred years later, the Negro lives on a lonely island of poverty in the midst of a vast ocean of material prosperity. One hundred years later, the Negro is still languished in the corners of American society and finds himself an exile in his own land. So we have come here today to dramatize an appalling condition.

In a sense we have come to our nation's capital to cash a check. When the architects of our republic wrote the magnificent words of the Constitution and the Declaration of Independence, they were signing a promissory note to which every American was to fall heir. This note was a promise that all men would be guaranteed the unalienable rights of life, liberty, and the pursuit of happiness.

It is obvious today that America has defaulted on this promissory note insofar as her citizens of color are concerned. Instead of honoring this sacred obligation, America has given the Negro people a bad check; a check which has come back marked 'insufficient funds'. But we refuse to believe that the bank of justice is bankrupt. We refuse to believe that there are insufficient funds in the great vaults of opportunity of this nation. So we have come to cash this check – a check that will give us upon demand the riches of freedom and the security of justice. We have also come to this hallowed spot to remind America of the fierce urgency of *now*. This is no time to engage in the luxury of cooling off or to take the tranquilizing drug of gradualism.

Now is the time to make real the promises of Democracy.

Now is the time to rise from the dark and desolate valley of segregation to the sunlit path of racial justice.

Now is the time to open the doors of opportunity to all of God's children.

Now is the time to lift our nation from the quicksands of racial injustice to the solid rock of brotherhood.

It would be fatal for our nation to overlook the urgency of the moment and to underestimate the determination of the Negro. This sweltering summer of the Negro's legitimate discontent will not pass until there is an invigorating autumn of freedom and equality. Nineteen sixty-three is not an end, but a beginning. Those who hope that the Negro needed to blow off steam and will now be content will have a rude awakening if the nation returns to business as usual. There will be neither rest nor tranquility in America until the Negro is granted his citizenship rights. The whirlwinds of revolt will continue to shake the foundations of our nation until the bright day of justice emerges.

But there is something that I must say to my people who stand on the warm threshold which leads into the palace of justice. In the process of gaining our rightful place we must not be guilty of wrongful deeds. Let us not seek to satisfy our thirst for freedom by drinking from the cup of bitterness and hatred. We must forever conduct our struggle on the high place of dignity and discipline. We must not allow our creative protest to degenerate into physical violence. Again and again we must rise to the majestic heights of meeting physical force with soul force. The marvelous new militancy which has engulfed the Negro community must not lead us to a distrust of all white people, for many of our white brothers, as evidenced by their presence here today, have come to realize that their destiny is tied up with our destiny and their freedom is inextricably bound to our freedom. We cannot walk alone.

And as we walk, we must make the pledge that we shall march ahead. We cannot turn back. There are those who are asking the devotees of civil rights, 'When will you be satisfied?' We can never be satisfied as long as the Negro is the victim of the unspeakable horrors of police brutality. We can never be satisfied as long as our bodies, heavy with the fatigue of travel, cannot gain lodging in the motels of the highways and the hotels of the cities. We cannot be satisfied as long as the Negro's basic mobility is from a smaller ghetto to a larger one. We can never be satisfied as long as a Negro in Mississippi cannot vote and a Negro in New York believes he has nothing for which to vote. No, no, we are not satisfied, and we will not be satisfied until justice rolls down like waters and righteousness like a mighty stream.

I am not unmindful that some of you have come here out of great trials and tribulations. Some of you have come fresh from narrow jail cells. Some of you have come from areas where your quest for freedom left you battered by the storms of persecution and staggered by the winds of police brutality. You have been the veterans of creative suffering. Continue to work with the faith that unearned suffering is redemptive.

Go back to Mississippi, go back to Alabama, go back to South Carolina, go back to Georgia, go back to Louisiana, go back to the slums and ghettos of our northern cities, knowing that somehow this situation can and will be changed. Let us not wallow in the valley of despair.

I say to you today, my friends, that in spite of the difficulties and frustrations of the moment I still have a dream. It is a dream deeply rooted in the American dream.

I have a dream that one day this nation will rise up and live out the true meaning of its creed: 'We hold these truths to be self-evident; that all men are created equal.'

I have a dream that one day on the red hills of Georgia the sons of former slaves and the sons of former slave owners will be able to sit down together at the table of brotherhood.

I have a dream that one day even the state of Mississippi, a desert state sweltering with the heat of injustice and oppression, will be transformed into an oasis of freedom and justice.

I have a dream that my four little children will one day live in a nation where they will not be judged by the color of their skin but by the content of their character.

I have a dream today.

I have a dream that one day the state of Alabama, whose governor's lips are presently dripping with the words of interposition and nullification, will be transformed into a situation where little black boys and black girls will be able to join hands with little white boys and white girls and walk together as sisters and brothers.

I have a dream today.

I have a dream that one day every valley shall be exalted, every hill and mountain shall be made low, the rough places will be made plains, and the crooked places will be made straight, and the glory of the Lord will be revealed, and all flesh shall see it together.

This is our hope. This is the faith with which I return to the South. With this faith we will be able to hew out of the mountain of despair a stone of hope. With this faith we will be able to transform the jangling discords of our nation into a beautiful symphony of brotherhood. With this faith we will be able to work together, to pray together, to struggle together, to go to jail together, to stand up for freedom together, knowing that we will be free one day.

This will be the day when all of God's children will be able to sing with new meaning

> My country, 'tis of thee,
> Sweet land of liberty,
> Of thee I sing:
> Land where my fathers died,
> Land of the pilgrims' pride,
> From every mountainside
> Let freedom ring.

And if America is to be a great nation this must become true. So let freedom ring from the prodigious hilltops of New Hampshire. Let freedom ring from the mighty mountains of New York. Let freedom ring from the heightening Alleghenies of Pennsylvania!

Let freedom ring from the snowcapped Rockies of Colorado!

Let freedom ring from the curvacious peaks of California!

But not only that; let freedom ring from Stone Mountain of Georgia!

Let freedom ring from Lookout Mountain of Tennessee!

Let freedom ring from every hill and molehill of Mississippi. From every mountainside, let freedom ring.

When we let freedom ring, when we let it ring from every village and every hamlet, from every state and every city, we will be able to speed up that day when all God's children, black men and white men, Jews and Gentiles, Protestants and Catholics, will be able to join hands and sing in the words of the old Negro spiritual, 'Free at last! free at last! thank God almighty, we are free at last!'

Nelson Mandela:

20 April 1964

'An ideal for which I am prepared to die'

These are the concluding words of a four-hour speech made by Mandela in Johannesburg when he was charged with being a Communist. His defence was that he was an African patriot, and an admirer of the Magna Carta and the Bill of Rights. He was sentenced to life imprisonment.

Our fight is against real, and not imaginary hardships, or, to use the language of the State Prosecutor, 'so-called hardships'. We fight against two features which are the hallmarks of African life in South Africa, and which are entrenched by legislation which we seek to have repealed. These features are poverty and lack of human dignity, and we do not need Communists, or so-called 'agitators', to teach us about these things.

The whites enjoy what may well be the highest standard of living in the world, whilst Africans live in poverty and misery. Forty per cent of the Africans live in hopelessly overcrowded and, in some cases, drought-stricken reserves, where soil erosion and the overworking of the soil make it impossible for them to live properly off the land. Thirty per cent are labourers, labour tenants, and squatters on white farms and work and live under conditions similar to those of the serfs of the Middle Ages. The other thirty per cent live in towns where they have developed economic and social habits which bring them closer, in many respects, to white standards. Yet forty-six per cent of all African families in Johannesburg do not earn enough to keep them going.

The complaint of Africans, however, is not only that they are poor and whites are rich, but that the laws which are made by the whites are designed to preserve this situation. There are two ways to break out of poverty. The first is by formal education, and the second is by the worker acquiring a greater skill at his work and thus higher wages. As far as Africans are concerned, both these avenues of advancement are deliberately curtailed by legislation.

The present Government has always sought to hamper Africans in their search for education. There is compulsory education for all white children at virtually no cost to their parents, be they rich or poor. Similar facilities are not provided for African children. In 1960–61, the per capita spending on African students at state-funded schools was estimated at R12.46. In the same year, the per capita spending on white children in the Cape Province (which are the only figures available to me) was R144.57. The present Prime Minster said during the debate in the Bantu Education Bill in 1953: 'When I have control of Native education, I will reform it so that Natives will be taught from childhood to realise that equality with Europeans is not for them ... People who believe in equality are not desirable teachers for Natives. When my Department controls Native education, it will know for what class for higher education a Native is fitted, and whether he will have a chance in life to use his knowledge.'

The other main obstacle to the economic advancement of the Africans is the industrial colour bar by which all the better jobs of industry are reserved for whites only. Moreover, Africans are not allowed to form trade unions, which have recognition under the Industrial Conciliation Act. The Government often answers its critics by saying that Africans in South Africa are economically better off than the inhabitants of the other countries in Africa. Our complaint is not that we are poor by comparison with people in other countries, but that we are poor by comparison with white people in our own country, and that we are prevented from altering this imbalance.

Hundreds and thousands of Africans are thrown into gaol each year under pass laws. Even worse than this is the fact that pass laws keep husband and wife apart and lead to the breakdown of family life.

Poverty and the breakdown of family life have secondary effects. Children wander about the streets of the townships because they have no schools to got to, or no money to enable them to go to school, or no parents at home to see that they go to school because both parents, if there be two, have to work to keep the family alive. This leads to a breakdown in moral standards, to an alarming rise in illegitimacy and to growing violence which erupts, not only politically but everywhere. Life in the townships is dangerous; there is not a day that goes by without somebody being stabbed or assaulted. And violence is carried out of the townships into the white living areas. People are afraid to walk alone in the streets after dark. House-breakings and robberies are increasing despite the fact that the death sentence can now be imposed for such offences. Death sentences cannot cure the festering sore. The only cure is to alter the conditions under which the Africans are forced to live, and to meet their legitimate grievances.

We want to be part of the general population, and not confined to living in our ghettos. African men want to have their wives and children to live with them where they work, and not to be forced into an unnatural existence in men's hostels. Our women want to be left with their men folk, and not to be left permanently widowed in the Reserves. We want to be allowed out after 11 p.m. and not to be confined to our rooms like little children. We want to be allowed to travel in our own country, and seek work where we want to, and not where the Labour Bureau tells us to. We want a just share in the whole of South Africa; we want security and a stake in society.

Above all, my lord, we want equal political rights, because without them our disabilities will be permanent. I know this sounds revolutionary to the whites in this country, because the majority of voters will be Africans. This makes the white man fear democracy. But this fear cannot be allowed to stand in the way of the only solution which will guarantee racial harmony and freedom for all. It is not true that the enfranchisement of all will result in racial domination. Political division, based on colour, is entirely artificial, and when it disappears, so will the domination of one colour group by another. The ANC has spent half a century fighting against racialism. When it triumphs, as it certainly must, it will not change that policy.

This then is what the ANC is fighting. Our struggle is a

truly national one. It is a struggle of the African people, inspired by our own suffering and our own experience. It is a struggle for the right to live.

During my own lifetime I have dedicated my life to this struggle of the African people. I have fought against white domination, and I have fought against black domination. I have cherished the ideal of a democratic and free society in which all persons live together in harmony with equal opportunities. It is an ideal which I hope to live for, and to see realised. But my lord, if needs be, it is an ideal for which I am prepared to die.

Coretta Scott King:

8 April 1968

We are concerned about the poor all over the world

Four days after Martin Luther King's assassination, his widow gave this speech in Memphis City Hall.

To my dear friends in Memphis and throughout this nation:

I come here today because I was impelled to come. During my husband's lifetime I have always been at his side when I felt that he needed me, and needed me most. During the twelve years of our struggle for human rights and freedom for all people, I have been in complete accord with what he stood for.

I came because whenever it was impossible for my husband to be in a place where he wanted to be, and felt that he needed to be, he would occasionally send me to stand in for him. And so today, I felt that he would have wanted me to be here.

I need not say to you that he never thought in terms of his personal welfare, but always in terms of the Cause which he dedicated his life to, and that Cause we shared with him. I have always felt that anything I could do to free him to carry on his work, that I wanted to do this, and this would be the least that I could do.

Three of our four children are here today, and they came because they wanted to come. And I want you to know that in spite of the times that he had to be away from his family, his children knew that Daddy loved them, and the time that he spent with them was well spent. And I always said that it's not the quantity of time that is important but the quality of time.

I have been deeply gratified, and my spirit has been uplifted, because of many thousands of persons and followers of my husband, like you, have done so many wonderful things and said so many kind things to lift my spirit and that of our family. Your presence here today indicates your devotion, and I would say your dedication to those things which he believed in, and those things that he gave his life for.

My husband was a loving man, a man who was completely devoted to nonviolence, and I don't need to say that. And he, I think, somehow was able to instil much of this into his family. We want to carry on the best we can in the tradition in which we feel he would want us to carry on.

And this hour to me represents much more than just a time to talk about and to eulogise my husband, who I can say was a great man, a great father and a great husband. We loved him dearly, the children loved him dearly. And we know that his spirit will never die.

And those of you who believe in what Martin Luther King, Jr., stood for, I would challenge you today to see that his spirit never dies and that we will go forward from this experience, which to me represents the Crucifixion, on towards the resurrection and the redemption of the spirit.

How many times I heard him say, that with every Good Friday there comes Easter. When Good Friday comes there are the moments in life when we feel that all is lost, and there is no hope. But then Easter comes as time of resurrection, of rebirth, of hope and fulfilment.

We must carry on because this is the way he would have wanted it to have been. We are not going to get bogged down. I hope in this moment we are going to go forward; we are going to continue his work to make all people truly free and to make every person feel that he is a human being. His campaign for the poor must go on.

Twelve years ago in Montgomery, Alabama, we started out with the bus protest, trying to get a seat, the right to sit down on the bus in any seat that was available. We moved through that period on to the period of desegregating public accommodations and on through voting rights, so that we could have political power. And now we are at the point where we must have economic power.

He was concerned about the least of these, the garbage collectors, the sanitation workers here in Memphis. He was concerned that you have a decent income and protection that was due to you. And this was why he came back to Memphis to give his aid.

We are concerned about not only the Negro poor, but the poor all over America and all over the world. Every man deserves a right to a job or an income so that he can pursue liberty, life, and happiness. Our great nation, as he often said, has the resources, but his question was: Do we have the will? Somehow I hope in this resurrection experience the will will be created within the hearts, the minds, and the souls, and the spirits of those who have the power to make these changes come about.

If this can be done, then I know that his death will be the redemptive force that he so often talked about in terms of one giving his life to a great cause and the things that he believed in.

He often said, unearned suffering is redemptive, and if you give your life to a cause in which you believe, and which is right and just – and it is – and if your life comes to an end as a result of this, then your life could not have been lived in a more redemptive way. And I think that this is what my husband has done.

But then I ask the question: How many men must die before we can really have a free and true peaceful society? How long will it take? If we can catch the spirit, and the true meaning of this experience, I believe that this nation can be transformed into a society of love, of justice, peace, and brotherhood where all men can really be brothers.

Mother Teresa:

10 June 1977

Christianity is Giving

Below is the address which Mother Teresa gave at the university parish of Cambridge, England, when she was awarded the *honoris causa* doctorate by the Duke of Edinburgh, the Chancellor of Cambridge University.

To the question, 'What is Christianity?' a Hindu gentleman answered, 'Christianity is giving.'

God so loved the world that he gave his Son. He gave him to Mary, that she would be his mother. Jesus became a person, just as you and I, except without sin. And he showed his love to us by giving us his life, his whole being.

He made himself poor though he was rich – for you and for me. He gave himself up completely. He died on the cross. But before dying he became the bread of life – in order to meet our hunger for love.

He said, 'If you do not eat the flesh of the Son of Man and drink his blood, you have no life in you' (John 6:53). The greatness of his love made him feel hunger. And he said, 'I was hungry and you gave me food. If you do not give me food, you cannot enter eternal life' (see Matthew 25:31–46).

Such is Christ's gift. God continues to love the world in our day. He sends you and me to show that he still loves the world and that he has not stopped having mercy on it. It is we who today have to be his love and mercy to the world.

But in order for us to be able to love we need to have faith because faith is love in action, and love in action is service. This is why Jesus became the bread of life: so that we may be able to eat and live and to see him in the faces of the poor. In order for us to love we have to be able to see and touch. And so Jesus made the poor the hope of salvation for you and for me. In fact, Jesus said, 'As often as you did it for one of my least brothers, you did it for me' (Matthew 25:40).

The Missionaries of Charity are not social activists but contemplatives in the very heart of today's world. We take literally the words of Jesus: 'I was hungry, I was naked, without a home, and you gave me food, you clothed me, you gave me shelter' (see Matthew 25:35–36). In this way we are in contact with him twenty-four hours a day. This contemplation, this touching of Christ in the poor, is beautiful, very real, and full of love.

Our poor do not need compassion and condescendence; what they need is love and aid. But we have to be aware that the poor are worthy of love, that they are great. This will lead us to love them and serve them.

Love Begins at Home

Do we know our poor here and now? There may be poor within our own family: let us not forget that love begins at home. Do we know them? Do we know those who live alone? The unwanted? The forgotten?

One day I found among the debris a woman who was burning with fever. About to die, she kept repeating, 'It is my son who has done it!'

I took her in my arms and carried her home to the convent. On the way I urged her to forgive her son. It took a good while before I could hear her say, 'Yes, I forgive him.' She said it with a feeling of genuine forgiveness, just as she was about to pass away.

The woman was not aware that she was dying, that she was burning with fever, that she was suffering. What was breaking her heart was her own son's lack of love.

Saint John says, 'How can you say that you love God, whom you do not see, if you do not love your neighbour, whom you do see?' He uses a strong expression for such an attitude: 'You are a liar if you say that you love God but do not love your neighbour' (see 1 John 4:20).

I think this is something we all have to understand: that love begins at home. In our day we see with growing clarity that the sorrows of the world have their origin in the family. We do not have time to look at each other, to exchange a greeting, to share a moment of joy. We take still less time to be what our children expect of us, what our spouse expects of us. And thus, each day we belong less and less to our own homes, and our contacts are less.

Where are our elderly people today? Usually in institutions. Where is the unborn child? Dead! Why? Because we do not want him.

I see a great poverty in the fact that in the West a child may have to die because we fear to feed one more mouth, we fear to educate one more child. The fear of having to feed an elderly person in the family means that this person is sent away.

One day, however, we will have to meet the Lord of the universe. What will we tell him about that child, about that old father or mother? They are his creatures, children of God. What will be our answer?

God has invested all his love in creating that human life. That is why we are not entitled to destroy it, especially we who know that Christ has died for the salvation of that life. Christ has died and has given everything for that child.

If we are really Christian, then for us too, as for that Hindu gentleman, 'Christianity is giving.' We have to give until it hurts. Love, in order to be genuine, has to have a cost. For Jesus the cost was loving us. Even God had a cost in loving: he gave us his Son.

There's nothing I can give you today because I have nothing. But what I desire from you is that when we look together and discover the poor in our families, we may begin to give love in our homes until it hurts. May we have a prompt smile. May we have time to devote to our people.

A few days ago, a man came toward me on the street and asked, 'Are you Mother Teresa?'

'Yes,' I answered.

He asked, 'Send one of your sisters to our home. I am half blind, and my wife is on the fringe of insanity. We long to hear the echo of a human voice. This is the only thing we miss.'

When I sent the sisters, they realized it was true. The couple lacked nothing materially. But they were being suffocated by the anguish of not having any relatives nearby. They felt unwanted, useless, unprofitable – doomed to die in utter loneliness.

This wounds Christ's heart. He loved to the point of suffering. But how will we be able to love the poor if we do not begin by loving the members of our own family?

Love – I will never get tired of saying it – *begins at home.*

God Provides

My sisters are very busy with the poorest poor, with the handicapped, the blind, the abnormal. We have homes for the seriously ill and for the dying.

We are about to celebrate the twenty-fifth anniversary of our House of the Dying in Calcutta. Through these twenty-five years we have picked up more than thirty-six thousand seriously ill people in the streets, of whom about sixteen thousand have died among us.

I feel that the most adequate way of commemorating this anniversary is by celebrating it on November 1, the feast of All Saints. I am more than sure that all these people who have died with us are in heaven. They are genuine saints. They are already in the presence of God. Perhaps they were not loved on earth, but they are favourite children of God.

Therefore I want to pray and to thank God for all the beautiful things that my sisters have done in the House of the Dying. Even though that house is a part of the temple of Kali, the goddess of terror, what reigns there above all is the joy of helping the ill to die in peace with God.

You would be amazed to see the calmness with which these people die. One day the sisters picked up a man who was already half eaten by worms. He said, 'I have lived in the streets like an animal, but I am going to die like an angel, surrounded by love and care.' He really died like an angel, with a very serene death.

Some time ago, we in Calcutta underwent a period when

sugar was very scarce. Somehow the story spread that Mother Teresa had no sugar for her orphans.

A child said to his parents, 'For three days I won't eat sugar: what I save I want to give to Mother Teresa.'

So his parents, who had never been to our house, brought the child with a can of sugar. He was four years old and could barely speak, but that small child had a great love: he loved with sacrifice.

We who know Jesus, who love Jesus, who are even consecrated to Jesus, have to love as Jesus loved. He has given us the bread of life so that we may love as he has loved us. He continues to say, 'As the Father has loved me, I have loved you' (John 15:9).

How has Jesus loved us? By giving himself to us. This is how we are to love each other: by giving ourselves to each other, giving ourselves to the point of feeling pain. I don't want you to give me your surplus. I want you to give with personal deprivation.

I and my sisters have deliberately chosen to be poor, depending exclusively on divine providence. It would take me a whole day and night to tell you the thousands of proofs of the loving providence and fatherhood of God toward us. We deal with thousands of people, and we have never had to tell anyone, 'We are sorry, but we have run out of everything.'

In Calcutta we care for some seven thousand people every day. If one day we don't cook, they will not eat. A sister came to me one day and said, 'Mother, there is no rice for Friday and Saturday. We should let the people know.' I was surprised because through twenty-five years I had never had to hear anything like that.

Friday morning, about nine o'clock, there came a truck full of thousands of small loaves of bread. No one in Calcutta knew why the government had closed the schools that day, but it had happened, and all the bread was brought to us. For two days the people we cared for were able to get enough bread.

I guessed why God had closed the schools: he wanted the people we care for to know that they were more important than grass, than birds, and than the lilies of the field – that they were his favourites. Those thousands of people needed proof that he loved them, that he cared for them. That was a clear proof of God's tenderness toward his children.

Prayer and Sacrifice

In order to be able to carry out her task, every sister consecrates her life to the Eucharist and to prayer. You might be surprised to hear that we have hundreds of young and generous vocations. Young women write to us wonderful things: 'I want a life of poverty, of prayer and sacrifice, to go along with my service to the poor.'

That's what our young women are like: full of love and generosity. In a moment they can be sent anywhere, to carry out the most humble task. We also have brothers – the Missionary Brothers of Charity – who carry out a task similar to ours in complete submission to God's will. It is exciting to see our young people so fully committed, overflowing in love toward Christ's poor.

Our congregation is fully devoted to feeding Christ who is hungry, clothing Christ who is naked, aiding Christ who is ill, offering shelter to Christ who is ousted. We profess the three vows of loving Christ with undivided love in chastity, through the freedom of poverty, in total commitment through obedience. We assume a fourth vow whereby we commit ourselves to offer from our hearts voluntary service to the poorest among the poor, that is to say, to Christ under the humble appearance of the poor.

We need prayers in order to better carry out the work of God. Pray for us, so that the work we do may be God's work and so that in every moment we may know how to be completely available to him.

The ideal of our congregation consists of quenching the thirst of Christ on the cross for the sake of souls. The spirit of the congregation is total commitment to God, a loving confidence in the superiors, and loving care. For without joy there is no possibility of love, and love without joy is not sincere and genuine love.

We have to take that love and that joy to today's world. We have no need of cannons or bombs to bring peace: we only need love and kindness. And we also need a deep union with God and prayer – prayer accompanied by sacrifice, and sacrifice accompanied by adoration.

A family that prays together stays together. As we are united at this moment, let us join also the prayer of all and everyone. What you can do I cannot do. And what I can do you cannot do. But all of us together are doing something beautiful for God.

Let us now pray thus:

Lord, make us worthy to serve our brothers,
men of all the world,
who live and die in poverty and hunger.
Give them this day, through our hands,
their daily bread,
And through our love and understanding,
give them peace and joy.
Amen.

Margaret Thatcher:
18 December 1979

The Foreign Policy of Great Britain

Margaret Thatcher, Britain's first woman prime minister (1979–1990), set out her radical thinking about international affairs in this speech. It resulted in her being able to say of Gorbachev, 'He was a man we could do business with.'

As I speak today, 1979 – and with it the 1970s – has less than two weeks to run. I myself will have some reason to remember both the year and the decade with affection. But in general few, I suspect, will regret the passing of either.

The last 10 years have not been a happy period for the Western democracies domestically or internationally. Self-questioning is essential to the health of any society. But we have perhaps carried it too far and carried to extremes, of course, it causes paralysis. The time has come when the West – above all Europe and the United States – must begin to substitute action for introspection.

We face a new decade – I have called it 'the dangerous decade' – in which the challenges to our security and to our way of life may if anything be more acute than in the 1970s. The response of Western nations and their leaders will need to be firm, calm and concerted. Neither weakness nor anger nor despair will serve us. The problems are daunting but there is in my view ample reason for optimism.

Few international problems today lend themselves to simple solutions. One reason is that few such problems can any longer be treated in isolation. Increasingly they interact, one between the other. Thanks to a still-accelerating technological revolution we become daily more aware that the earth and its resources are finite and in most respects shrinking.

The fact of global interdependence – I apologize for the jargon – is nothing new. Four hundred years ago South American gold and silver helped to cause inflation in Europe – an early example of the evils of excess money supply. Two hundred years ago men fought in India and along the Great Lakes here in America in order that, as Macaulay put it, the King of Prussia might rob a neighbour whom he had promised to defend.

But the popular perception of interdependence lagged far behind the fact. When I was in my teens a British Prime Minister could still refer to Czechoslovakia as 'a far-away country' of whose quarrels the British people knew nothing; and an American President could still experience difficulty in persuading his people of the need to concern themselves with a European war.

Today it is painfully obvious that no man – and no nation – is an island. What President Cleveland once described as 'foreign broils' are brought into every home. The price of oil in Saudi Arabia and Nigeria, the size of the grain harvest in Kansas and the Ukraine – these are of immediate concern to people all over the world. The Middle East and the middle West have become neighbours and will remain so, uncomfortable though they may on occasion find it. The bell tolls for us all.

This has been tragically underlined in recent weeks. The world has watched with anger and dismay the events of Tehran. We have all felt involved with the fate of the hostages. Nothing can excuse the treatment they have received; for hundreds of years the principle of the immunity of the messenger and the diplomat has been respected. Now this principle, central to the civilized conduct of relations between states, is being systematically flouted.

We in Britain have respected and supported the calmness

and resolution with which President Carter has handled an appalling situation. With our partners in Europe we have given full public and private support to his efforts to secure the unconditional release of the hostages. We will continue to support and to help in any way we can. Above all we have admired the forbearance with which the American people have responded to the indignities inflicted upon their fellow citizens. That restraint has undoubtedly been in the best interests of the captives.

The Iranian crisis epitomises the problems which we face in trying to co-exist in a shrinking world where political, economic and social upheavals are endemic. Some would add religious upheavals to that list. But I do not believe we should judge Islam by events in Iran. Least of all should we judge it by the taking of hostages. There is a tide of self-confidence and self-awareness in the Muslim world which preceded the Iranian Revolution, and will outlast its present excesses. The West should recognize this with respect, not hostility. The Middle East is an area where we have much at stake. It is in our own interests, as well as in the interests of the people of that region, that they build on their own deep religious traditions. We do not wish to see them succumb to the fraudulent appeal of imported Marxism.

Because, to look beyond the Middle East, I am convinced that there is little force left in the original Marxist stimulus to revolution. Its impetus is petering out as the practical failure of the doctrine becomes daily more obvious. It has failed to take root in the advanced democracies. In those countries where it has taken root – countries backward or, by tradition, authoritarian – it has failed to provide sustained economic or social development. What is left is a technique of subversion and a collection of catch-phrases. The former, the technique of subversion, is still dangerous. Like terrorism it is a menace that needs to be fought wherever it occurs – and British Prime

Ministers have had reason to speak with some passion about terrorism in recent years. As for the catch-phrases of Marxism, they still have a certain drawing power. But they have none in the countries which are ruled by the principles of Marx. Communist regimes can no longer conceal the gulf that separates their slogans from reality.

The immediate threat from the Soviet Union is military rather than ideological. The threat is not only to our security in Europe and North America but also, both directly and by proxy, in the third world. I have often spoken about the military challenge which the West faces today. I have sometimes been deliberately misunderstood, especially by my enemies who have labelled me the 'Iron Lady'. They are quite right – I am. Let me, therefore, restate a few simple propositions.

The Soviet Union continues to proclaim the ideological in its struggle. It asserts that the demise of the Western political system is inevitable. It neglects the fact that few indeed who live in Western democracies show any sign of wanting to exchange their system for that operated by the Russians. In 1919, Lenin said: 'World imperialism cannot live side by side with a victorious Soviet revolution – the one or the other will be victorious in the end.'

The Soviet government have not repudiated this threatening prediction. Indeed they broadcast their ambitions wholesale. They should not be surprised if we listen and take note.

Meanwhile they expand their armed forces on land, sea and air. They continually improve the quality of their armaments. They and their allies outnumber us in Europe. Their men, their ships, and their aircraft appear ever more regularly in parts of the world where they have never been seen before. Their Cuban and East German proxies likewise.

We can argue about Soviet motives. But the fact is that the

Russians have the weapons and are getting more of them. It is simple prudence for the West to respond. We in Britain intend to do that to the best of our ability and at every level including the strategic. President Carter has shown that he intends to do likewise. And the Alliance last week decided to modernize its long-range theatre nuclear weapons. This in due course will help to balance the new and sophisticated weapons the Russians already have targeted on Europe. The strategic power of the USA in the Western Alliance remains paramount. But I would underline the contribution of the European members of NATO – a contribution which is never overlooked by the Russians.

Modern weapons are totally destructive and immensely expensive. It is in nobody's interest that they should be piled up indefinitely. It makes good sense for both sides to seek agreements on arms control which preserve the essential security of each. We in Britain have therefore supported the talks on Strategic Arms Limitation and on Mutual and Balanced Force Reductions. The British Government hopes that the SALT II agreement can be ratified.

I have been attacked by the Soviet Government for arguing that the West should put itself in a position to negotiate from strength. But in saying this, I have done no more than echo the constant ambition of the Soviet Government itself. I am not talking about negotiations from a position of superiority. What I am seeking is a negotiation in which we and they start from the position of balance, and if both sides can negotiate, genuinely, to maintain that balance at lower levels, I shall be well content. It is in that spirit that I approach the proposals which have recently been made by President Brezhnev and others.

The East/West conflict permeates most global issues. But other equally pressing problems have arisen. These affect above all the world economy and the relationship between the developed Western world and the newly emerging countries of Latin America, Africa and Asia.

No country can today escape economic involvement with the economies of others. In the UK external trade has always been of central importance to our economy. In the USA this has been less so. But recently you have become much more dependent on overseas countries. 10 years ago you imported 5 per cent of your oil. Now it is 50 per cent. But it is not just oil – this has obvious consequences for your foreign policy. So, rich and poor, communist and noncommunist, oil-producers and oil-consumers – our economic welfare is increasingly affec-ted by the operation of the market. Increasingly affected by the growing demand of complex industries for scarce materials and by the pressure on the world's finite resources of fossil fuels.

All of this has coincided with a prolonged period of uneasiness in the world's economy. The immediate prospects are sombre: inflation will be difficult to eradicate; growth has fallen sharply from its earlier levels; there is a constant threat of disorder in the world oil market. News of recent price rises can only have added to the general uncertainty which is one of the most damaging consequences of the present oil situation. The task of economic management, both nationally and internationally, is becoming more and more difficult. The precarious balance of the world economy could at any time be shaken by political upheavals in one or more countries over which the rest of us might have very little influence.

In these circumstances, we all have a direct practical interest in the orderly settlement of political disputes.

These were some considerations which, in addition to the obvious ones, persuaded the new British Government of the need for a decisive effort to secure a settlement in Zimbabwe Rhodesia. As you know, after months of strenuous negotiation, overall agreement was finally reached yesterday on the new Constitution, arrangements for free and fair elections, and a cease-fire. The agreement secured in London showed that even the most intractable problem will yield to the necessary combination of resolve and imagination. Concessions were made by all sides. Many difficult decisions were involved – not least for the British Government, which found itself acquiring a new colony, albeit for a short period. We are grateful for the forceful and timely support we received throughout the negotiations from the United States Government, and from President Carter personally, especially in the final stages.

We have no illusion about the practical problems of implementing this agreement on the ground, against a background of years of bitter conflict. But now is a time for reconciliation, and for restoring normal relations between all the states in the area. The Lancaster House agreement could prove a major step toward peaceful evolution and away from violent revolution in Southern Africa. We are encouraged to persevere with the Five Power initiative to achieve an all-party settlement in Namibia.

In this context I want to say a particular word about South Africa. There is now a real prospect that the conflicts on South Africa's borders, in Rhodesia and Namibia, will shortly be ended. This, combined with welcome initiatives in South African domestic policies, offer a chance to defuse a regional crisis which was potentially of the utmost gravity, and to make progress toward an ending of the isolation of South Africa in world affairs.

We must not regard these problems as insoluble. The West has immense material and moral assets. To those assets must be added the clarity to see where our strengths should be used; the will and confidence to use them with precision; and the stamina to see things through.

Let us never forget that despite the difficulties to which I have referred, the Western democracies remain overwhelmingly strong in economic terms. We are, it is true, more vulnerable than before. Vulnerable because of our reliance on raw materials; vulnerable because of the specialization and complexity of our societies. It is vital therefore, that we keep a steady nerve and that we concert our policies. We already agree on the basic requirements – on the need to defeat inflation; to avoid protectionalism: to use our limited energy resources better. And as we deal with the problems our inherent vitality will reassert itself. There is, after all, no discernible challenge to the role of the Western democracies as the driving force of the world economy.

The political strength and stability of the West is equally striking. Preoccupied by passing political dramas, we often overlook the real sturdiness of our political institutions. They are not seriously challenged from within. They meet the aspirations of ordinary people. They attract the envy of those who do not have them. In the 35 years since the last war, they have shown themselves remarkably resistant to subversive influences.

Our democratic systems have made it possible to organize our relationships with one another on a healthy basis. The North Atlantic Alliance and the European Community are – and remain – free associations of free peoples. Policies are frankly debated. Of course the debates are often lively and occasionally heated. But those debates are a sign of strength just as the regimented agreements of the Communist alliances are a mark of weakness.

The argument now going on in the European Community is a case in point. The Community is used to debate, often difficult and prolonged. We are seeing at present something more serious than many of the disputes which have taken place in the past. But the interests that unite the members of the Community are stronger than those which divide them – particularly when viewed in the light of other international problems. I believe that these common interests will assert themselves. I am confident that an acceptable solution will be found and that the European Community will emerge fortified from the debate. And a strong Europe is the best partner for the United States. It is on the strength of that partnership that the strength of the free world depends.

The last asset I want to mention today is the West's relationship with the countries of the Third World. Neither recent events; nor past injustices; nor the outdated rhetoric of anti-colonialism can disguise the real convergence of interest between the Third World and the West.

It is we in the West who have the experience and contacts the Third World needs. We supply most of the markets for their goods and their raw materials. We supply most of the technology they require. We provide them with private investment as well as Government aid.

We do this not only for our own sake but also because we support the efforts of the countries of the Third World to develop their own economies.

I have only been able to touch on a few current international issues. There are many I have not mentioned. Nor would I wish anyone to think that I underestimate the difficulties, particularly on the domestic economic front, faced by Britain and our Western partners, including the United States. But these difficulties can and will be overcome provided we do not undervalue ourselves nor decry our strength. We shall need self-confidence to tackle the dangerous decade.

It is a time for action, action for the eighties:
– we must restore the dynamic to our economies
– we must modernize our defence

– we must continue to seek agreement with the East
– we must help the developing countries to help themselves
– we must work together to improve the world economy through our international trading and financial institutions
– we must conserve our resources of energy and especially fossil fuels
– we must achieve an understanding with the oil producers which benefits us all
– we must never fail to assert our faith in freedom and our belief in the institutions which sustain it.

The cynics among you will say that none of this is new. Quite right. It isn't. But there are no new magic formulae. We know what we have to do. Our problems will only yield to sustained effort. That is the challenge of political leadership.

Enduring success never comes easily to an individual or to a country. To quote Walt Whitman: 'It takes struggles in life to make strength; it takes fight for principles to make fortitude; it takes crisis to give courage and singleness of purpose to reach an objective.' Let us go down in history as the generation which not only understood what needed to be done but a generation which had the strength, the self-discipline and the resolve to see it through. That is our generation. That is our task for the eighties.

Mother Teresa:

1995

'I address you on behalf of the unborn child'

The following *amicus curiae* brief was filed by Mother Teresa before the US Supreme Court in the cases of Loce v. New Jersey and Krail et al. v. New Jersey.

I hope you will count it no presumption that I seek your leave to address you on behalf of the unborn child. Like that child I can be considered an outsider. I am not an American citizen. My parents were Albanian. I was born before the First World War in a part of what was not yet, and is no longer, Yugoslavia. In many senses I know what it is like to be without a country. I also know what is like to feel an adopted citizen of other lands. When I was still a young girl I traveled to India. I found my work among the poor and the sick of that nation, and I have lived there ever since.

Since 1950 I have worked with my many sisters from around the world as one of the Missionaries of Charity. Our congregation now has over four hundred foundations in more than one hundred countries, including the United States of America. We have almost five thousand sisters. We care for those who are often treated as outsiders in their own communities by their own neighbors – the starving, the crippled, the impoverished, and the diseased, from the old woman with a brain tumor in Calcutta to the young man with AIDS in New York City. A special focus of our care are mothers and their children. This includes mothers who feel pressured to sacrifice their unborn children by want, neglect, despair, and philosophies and government policies that promote the dehumanization of inconvenient human life. And it includes the children themselves, innocent and utterly defenseless, who are at the mercy of those who would deny their humanity. So, in a sense, my sisters and those we serve are all outsiders together. At the same time, we are supremely conscious of the common bonds of humanity that unite us and transcend national boundaries.

In another sense, no one in the world who prizes liberty and human rights can feel anything but a strong kinship with America. Yours is the one great nation in all of history that was founded on the precept of equal rights and respect for all humankind, for the poorest and weakest of us as well as the richest and strongest. As your Declaration of Independence put it, in words that have never lost their power to stir the heart: 'We hold these truths to be self evident: that all men are created equal; that they are endowed by their creator with certain inalienable rights; that among these are life, liberty, and the pursuit of happiness ...' A nation founded on these principles holds a sacred trust: to stand as an example to the rest of the world, to climb ever higher in its practical realization of the ideals of human dignity, brotherhood, and mutual respect. Your constant efforts in fulfillment of that mission, far more that your size or your wealth or your military might, have made America an inspiration to all mankind.

It must be recognized that your model was never one of realized perfection, but of ceaseless aspiration. From the outset, for example, America denied the African slave his freedom and human dignity. But in time you righted that wrong, albeit at an incalculable cost in human suffering and loss of life. Your impetus has almost always been toward a fuller, more all embracing conception and assurance of the rights that your founding fathers recognized as inherent and God-given. Yours has ever been an inclusive, not an exclusive, society. And your steps, though they may have paused or faltered now and then, have been pointed in the right direction and have trod the right path. The task has not always been an easy one, and each new generation has faced its own challenges and temptations. But in a uniquely courageous and inspiring way, America has kept faith.

Yet there has been one infinitely tragic and destructive departure from those American ideals in recent memory. It was this Court's own decision in Roe v. Wade (1973) to exclude the unborn child from the human family. You ruled that a mother, in consultation with her doctor, has broad discretion, guaranteed against infringement by the United States Constitution, to choose to destroy her unborn child. Your opinion stated that you did not need to 'resolve the difficult question of when life begins.' That question is inescapable. If the right to life is an inherent and inalienable right, it must surely exist wherever life exists. No one can deny that the unborn child is a distinct being, that it is human, and that it is alive. It is unjust, therefore, to deprive the unborn child of its fundamental right to life on the basis of its age, size, or condition of dependency. It was a sad infidelity to America's highest ideals when this Court said that it did not matter, or could not be determined, when the inalienable right to life began for a child in its mother's womb.

America needs no words from me to see how your decision in Roe v. Wade has deformed a great nation. The so-called right to abortion has pitted mothers against their children and women against men. It has sown violence and discord at the heart of the most intimate human relationships. It has aggravated the derogation of the father's role in an increasingly fatherless society. It has portrayed the greatest of gifts – a child – as a competitor, an intrusion, and an inconvenience. It has nominally accorded mothers unfettered domination over the independent lives of their physically dependent sons and daughters. And, in granting this unconscionable power, it has exposed many women to unjust and selfish demands from their husbands or other sexual partners.

Human rights are not a privilege conferred by government. They are every human being's entitlement by virtue of his humanity. The right to life does not depend, and must not be declared to be contingent, on the pleasure of anyone else, not even a parent or a sovereign. The Constitutional Court of the Federal Republic of Germany recently ruled that 'the unborn child is entitled to its rights to life independently of acceptance by its mother; this is an elementary and inalienable right that emanates from the dignity of the human being.' Americans may feel justly proud that Germany in 1993 was able to recognize the sanctity of human life. You must weep that your own government, at present, seems blind to this truth.

I have no new teaching for America. I seek only to recall you to faithfulness to what you once taught the world. Your nation was founded on the proposition – very old as a moral precept, but startling and innovative as a political insight – that human life is a gift of immeasurable worth, and that it deserves, always and everywhere, to be treated with the utmost dignity and respect. I urge the Court to take the opportunity presented by the petitions in these cases to consider the fundamental question of when human life begins and to declare without equivocation the inalienable rights which it possesses.

Hillary R. Clinton:

5 September 1995

'Give voice to women everywhere whose words go unnoticed'

This speech was made by America's first lady at the United Nations Fourth World Conference on Women, held in Beijing, China.

Mrs. Mongella, distinguished delegates and guests:

I would like to thank the Secretary General of the United Nations for inviting me to be part of the United Nations Fourth World Conference on Women. This is truly a celebration – a celebration on the contributions women make in every aspect of life: in the home, on the job, in their communities, as mothers, wives, sisters, daughters, learners, workers, citizens and leaders.

It is also a coming together, much the way women come together every day in every country.

We come together in fields and in factories. In village markets and supermarkets. In living rooms and board rooms.

Whether it is while playing with our children in the park, or washing clothes in a river, or taking a break at the office water cooler, we come together and talk about our aspirations and concerns. And time and again, our talk turns to our children and our families.

However different we may be, there is far more that unites us than divides us. We share a common future. And we are here to find common ground so that we may help bring new dignity and respect to women and girls all over the world – and in so doing, bring new strength and stability to families as well.

By gathering in Beijing, we are focusing world attention on issues that matter most in the lives of women and their families:

access to education, health care, jobs, and credit, the chance to enjoy basic legal and human rights and participate fully in the political life of their countries.

There are some who question the reason for this conference. Let them listen to the voices of women in their homes, neighborhoods, and workplaces.

There are some who wonder whether the lives of women and girls matter to economic and political progress around the globe. ... Let them look at the women gathered here and at Huairou ... the homemakers, nurses, teachers, lawyers, policymakers, and women who run their own businesses.

It is conferences like this that compel governments and peoples everywhere to listen, look and face the world's most pressing problems.

Wasn't it after the women's conference in Nairobi ten years ago that the world focused for the first time on the crisis of domestic violence?

Earlier today, I participated in a World Health Organization forum, where government officials, NGOs, and individual citizens are working on ways to address the health problems of women and girls.

Tomorrow, I will attend a gathering of the United Nations Development Fund for Women. There, the discussion will focus on local – and highly successful – programs that give hard-working women access to credit so they can improve their lives and the lives of their families.

What we are learning around the world is that, if women are healthy and educated, their families will flourish. If women are free from violence, their families will flourish. If women have a chance to work and earn as full and equal partners in society, their families will flourish. And when families flourish, communities and nations will flourish. That is why every woman, every man, every child, every family, and every nation on our planet has a stake in the discussion that takes place here.

Over the past 25 years, I have worked persistently on issues relating to women, children and families. Over the past two-and-a-half years, I have had the opportunity to learn more about the challenges facing women in my country and around the world.

I have met new mothers in Jakarta, Indonesia, who come together regularly in their village to discuss nutrition, family planning, and baby care.

I have met working parents in Denmark who talk about the comfort they feel in knowing that their children can be cared for in creative, safe, and nurturing after-school centers.

I have met women in South Africa who helped lead the struggle to end apartheid and are now helping build a new democracy.

I have met with the leading women of the Western Hemisphere who are working every day to promote literacy and better health care for the children of their countries.

I have met women in India and Bangladesh who are taking out small loans to buy milk cows, rickshaws, thread and other materials to create a livelihood for themselves and their families.

I have met doctors and nurses in Belarus and Ukraine who are trying to keep children alive in the aftermath of Chernobyl.

The great challenge of this conference is to give voice to women everywhere whose experiences go unnoticed, whose words go unheard.

Women comprise more than half the world's population. Women are 70 per cent of the world's poor, and two-thirds of those who are not taught to read and write.

Women are the primary caretakers for most of the world's children and elderly. Yet much of the work we do is not valued –

not by economists, not by historians, not by popular culture, not by government leaders.

At this very moment, as we sit here, women around the world are giving birth, raising children, cooking meals, washing clothes, cleaning houses, planting crops, working on assembly lines, running companies, and running countries.

Women are also dying from diseases that should have been prevented or treated; they are watching their children succumb to malnutrition caused by poverty and economic deprivation; they are being denied the right to go to school by their own fathers and brothers; they are being forced into prostitution, and they are being barred from the ballot box and the bank lending office.

Those of us with the opportunity to be here have the responsibility to speak for those who could not.

As an American, I want to speak up for women in my own country – women who are raising children on the minimum wage, women who can't afford health care or child care, women whose lives are threatened by violence, including violence in their own homes.

I want to speak up for mothers who are fighting for good schools, safe neighborhoods, clean air and clean airwaves ... for older women, some of them widows, who have raised their families and now find that their skills and life experiences are not valued in the workplace ... for women who are working all night as nurses, hotel clerks, and fast food chefs so that they can be at home during the day with their kids ... and for women everywhere who simply don't have enough time to do everything they are called upon to do each day.

Speaking to you today, I speak for them, just as each of us speaks for women around the world who are denied the chance to go to school, or see a doctor, or own property, or have a say about the direction of their lives, simply because they are women. The truth is that most women around the world work both inside and outside the home, usually by necessity.

We need to understand that there is no formula for how women should lead their lives. That is why we must respect the choices that each woman makes for herself and her family. Every woman deserves the chance to realize her God-given potential.

We must also recognize that women will never gain full dignity until their human rights are respected and protected.

Our goals for this conference, to strengthen families and societies by empowering women to take greater control over their own destinies, cannot be fully achieved unless all governments – here and around the world – accept their responsibility to protect and promote internationally recognized human rights.

The international community has long acknowledged – and recently affirmed at Vienna – that both women and men are entitled to a range of protections and personal freedoms, from the right of personal security to the right to determine freely the number and spacing of the children they bear.

No one should be forced to remain silent for fear of religious or political persecution, arrest, abuse or torture.

Tragically, women are most often the ones whose human rights are violated. Even in the late 20th century, the rape of women continues to be used as an instrument of armed conflict. Women and children make up a large majority of the world's refugees. And when women are excluded from the political process, they become even more vulnerable to abuse.

I believe that, on the eve of a new millennium, it is time to break our silence. It is time for us to say here in Beijing, and the world to hear, that it is no longer acceptable to discuss women's rights as separate from human rights.

These abuses have continued because, for too long, the history of women has been a history of silence. Even today, there are those who are trying to silence our words.

The voices of this conference and of the women at Huairou must be heard loud and clear.

It is a violation of human rights when babies are denied food, or drowned, or suffocated, or their spines broken, simply because they are girls.

It is a violation of human rights when women and girls are sold into the slavery of prostitution.

It is a violation of human rights when women are doused with gasoline, set on fire and burned to death because their marriage dowries are deemed too small.

It is a violation of human rights when individual women are raped in their own communities and when thousands of women are subjected to rape as a tactic or prize of war.

It is a violation of human rights when a leading cause of death worldwide among women ages 14 to 44 is the violence they are subjected to in their own homes.

It is a violation of human rights when young girls are brutalized by the painful and degrading practice of genital mutilation.

It is a violation of human rights when women are denied the right to plan their own families, and that includes being forced to have abortions or being sterilized against their will.

If there is one message that echoes forth from this conference, it is that human rights are women's rights. ... And women's rights are human rights.

Let us not forget that among those rights are the right to speak freely. And the right to be heard.

Women must enjoy the right to participate fully in the social and political lives of their countries if we want freedom and democracy to thrive and endure.

It is indefensible that many women in non-governmental organizations who wished to participate in this conference have not been able to attend – or have been prohibited from fully taking part.

Let me be clear. Freedom means the right of people to assemble, organize, and debate openly. It means respecting the views of those who may disagree with the views of their governments. It means not taking citizens away from their loved ones and jailing them, mistreating them, or denying them their freedom or dignity because of the peaceful expression of their ideas and opinions.

In my country, we recently celebrated the 75th anniversary of women's suffrage. It took 150 years after the signing of our Declaration of Independence for women to win the right to vote. It took 72 years of organized struggle on the part of many courageous women and men.

It was one of America's most divisive philosophical wars. But it was also a bloodless war. Suffrage was achieved without a shot fired.

We have also have been reminded, in VJ Day observances last weekend, of the good that comes when men and women join together to combat the forces of tyranny and build a better world.

We have seen peace prevail in most places for a half century. We have avoided another world war.

But we have not solved older, deeply rooted problems that continue to diminish the potential of half the world's population.

Now it is time to act on behalf of women everywhere.

If we take bold steps to better the lives of women, we will be taking bold steps to better the lives of children and families too. Families rely on mothers and wives for emotional support and care; families rely on women for labor in the home; and increasingly, families rely on women for income needed to raise healthy children and care for other relatives.

As long as discrimination and inequities remain so commonplace around the world – as long as girls and women are valued less, fed less, fed last, overworked, underpaid, not schooled and subjected to violence in and out of their homes – the potential of the human family to create a peaceful, prosperous world will not be realized.

Let this conference be our – and the world's – call to action.

And let us heed the call so that we can create a world in which every woman is treated with respect and dignity, every boy and girl is loved and cared for equally, and every family has the hope of a strong and stable future.

Thank you very much.

God's blessings on you, your work and all who benefit from it.

Acknowledgements

The following writers and publishers have kindly given permission for the reprinting of copyright material:

Winston Churchill: 'We shall defend our island whatever the cost', reproduced by permission of Curtis Brown Ltd, London, on behalf of the Estate of Sir Winston S. Churchill. Copyright Winston S. Churchill.

Adolf Hitler: 'The annihilation of the Jewish race in Europe', from *The Speeches of Adolf Hitler, April 1892–August 1939*, Vol. 1., pp 740–1, published by Oxford University Press for the Royal Institute of International Affairs, 1942. By permission of the Royal Institute of International Affairs.

Martin Luther King: 'I have a dream', from *The Words of Martin Luther King*, edited by Coretta Scott King, pp. 95–8, published by Fount Paperbacks, 1985.

Nelson Mandela: 'An ideal for which I am prepared to die', used by permission of the South African Government.

Mother Teresa: 'Christianity is giving', from *Heart of Joy: The Transforming Power of Self-giving*, by Mother Teresa, pp. 31–8, first published by Servant Books, Ann Arbor, Michigan, 1987. By permission of Servant Publications, USA.